OCT 2 0 1981 ✓

3 1336 00211 2473

D0978974

428   Quinn, Jim.   Cop. a

American tongue and
cheek

11 95

DATE			

San Diego Public Library

© THE BAKER & TAYLOR CO.

American Tongue and Cheek

American
Tongue
and
Cheek

A Populist Guide to
Our Language

by Jim Quinn *Cop a*

Pantheon Books, New York

Copyright © 1980 by Jim Quinn

Introduction Copyright © 1980 by Random House, Inc.

*All rights reserved under International and Pan-American Copyright
Conventions. Published in the United States by Pantheon Books, a division of
Random House, Inc., New York, and simultaneously in Canada by Random
House of Canada Limited, Toronto.*

Grateful acknowledgment is made to the following for permission to reprint
from previously published material:

Harcourt Brace Jovanovich, Inc., and Faber & Faber Ltd.: Excerpt from "The
Love Song of J. Alfred Prufrock" from *Collected Poems 1909–1962* by T.S.
Eliot.

Edna St. Vincent Millay: Excerpt from "Passer Mortuus Est" from *Collected
Poems* by Edna St. Vincent Millay. Published by Harper & Row Publishers,
Inc. Copyright 1921, 1949 by Edna St. Vincent Millay.

Universal Press Syndicate: *Dear Abby* letter and reply. Copyright © 1978 by
Universal Press Syndicate. All rights reserved.

Library of Congress Cataloging in Publication Data

Quinn, Jim.
  American tongue and cheek.

Includes index.
  1. English language in the United States. 2. English language—Usage. 3. English language—Standard-
ization. I. Title.
PE2808.Q5   428'.00973   80–7716
ISBN 0–394–50905–6

Design by Stephanie Tevonian of Works

Manufactured in the United States of America
FIRST EDITION

This book is for Eliza and Charlotte and Freedom (I mean Mike).

Contents

Contents

Foreword

With introducers like me, Jim Quinn may not need enemies. I'm prepared to grant (whether granted by me or not it will be instantly apparent to every sane reader) that *American Tongue and Cheek* is a wonderfully lively send-up of contemporary language correctors—Edwin Newman, William Safire, John Simon, that lot. But some themes in the book bother me. To begin with, I don't buy Quinn's denial of the connection between bad thinking and bad writing. The reasoning behind the denial is familiar: Pound, Eliot, and Yeats, good writers, flirted or worse with fascism, therefore they must be bad thinkers, therefore quality of writing and quality of thought aren't related. (For the edification of left-leaning radicals Quinn extends his point, using Auden as his example of a good writer who flirted or worse with communism.) This is, I think, shaky stuff. Wrong-headed they were on occasion, even cruel—the poets Quinn names—but they weren't negligible as interpreters of history or as critics of the cultural life of mass urban-democratic society. The edge they have on some authors who, unlike themselves, remained skeptical of totalitarianism derives from the intensity of their responsiveness—both as thinkers and as writers—to the social change occurring in front of their eyes. And dismissing the results of that responsiveness—Eliot's admittedly sniffish but everywhere provocative *Notes Toward the Definition of Culture,* for instance—as bad thinking but good writing is foolishness.

Count one: here and there Jim Quinn oversimplifies.

Count two: Quinn often seems to deny the existence of any substantial ground for preferring one usage to another. I have no quarrel, as I say, with the case the author brings against the prissy purists he calls pop grammarians. These fellows, who've been in contempt of the history of language for years, make out like bandits by arguing that perfect English was discovered—like the Galápagos—at a particular date in yesteryear, and that its forms should be as unchangeably fixed in the cultivated mind as the Rembrandts on the Rijkmuseum walls. Drawing on his trusty OED to prove that idioms and usages deemed repugnant by Newman et al. were approved by Shakespeare or Mill or Dickens or a dozen others of nearly equal repute, and guided philosophically by a linguistic tradition of exemplary scholarship and admirable humanity—Jespersen, Lounsbury, Bergen Evans, others—Quinn shows the absolutists up for what they are: pompous opportunists with a weak grasp of the nature of language, and a pathetic longing to be perceived as the last true gentlemen of Western Culture.

But it's one thing to be sympathetic with an attack on priggish decline-of-culture mongers, and another altogether to conclude that, in the field of usage, preferences are impossible to justify. The reason the phrase *oddly enough,* much favored by Jim Quinn, seems inelegant to me is that once somebody I admired for grace and wit asked why I needed *enough:* Wouldn't *oddly* by itself do? A fair question, style and economy being near allies. The reason I'm less inclined than Quinn to speak up for Watergate English is that we remember different phrases from the period. He remembers, fondly, *go the hangout route,* a phrase he links to a fine old joke. I remember, irritably, *at this point in time,* a phrase I interpret as an evasive maneuver conducted by persons bent on using language not as an instrument of truthseeking but as a means of saving their donkey. And the reason I don't share Quinn's high enthusiasm for *like* as a conjunction—"Write like you talk [he says], talk like you think. Think like you want"—is that I have a vision of the process by which the famous Winston cigarette slogan was arrived at, and think the process stinks. (At center-stage I see an Ivy League–educated copywriter trying to imagine ways to cosy up to a crowd with whom, except for the exigencies of his work situation, he'd never dream of breaking bread. —"Hmm," I hear the adman say, *"Tastes as good as . . .* Nah, *They* don't say that. Gotta muss it up a little. Fuck it up for the folk. The great unwashed would say—*like.* Yeah! *Winston tastes good like a cigarette should.* Rhymes! Check. Got it.") For me, in short, the trouble with *like* is that it's associated with efforts to adopt the mucker pose. I hate mucker poses.

Which brings me to *hopefully.*

Quinn sees the *hopefully* flap as a key to the new language correctors' con. He says the correctors enjoy crusading against a term already in general use because they thereby gain the epic elevation of a Roland, or the boy at the dike. . . . I agree about the lure of lost causes for Tories, but my prejudice against *hopefully* survives. Once upon a day, when my two sons were kids, they were beaten up with baseball bats, on a basketball court at the college where I teach, by seven bruisers from the city of Springfield, Mass. —figures on campus for an "enrichment summer." An anguish-making episode, and the bruisers went unpunished. A day or two after my sons were out of the hospital, I crossed the path of the college's chief PR man, a preternaturally smooth customer (one of his roles was that of choragus at old grads' reunions). The fellow said to me: "Ah, uh, er, Ben, I was sorry to hear of that ah-er-uh *fracas* your boys were in."

No *hopefully?* No, but it happens that the *fracas*-fellow was a *hopefully* addict, given to dropping the word into every PR announcement. *"Hopefully* we'll have a schedule soon." "We'll *hopefully* be able to give you something on that tomorrow." *"Hopefully* the protesters occupying the physics building will accept our offer to negotiate." I'm saying that I connect *hopefully* with a certain paint-out-the-unpleasantness attitude toward life —with hope that's too easy, too manipulative, too clearly an instrument of what the new anthropologists contentedly call "impression management."

And, more important, I'm implying that usage preferences tend to be rooted in decisions about the kind of person you do and don't want to be. The demeanor that a William F. Buckley turns toward the world strikes me as affectedly toplofty, so I avoid Buckleyisms—words that say to the listener: Look it up, serf. (Example? *Nugatory.*) Language fanciers like Tony Randall who while away a guest spot on the Johnny Carson show with chat about the beauty of some rare word meaning peacock-like seem to me foppish. No fan of foppishness, I am not going to drop synonyms for peacock-like into my conversation. So it goes. I believe I've built a fair and consistent system of exclusions and inclusions on this basis—rules of usage reasonable to me and to any others who share my views of the world. Hence, when Quinn tells me there *are* no grounds for rejecting this or that idiom—no acceptable rationales for personal acts of discrimination—I think he is (reverting to a vanished form) out to lunch.

With introducers like me . . .

What, then, am I doing at this front of this book? If I have no sympathy with dismissals of standards, what makes me eager to win an audience for *American Tongue and Cheek?* I've already said I think Quinn is incontrovertibly right in his overall assessment of the language correctors: they're ignorant of the history of language, and (with the exception of Safire) repressive-authoritarian in mode of address, and mean and humorless in temper. They deserve the lumps Quinn gives them.

But the author has other virtues besides his smarts about pop grammarians. He's a splendid parodist—witness the marvelous collection of "corrected" sentences mocking the prissy-purist line that *less* must be used with quantity and *fewer* with number. He has, furthermore, an instinctive feeling for the connection between powerful imagining and good writing—a concern for the damage people wreak when they begin fixing up strongly imagined observation in the name of orderliness. (Witness his penetrating comment on Wilson Follett's revision of a passage from a work of Arctic exploration.) He's alert to the truth that the finicky often take out after a word (*giftable* is his example) when they ought to be taking out after the culture of commercialization of which the word is merely a symptom. And his pages are filled with lore that you won't be able to turn away from for a minute even if you can't bear all the Quinnian assumptions. Think of Noah Webster struggling those many years to persuade people to adopt *bridegoom* and outlaw *bridegroom.* Think of Landor's attempt to abolish *rewrite.* Or Fowler's attempt to ban *amoral, bureaucrat, coastal, gullible,* and other perfectly decent terms. Think of the past of *occupy:*

> *From the late fourteenth century until the beginning of the eighteenth, occupy was a euphemism: to occupy someone meant to have sex with them. Kind of a nice euphemism, as a metaphor for the way troops occupy a town sometimes after a battle, sometimes without a struggle. When the word stopped being used to mean sex, it came back into use again—its meaning unchanged, and the language unharmed. Remember to tell your friends about the verb* occupy *when they complain about* gay *being ruined forever because it is now used to mean* homosexual.

As a sometime social critic, I envied Quinn's insight into the element of fad in contemporary anti-usage campaigns, shared his doubt about the back-to-basics movement (to which the language correctors have lent support), and was moved by his remarks on the Black English controversy:

> ... there is a way of writing that is necessary to success. Just as there are rules about which fork to use at an expensive restaurant. And preparing children for success means preparing them to manipulate those rules, just as they have to be taught to manipulate the salad fork and demitasse spoon. There is really no argument about teaching children to read and write Standard English—only about how it is to be done. With humanity and with understanding or with drills that children cannot understand.

I may as well add, in superhuman fairness, that on occasion Quinn does seem to glimpse the possibility that prejudice against a usage can be justified if one antes up a frank account of why one doesn't hold with those enamored of it. (See the paragraph commending Bergen Evans's hostility to the adjective *fun*. "What a fun thing to do!")

Hard not to end this advertisement on a jingo note. Time and again the sense of despair rises about American cultural life—about, that is, the seeming incapacity of our country, as it advances from youth into something else, to remember what it was created for, the nature of its initial aspirations, the dream of ideal human relationships and ideal fraternity that haunted us when we were closer to our origins. No small portion of that despair has been stimulated lately by initiatives of the managers of the official culture—the establishmentarian Humanities Endowment deciding all will be swell in the U. S. of A. provided the nation floats an overstuffed BBC-style series of dramatic productions of short stories by dead American authors ... or the foundation-supported college presidents of America announcing it's time to cut the throat of Affirmative Action ... or. ... But despair never fully takes hold, partly because our culture goes on producing special beings: men and women who could not, I want to believe, breathe deeply in any air but our own. One year it's Studs Terkel. The next it's the greatly gifted Mina Shaughnessey, the subtlest (because most loving) writing teacher of her time. Now it's Jim Quinn. I don't, to repeat, buy the whole of this book's argument, but I love its tone and its feeling for what's right in and for our impious society. And as for the authorial self . . . Friends, you are about to meet one of our current best, a rude, shrewd, funny, solidly knowledgeable, exhilaratingly good-hearted American. *Go.*

Benjamin DeMott

A Special Preface for You, The Lover of Our Language,

and Kind of a Sincere Apology

If this book doesn't make you angry, it wasn't worth writing.

This is a book on language that is not like the usual language books:

It attacks no use of language.

It defends all the words and phrases and sentences you have been trying to stamp out:

Finalize.

Hopefully.

Between you and I.

You know?

Giftable.

Winston tastes good—like a cigarette should.

There's two of you.

Anybody can do what they want.

Different than.

Dangling participles.

Just about everything you've ever heard was illiterate, barbarous, illogical, and a threat to the future of English.

This book defends all those constructions—not on the grounds that anyone can say what they please (though of course they can)—but on the grounds that all those constructions are *grammatically* correct.

Nothing in this book is really new. Most of the arguments, and the facts on which the arguments are based, have appeared in the works of scholars for the past century—works read largely by other scholars. Scholars generally do not get into fights with media grammar experts—because they have nothing to win in terms of reputation, and because they generally lack a talent for name-calling and abuse.

Popular language experts—pop grammarians like Edwin Newman and John Simon, to name only two—ordinarily use no arguments at all but name-calling and abuse.

This book is a propaganda piece—written as polemic. But the arguments are based on facts, and on the scholar's contention that there are discoverable facts of English usage. We know how a word is used now, we know how a word was used historically. However angry the facts of usage make pop grammarians—the facts are more important than their opinion, or than anyone's opinion.

It may be difficult for you to believe that information about language can make you, who love the language, angry. So let's start with a couple samples; just test your grammar against the usage of some of our greatest writers:

All debts are cleared between you and *(I, me)*. (Shakespeare, *Merchant of Venice,* III, ii, 321)

So far had this innocent girl gone in jesting between her and *(I, me)*. (Defoe, *Roxanna,* p. 40)

Nobody will miss her *(like, as)* I do. (Dickens, Letter, July 1, 1841)

If you read these *(kind, kinds)* of things. (Swift, *Journal to Stella,* p. 150)

(Who, whom) are you speaking of? (Hardy, *Far from the Madding Crowd,* p. 170)

In fact, Shakespeare used *between you and I,* and Defoe used the equivalent; Dickens used *like* as a conjunction; Swift wrote *these kind of things;* and Hardy wrote *Who are you speaking of.*

Hopefully, those facts are capable of shaking your certainty that you learned everything there is to know about our language from your high-school grammar book. If so, this book will try shaking you loose from many more prejudices.

It will try to convince you not only that protecting the language is impossible—but also that the protectors themselves are faddish know-nothings. This is a book against plain English. It questions the basic facts of the back-to-basics movement. It defends the language of Watergate conspirators, of Black children, of Madison Avenue, of slangy college students . . . all the language attacked by the pop grammarians.

But it is possible—even, alas, probable—that as a lover of language you are impervious to facts about language. A few years ago I wrote an article for *The Washington Post Sunday Magazine* defending many idioms condemned by pop grammarians. Among them was the phrase *kind of a,* which is condemned by Theodore Bernstein in *Dos, Don'ts & Maybes of English Usage* (1977). This particular idiom has been used by many writers, including William James and Defoe—and Shakespeare, who I quoted in the article:

> I have the wit to think my master is a kind of a knave. *(Two Gentlemen of Verona,* III, i, 262)

Among the very many angry letters I got about that article, one came from a woman who had gone to the trouble to look up the quote in her edition of Shakespeare. There the line was

> I have the wit to think my master is a kind of knave.

"How dare you change Shakespeare's lines and make him appear to agree with such awful expression!" she wrote. "This quotation calls your whole method into question."

I went back to the *Oxford English Dictionary,* where I had found the justification for the idiom and the quote itself—and discovered that the earliest and also the best editions of the play had the line as *kind of a.* It was the editor of the woman's edition who had changed Shakespeare to conform to *his* ideas of what was good English. "If you will send me the name of the editor," I wrote, "I will join you in writing him a letter of protest. How dare he change Shakespeare!"

Here is the woman's answer:

> *Oh dear! I think you're right. After reading your letter I "have the wit" to see that I, like many English speaking persons, have deified Shakespeare to the point where I thought he could do no wrong. I'm sure now that he must have made many grammatical errors, and was probably later corrected by many editors of many different editions. May he rest in peace!*

> *The edition I use is the one I purchased as a bride, some forty years ago, for 50¢ and a "White King" boxtop, published by World Syndicate Publishing Company, Cleveland O. and New York, N. Y. (no date and no editor listed). How's that for a bargain? It is an indexed edition* in one volume *[underlined twice] and includes The Temple Notes, Plays, Poems, History of Shakespeare's Life, His Will, Introduction to Each Play and an Index to The Characters; and, yes, it is a thick volume, but well bound and holding up very well after 40 years use!*

There is a reproof in that nice letter—and kind of an important one. For some people the rules of good English are permanent and immutable. Grammar is as fixed and settled a subject as addition and subtraction. Two plus two is always four, *kind of a* is always wrong. Demonstrate that very few people today follow those rules, and these people respond by talking about the decay of language. Demonstrate that many writers, even the greatest writers, of the past did not follow those rules, and these people respond by saying that great writers can make mistakes, too. The rules, got from who knows where, first promulgated by who knows who and who knows why—the rules are the rules.

Some of those people are pop grammarians and arrogant language lovers who enjoy embarrassing other people about their language. Some of them are as delightful as the woman with the White King Shakespeare.

It is kind of a shame that you can't fight the first bunch without disillusioning the second. But you can't.

Hopefully, however, both kinds will have stopped reading this book the minute they learned that Dickens used *like* exactly like it's used in the Winston ad.

So there's no reason for the rest of us not to talk frankly.

Oddly enough, writers never seem to thank their agents. However, Knox Burger was, in every sense, the person who made this book possible: reworking and revising many, many outlines, enduring bad-tempered remarks about the decay of English from old friends, and encouraging and sometimes hectoring this book into preliminary shape. Thanks, Knox. Thanks also to his associate Kitty Sprague for her help. Thanks, Phil Pochoda, editor of this book, for making order out of chaos and for lots of patience. Thanks, William Golightly, who did the copyediting and endless checking of quotes and references.

The Road to Ruin

The Standard of Nineteenth-Century Usage

Of all the corners of any old bookstore, the dustiest and most neglected is the one filled with language books: big fat home and school dictionaries, all with the name Webster prominently displayed, spines split and pages dirtied by lots of little hands, smelling old and dead and chalky; Warriner's grammars appropriate to each and every year of school from third grade through College English, patiently explaining the same rules over and over in more and more complicated and less and less interesting language; jokebooks for public speakers written in the 1920s, that turn out to be depressing storehouses of racism, anti-Semitism, and anti-immigrant prejudice; books of popular etymology full of pages of misinformation on the origin of sayings like *independent as a hog on ice;* the all-natural way to improve your word power by J. I. Rodale, the famous organic farmer; at least one copy of Mario Pei's *The Story of Language;* at least two of the unrevised edition of Fowler's *Modern English Usage;* sometimes, in recent years, a copy of Edwin Newman's *Strictly Speaking.* Books on language, from the evidence here, seem to get bought but not read—all of the books, except for the dictionaries and the jokebooks, are in pristine, never-used condition. It was in one of the dustiest and most neglected of all these corners that I found my copy of *The Standard of Usage in English,* published in 1908, by Thomas R. Lounsbury, then "Emeritus Professor of English in Yale University."

From the title, and the old-fashioned use of *"in* Yale University," I expected an old-fashioned prescriptive grammar book, and read the first few sentences with surprise:

> *No one who is interested in the subject of language can have
> failed to be struck with the prevalence of complaints about the
> corruption which is overtaking our own speech. The subject comes
> up for consideration constantly. Reference to it turns up not
> infrequently in books: discussion of it forms the staple of articles
> contributed to magazines, and of numerous letters written to
> newspapers. Lists of objectionable words and phrases and
> constructions are carefully drawn up. The frequency of their use is
> made the subject sometimes of reprobation, sometimes of
> lamentation. There exists, it appears, a class of persons who,
> either through ignorance or indifference, or often through both
> combined, are doing all in their power to corrupt the English
> tongue. Their efforts are too largely successful.*

Thomas R. Lounsbury, the dean of American grammarians in
his day, was writing a book that poked fun at language correctors.
Except for a pleasantly antiquated turn of phrase—natural in a
scholar then in his seventies—Lounsbury could be writing today,
and describing the work of Edwin Newman, Thomas Middleton,
and John Simon.

Somehow all of us, from the protectors of the purity of language down to those of us language has to be protected from,
imagine that corruption is something that happened only recently—and was discovered by chance. Newman heard a teenager
or presidential co-conspirator talk out loud, and a crusade (and an
industry) was born.

But like most of the things that all of us always imagined
about language, that just isn't so. In fact, as Lounsbury points out,
even in 1908, the worry about corruption was nothing new:

> *There seems to have been in every period of the past, as there is
> now, a distinct apprehension in the minds of very many worthy
> persons that the English tongue is always in the condition
> approaching collapse, and that arduous efforts must be put forth,
> and put forth persistently, in order to save it from destruction. . . .
> From an early period there has existed a vague fear that the
> language is on the road to ruin. . . . These foretellers of calamity
> we have always had with us; it is in every way possible that we
> shall always have them.*

To Lounsbury, the notion of calamity was nonsense—he believed, like many other scholarly grammarians trained in the
nineteenth century, that the standard of usage in English was to
be found in the words of the great writers of our language. This

is an extremely conservative position, rejected by the major twentieth-century grammarians—who base correctness on actual usage of the language by the people who speak it. Still, Lounsbury is interesting even today. First of all, he spends a lot of time debunking wrong-headed "corrections" that are still part of popular lists of word peeves. And second, he treats the language corrector as a kind of pathological personality, drawing up features of their writing that demonstrate "a certain uniformity in their attitudes." The portrait of the corrector turns out to be as true today as it was in 1908, and just as quietly funny. Here are the eight signs of the corrector:

1 A Great Sorrow

No matter how angry the correctors get, no matter how careful they are about preserving the "fine points and subtleties" of the language, they seem to be convinced they are doomed to failure:

> *An undertone of melancholy, indeed, pervades most of the*
> *utterances of those who devote themselves to the care of*
> *the language. Though precautions of every sort may be taken, it is*
> *implied that in all probability they will turn out to be ineffectual.*

2 The Passing of a Golden Age

This is one of the oddest, and most universal, of all the articles of corrector faith:

> *They are always pointing to the past with pride. In some*
> *preceding period, frequently not very remote, they tell us that the*
> *language was spoken and written with the greatest purity. . . .*
> *But since that happy time it has been degenerating. . . .*
> *Corruptions of all kinds are not merely stealing in, they are*
> *pouring in with the violence of a tidal wave.*

For Jonathan Swift, the golden age was the Restoration. He wrote that the English language was deteriorating so quickly that "in a few years" no one would be able to read for pleasure at all—the glossaries required to explain good writing would be so long and cumbersome.

For James Beattie, a minor Scottish writer who became a famous defender of pure English in the reign of George III—and for the king himself, who loved to commiserate with Mr. Beattie about the the degeneracy of the modern tongue—the golden age was the age of Swift, when language had finally attained the peak of perfection (and had, of course, begun its swift decline).

Throughout the history of correction, the degeneracy of one set of correctors has turned out to be the golden age of the next —right down to our own time.

If you remember the correctors of the 1950s, their golden age was some vague prewar period when language, like everything else prewar, had yet to be corrupted by the hucksterism of television and Madison Avenue.

For Edwin Newman, the 1950s (corrupt as they seemed then) were the new golden age. It was the 1960s, and the protests against the war in Vietnam, that did English in: ". . . age, experience, and position were discredited, there was a wholesale breakdown in the enforcement of rules, and in the rules of language more than most."

It's doubtful that the rules of language were ever enforced at all—that's like enforcing the rules of gravity: both pointless and impossible. But for the moment that's beside the point: Newman's golden age saw itself as corrupt, Beattie's golden age saw itself as corrupt—and so on and on, back through mournful generations of worriers who misunderstood the meaning and process of linguistic change.

---

3 Evil Groups Pervert Language for Their Own Evil Ends

Jonathan Swift, the greatest and one of the most wrongheaded of all the language worriers, ascribed all the words he despised to "bullies of Whitefriars . . . certain pretty boys . . . and pedants," that is, to pimps, dandies, faddists, and members of the Royal Academy of Sciences. A few years later it became fashionable to blame political writers and pamphleteers (such as Swift had been).

But by the beginning of the nineteenth century, the most popular villain was the penny press. The increasing circulation of newspapers, which historians see as evidence of increasing literacy, was described as a threat to literacy, literature, language, and orderly government. Anymore, the conscious and evil perverters include not only newspaper writers (especially headline writers), but ad men, television news commentators, the Watergate gang, student radicals, and—most insidious and dangerous of all—advocates of Women's Liberation. That is, everyone and everything, on the Right or Left, that threatens comfortable middlebrow middle-class middle-of-the-road journalists and their audience.

4 Ignorance Is Equally to Blame

Some poor or despised ethnic group or class is frequently used as a whipping boy:

> *[The] so-called Scotticism . . . , and to a less extent Irishism, were the . . . [terms] commonly employed before the discovery or invention of Americanism to designate any particular locution, no matter from what quarter coming, to which exception was taken by any Englishman to whom it chanced to be unfamiliar. Consequently the epithet was not infrequently applied to words and phrases which had never been heard of in the region in which they were supposed to have sprung up.*

The Scots, says Lounsbury, seemed particularly affected by the criticism:

> *That an expression should be stigmatized as a Scotticism by any half-educated Englishman was sufficient to induce the best-educated Scotchman to abandon the use of it. Hume's anxiety on this point is well known. He bowed with abject submission to the injunctions of obscure men who possessed not a tithe of his ability nor one-fourth of his familiarity with the usage of the best English writers. He revised his writings constantly in order to expunge any assumed latent traces of the peculiar speech of his native land.*

The Irish, possibly because they proved insufficiently conscience-stricken, never took the place of the Scots. The Americans proved a better choice.

And many Americans are habitually conscience-stricken about their own language. In fact, according to pop grammarians, the newest threats to our language are subgroups of Americans:

deprived Blacks and "illiterate" young people. Neither group seems especially disturbed by their role—though Edwin Newman has some hope for the (white) young. He claims he has been able to embarrass a few out of saying *Y'know?* (though of course he may only have succeeded in embarrassing them out of talking naturally when they talk to him, which he may see as a kind of victory).

As an oddity of worry about language corruption, it never seems to bother worriers when new words come from England to America: British slang like *fab* and *gear,* though it is just as outlandish in sound to outsiders, seems somehow less threatening to the right order of things than Black or teenage slang.

5 The Worriers Are Likely to Be Workaday Journalists

Just as it was the Scots who most avoided real or imagined Scotticisms, so it is journalists who complain about headlinese and writers of pop science articles who complain about jargon. "The authors of the first rank," wrote Lounsbury, "are as little disposed to originate artificial restraints upon expression as they are to respect them. . . . It is mainly by the semi-educated in language that all recommendations or denunciations found in [manuals of good English] are religiously heeded."

Lounsbury, who believed that the great writers of the language were always right about grammar, may have overstated his case—from the days of Swift to the days of W. H. Auden, there have always been great writers willing to complain about the way people talk and write. But it is true current attacks are led by columns and articles written by a TV newscaster (Newman), a drama critic (Simon), a presidential speech writer (William Safire), all workaday writers of one sort or another. As a workaday writer myself, and a journalist, I find this one of Lounsbury's marks of the amateur language writer a little more uncomfortable than the others. But I think I can explain the fascination of the journalist corrector—here's a guy who makes his living making language express his opinions. Of course, he considers himself an expert—and he is, in the practical use of language. You could have worse models, in the clear use of English prose, than William

Safire, for example. The problem with the journalist language critic is, says Lounsbury:

6 They Know Nothing of History

> *The experience of the past furnishes a most significant corrective to those who look upon the indifference manifested by the public to their warnings and to the awful examples they furnish as infallible proof of the increasing degeneracy of the speech. It would save them hours of unnecessary misery were they to make themselves acquainted with the views of the prominent men of former times, who felt as did they and talked as foolishly.*

And it is because they know nothing of the history of language that they fall into the final trap of correction:

7 They Try to Fix the Language Forever

> *There was one aim in particular. . . . This was to render the language what they called fixed. If that were once accomplished, the speech would undergo no further change. . . . The tide of corruptions, real or assumed, would thus be permanently stayed.*

Possibly the saddest of the many little sorrows that go to make up the great sorrow of language corruption is the sorrow over the loss of a word, the necessity to add a footnote more to the great literature of the past.

But as Lounsbury points out:

> *There was a certain excuse for the utterance, in the past, of these doleful forebodings. The nature of language and of the influences that operate upon it was then but little understood. . . . [Men] did not have the slightest conception out of what impurity had sprung much of the vaunted purity in which they rejoiced. To them the language seemed a sort of intellectual machine which had come into their possession with all its parts finished and elaborated. They were consequently solicitous that nothing should be brought in to impair its imagined perfection; they lived in perpetual dread of the agencies that might threaten its integrity.*

But now, to Lounsbury, there was no excuse—the twentieth century would be capable of convincing most (if not all) of the language worriers that there was nothing to worry about because of the *Oxford English Dictionary* (OED), then being published, a monumental work of scholarship that defines words according to historical principles—by giving examples of how the words were actually used in the literature of our language. The OED used quotations from great writers when it could find them—very satisfactory for Lounsbury's method of attacking the correctors. The twentieth-century supplements that have appeared since 1968 use all sorts of quotations—from newspapers, rock record jackets, and speeches of the queen of England.

The OED remains one of the best weapons against the ignorant corrector of good traditional English.

The OED, with its supplements, covers English almost up to the present day—but spends much more time on definition than on grammar. So I also use Otto Jespersen's *A Modern English Grammar on Historical Principles* (first printed 1909–31, revised edition 1947), which is considered the best scholarly grammar of our language.

Besides this, I frequently use Sterling A. Leonard's famous monograph, the first monograph published by the National Council of Teachers of English, *Current English Usage* (1932), and a sequel to that, *Facts About Current English Usage,* by Albert H. Marckwardt and Fred G. Walcott (1938).

And finally, I quote from the work of Bergen Evans, especially *A Dictionary of Contemporary American Usage* (1957), which Evans wrote with his sister Cornelia.

The OED is a prescriptive dictionary. When the editors believed something to be a "grammatical error" they said so. More often, they simply say "considered ungrammatical" or "widely regarded as incorrect"—indicating that there was a difference of opinion about usage. Sometimes, the editors justify the supposed error on the grounds of history and tradition. Sometimes, they leave it up to the reader to decide. Here are two quotes, used to illustrate the use of *between* for more than two (a practice the OED favors):

> *1755 Samuel Johnson,* Dictionary: Between *is properly used of* two, *and* among *of more; but perhaps this accuracy is not always preserved. 1771 Samuel Johnson in* Boswell's Life: *Book II, p. 127: I hope that, between publick business, improving studies, and domestick pleasures, neither melancholy nor caprice will find any place for entrance.*

This is a little bit of scholarly fun with the maker of the great prescriptive dictionary—who himself finally decided that improving the language was not possible.

The Evanses are also prescriptive writers about language; i.e., believers in an absolute standard of correctness: ordinary usage of educated people. But because they know so much more about language than any of our more recent writers of usage dictionaries, and because they are much more humane and tolerant, their work is considerably more open to real language. Beside the Evanses, both Newman and Bernstein, though they are writing years later, seem hopelessly dated and old-fashioned.

Lounsbury, who also sounds like a linguistic radical compared to the language worriers of today, was even more conservative than the Evanses. His absolute standard of correctness was not any kind of contemporary speech—but the usage of the "great writers of the past."

I emphasize how conservative the conservative sources of this book are, because Otto Jespersen, who first published *A Modern English Grammar* in 1909–31, is—in pop grammar jargon—a permissive radical.

Jespersen refused to judge English usage, and insisted that he simply reported what he found to be actual usage. That attitude is the basis of all contemporary scholarly study of the language —which has long since concluded that if you are a native-born speaker of English you never make a mistake in grammar, because you don't know how: grammar is what you say.

That's what I believe. For me, the only sensible standard of correctness is usage by ordinary people. We are the ones who do almost all of the inventing and changing, we are the ones who make English the living and exciting language it is. Language rules that try to tell us how to talk make about as much sense as rules telling us how to breathe, or how to walk.

We talk—that's English. And we know how to talk long before we go to school; in fact, except for vocabulary, a six-year-old child is essentially a language adult, who can use all the grammatical forms of English competently. We go to school not to learn English, but to learn that relatively rarer activity, called writing.

We don't go to school to learn how to talk—luckily. Luckily —as somebody once pointed out—we don't have to go to school to learn how to walk either.

Or we'd be a nation of cripples.

We do go to school to learn how to write. And thanks to what we learn, and how we're taught, most Americans write like cripples. So they go to books like *Strictly Speaking* or *The Careful Writer* to straighten out their writing—and come away with advice about as useful and sensible as shortening a short leg.

This is a book against all those prescriptive style manuals. But it is a conservative book. It defends the traditional use of English. It defends our language against ignorant corrections, self-proclaimed experts, and pointless logic chopping.

It is the stylebooks that are radical—since they are written without any understanding of history, or language, and are trying to change English into some new kind of lingo that never was, and, incidentally, never could survive as a living language.

There is a name, a traditional name, for people without a sense of history: barbarians.

So this is a book against Edwin Newman, Theodore Bernstein, the *Harper Dictionary of Contemporary Usage, The American Heritage Dictionary,* John Simon, Wilson Follett, Jacques Barzun, H. W. Fowler, and all the petty nuisances who write letters to the paper whenever they see the word *finalize* or *hopefully* or *less* instead of *few*. They are all linguistic barbarians.

These pop grammarians bear the same relation to scholarly work on language as pop sociologists do to serious study of our society. From pop sociologists we get articles in shiny page magazines that ask very important questions, like "Does TV Teach Kids to Kill?" From pop grammarians we get articles with equally important questions as titles: "Will America Be the Death of English?"

Professionals in the journalism of despair are pretty much alike, no matter what subject they are being paid to worry about. But pop grammarians are different than any other kind of pop writer. Pop sociologists, for instance, always manage to find a real sociologist to quote, or a real set of figures to misinterpret. Pop grammarians rarely quote grammar books or dictionaries; they frequently abuse the work done by scholars in the past century or so; and they provide little or nothing in the way of real information about language or language history. Instead, they rely on tone, a tone of absolute, and frequently bad-tempered, authority.

From the pop sociologist, it's possible to learn at least what some professional sociologists are thinking about. From pop grammar articles all we learn is that the author can't stand people who say *input* or *finalize* or who use the word *hopefully* to mean "it is to be hoped."

Unlike your favorite pop grammar book, this book is full of quotes from famous writers, opinions from scholars, references to authoritative grammars. And unlike pop grammar books, this book will give you facts about language.

But let's start, in a book about the facts of language, with the facts of pop grammar. Let's start with a quote from two writers who get the tone, the all-important tone, of pop grammar down exactly:

> *Dear Abby,*
>   *My mother-in-law taught English in a little country school in Idaho about forty years ago, so she considers herself an authority on grammar and word usage. Every time LeRoy gets a letter from his mother she encloses LeRoy's latest, all marked up with corrections she's made in red pencil. We just laugh and toss it in the wastepaper basket. LeRoy and I are both college graduates, and we know as much about writing as his mother. Should we tell her to go jump in the lake?*
>   *HAD IT, IN RUPERT, IDAHO*
>
> *Dear Had It,*
>   *If you and LeRoy knew as much about writing as his mother, you would tell her to go jump into the lake. If one jumps in the lake, it indicates that he was already in the water before he jumped.*
> *PS I don't want to be picky, but the same rule applies when tossing something in the wastepaper basket.*

Poor LeRoy. Poor Had It. Poor Abby.

What seems so sad about that letter—and the answer—is that Abby is one of the most broad-minded of all the agony columnists. She's always telling wives it's okay if their husbands want to dress up in women's underwear. She encourages husbands to work out their wives' sexual fantasies by pretending to be Paul Newman or Woody Allen or the Boston Strangler in bed. Read Dear Abby for a couple months and you get the idea that everything is alright—except child molesting, teen sex, incest, and bad grammar.

The first sign of pop grammar is that it's likely to be much more intolerant than any other kind of pop writing. And the second sign is that it's likely to be written by people who are ignorant of language, and language history.

The *Oxford English Dictionary* points out that *in* rather than *into* has been used with words like *throw, fall, put,* and *toss* for five centuries.

> "Hoar-headed frosts fall *in* the lap of the crimson rose."
> (Shakespeare, *A Midsummer Night's Dream*)
> "He *in* the billows plunged his hoary head." (Dryden,
> translating Vergil's *Georgics*)

And the use continues up to contemporary times.

As for *go jump in the lake*—a wonderful phrase because it's extremely derisive, and at the same time extremely affectionate; you never say *go jump in the lake* to somebody you hate, it's always to somebody you really *like:* ideal for telling off your mother-in-law. *Go jump in the lake* was first collected by Mathews in *A Dictionary of Americanisms* in 1912. Every time it has been cited by him, or by anybody else, it has been cited as *go jump in the lake.* Dear Abby's correction, *go jump into the lake,* is first of all so unidiomatic that it sounds funny in your mouth. And second, it has never appeared in print anywhere else that I can find.

So another thing about pop grammar is that it's likely to propose solutions for which there are no problems.

Pop grammar's tone is probably innocent enough, when it's confined to the newspapers and magazines. But it gets nastier when it begins to work its way into our schools.

L. Pearce Williams, a history professor at Cornell University, managed to accumulate so much pop grammar anger at the school's permissive introductory English course that he proposed to take it over and teach it himself. I quote Professor Williams, from an article in *The Washington Post:*

> *My method is the same as that used by the Marine Corps Drill Sergeant. I take the Freshmen apart and put them together as literates. You might say I destroy them. I'm a believer in the total assault method.*

We all know what the total assault concept means—that's the kind of English teacher who ridicules and abuses students by pretending to misunderstand sentences if they lack a comma or violate a textbook pronoun reference; the kind of teacher who produces two kinds of graduates: the ones who will absolutely refuse, from fear, to ever write anything again; and the ones who are as snotty and brutal as he is.

But that's beside the point. The point is that if a professor of history wanted to take over the introductory mathematics course at Cornell University, and announced that fact, his friends—after they sobered him up—would say, "Look, we know you believe in reciting the multiplication tables, and drill in long division. We know you're against teaching this highfalutin stuff called calculus. But it's probably better to leave the introductory courses to professionals. Or at least to get a little professional training before proposing to take over the *entire* mathematics program."

But there are no professionals in pop grammar—pop grammar's only prerequisite, it seems, is that you have no language training at all.

Just a little more about Professor Williams's teaching methods. Imagine a professor at a school with the reputation of Cornell —or any university, with any kind of reputation—saying he was going to teach chemistry by totally destroying the student and reconstituting him as someone who knows the atomic number of argon. Imagine anyone, in any kind of school, proposing to teach any kind of language by the total assault method.

If you go to any kind of school and want to learn a language —from Berlitz to your local community college—you'll be told that the concentration is on conversation: no boring grammar drills, no emphasis on rules. . . . You'll be told that learning a language is fun, that you learn by using it. Many private language schools provide a little wine and cheese for their students. If you want to learn any language except English, everybody will tell you you can have a good time learning. You can even have a good time learning English—if you don't know any English at all. It's only if you already know English, and were born in this country, and have been speaking it all your life—and you want to learn the pop grammar version—that you have to suffer, and learn the fear of God, and the limiting clause, and Professor Williams, and the Marine Drill Sergeant—whichever is more important.

The real home of pop grammar is the newspapers and magazines. Here's an editorial from *The Washington Star,* entitled "Unpalatable." The original took up a third of a page—showing how important the editors thought the subject was. It is a complaint against the use of the word *giftable.* One of the editors was riding home in his car and heard somebody on the radio say, "All the items in our store are giftable at Christmas." First of all, of course, he found the word *giftable* to be ugly. This is often the pop grammarian's standard reaction to a word he's never heard before —and the idea of ugly words is a curious one. We rarely stop to think, for example, if *bobolink* is an ugly word—or if it's more or less beautiful than *lizard* or *aposiopesis;* or if *murder* is an uglier word than *rape* or *torture.* But let that go, that's not the important problem with *giftable,* says the editorial:

> *The trouble with giftable is that, unlike other -able words, it's formed with a noun. Unless we stomp on it, it will surely multiply. Others like it will follow. So we say, "Stop it. Stop it now, whoever you are." Before language becomes unlanguageable, not to say unbearable.*

First of all, *gift* is often used as a verb. We use the past participle of that verb, as an adjective, whenever we say *a gifted writer, a gifted painter.* But even if *gift* wasn't a verb, it would be too late for us to stomp on the practice of adding *-able* to nouns: *actionable, charitable, companionable, dutiable, fashionable, impressionable, knowledgeable, marriageable* are among a few of the words formed by adding *-able* to nouns. Another word formed by adding *-able* to a noun is *unpalatable,* the very word the editor chose for the title of the editorial complaining about the process.

One more sign of pop grammar: it's often a contradiction in terms.

There have been many scholarly attacks on pop grammar: Thomas Lounsbury in *The Standard of Usage in English;* to Albert Marckwardt and Fred Walcott in *Facts About Current English Usage.* What these scholars tried to do was examine the shibboleths of pop grammar in the light of historical usage.

This is a very conservative way to argue with pop grammar. I want to emphasize that because what I'm writing, I believe, is a very conservative book about language, a return, if you will, to fundamentals. Pop grammarians like to rally round certain catchphrases, like "the need for standards," the "great history of our language." And they sometimes confess, with the shamefacedness we have come to recognize as arrogance, to being "a bit of a purist—even a pedant—but somebody has to keep up the fight to preserve the elegance and subtlety of our native tongue."

The usual reply is that language changes, language is determined by the people who speak it, and the rules of language must be derived from actual practice—not abstract principles of logic or etymology or literary felicity. Consider the Ptolemaic system, for example. It is deduced from first principles: that the earth is the center of the universe, and that the sun and stars should move in perfect circles because . . . well, because that's the way the astronomer would have done it if he was god. The Ptolemaic system was rigorous, beautiful, logical, elegant—and it did not work. The stars, which are not dependent on human systems, would not go where the Ptolemaic astronomers predicted they would go. With the invention of the telescope, and the possibility of more and more accurate observation, it became more and more clear that the beautiful system of Ptolemy had a serious defect: it did not work.

The astronomers who produced the new system started with the positions of the stars themselves, and did not try to impose their own sense of order on the universe. As a result, they came up with a solar system in which the sun was the center, in which orbits were not perfect circles; a system that had none of the old logic and beauty, but which did have one great advantage: it worked. Of course they were called atheists, those old astronomers, and given all sorts of trouble by the orthodoxy of their day— because some people can never admit any contradiction of their own beliefs without feeling that all the gods that be are reeling with horror at the blasphemy.

Language study, so this argument goes, is at the point that astronomy was around Galileo's time. There are new and objective ways to look at language. They describe what is actually happening. They are not concerned with imposing an outside sense of order on what people say. They have found a new kind of order—one that looks as odd, at first glance, as the orbit of earth must have looked to a confirmed Ptolemaist. And they work.

The people who believe in the old schoolbook grammars call the new rules chaos, of course. They cannot believe that an order that is different than the one they were taught is anything but an attack on elegance and subtlety and precision . . . enough to set all the gods reeling with horror once again. Trying to argue with these old-fashioned grammarians is difficult—it's like Galileo asking an archbishop to look though a telescope and see for himself that the planets are where they are in the sky. To the archbishop, the telescope is part of the problem—an instrument of the devil, to begin with.

To the pop grammarian, the study of language itself is part of the problem—and sure to lead to a breakdown of order. Don't we have grammar books enough already? Let the kids be taught to speak and write correctly!

"People's language has nothing to do with the grammar of the textbooks," says the new grammarian in despair.

"My language does!" roars the pop grammarian. "And everybody's language should."

Arguing about popular usage only feeds the ego of the pop grammarian—and the more you demonstrate that most people do not follow the rules, the more he congratulates himself that he, at least, is holding back the tides of change, single-handed and alone though he be.

Accusing the pop grammarian of being old-fashioned is like accusing a bully of being overbearing—all you do is demonstrate that he's succeeded in scaring you. Accusing pop grammarians of being elitists and snobs is in fact complimenting them on the very character traits they are most likely to cherish.

So instead, I'm going to accuse them of being know-nothings, who, in the name of defending the language, are actually trying to change the language from what it is, and has been all through its history, into a strange new kind of language that has never existed anywhere at all.

First of all, that's true. Second, maybe it will work.

A language conservative like myself resists change—for example, I still use the word *irregardless.* I grew up using it. Other language conservatives I can think of are people who still say either *Gramophone* or *Victrola* for the object you once called a *phonograph* and then a *record player* and then a *hi-fi* and then a *stereo* and which you now, if you are a language radical, probably call a *sound system.*

But there are also language reactionaries—people who want to write and talk only the way they did in the nineteenth century. This is an interesting and possibly even an admirable ambition— like deciding to dress in nineteenth-century costume, with spats and Celluloid collars fastened with gold studs, and buttoned shoes. But to be a genuine reactionary, you have to know something about the period you want to imitate. If you just walk into an old clothes store and put on whatever you find—and wind up wearing spats as gloves and collars as headbands—all you do is make yourself ridiculous.

Pop grammarians have rifled the old clothes stores of language—the grammar books still in use in many of our schools—and have wound up with the equally ridiculous idea that nineteenth-century English was a language based on logic and Latin grammar. In fact, no English, in any century, was ever based on logic or Latin.

two

Edwin Newman

Edwin Newman is our leading, but not only, linguistic Chicken Little. Sometimes there seems to be a whole chorus of voices shouting, "Standards are threatened! Language is dead! English is falling!" Every shiny paper magazine, every edition of the Sunday *New York Times,* every human interest commentary on the six o'clock news, seems to present us with new evidence— a sentence in a presidential press conference, a phrase in a cigarette ad, a word teenagers use—that all is up (or fallen down) semantically.

Well, despair sells—especially as pop social criticism. There is hardly an aspect of American life that has not made the best-seller list after somebody was lucky enough to discover it was in the last stages of decline.

But language decline, even in the literature of decline, is special; so little seems to be required of it.

Consider pop history. Consider Alex Haley. Haley went to great pains to convince us that he had searched obscure records, shipping lists, biographies of slaves and owners alike. He even visited Africa and found an oral historian. His book became a best seller and then he found that a number of professional historians —both Black and white—questioned his facts, his scholarship, and his basic honesty. Historians apparently do not like best sellers by amateurs. Or at least professionals like checking out the facts in best sellers by amateurs—and pointing out the unprofessionalism.

Now, consider Edwin Newman. He has written two best sellers about language. He does not in either book mention a single grammarian, a single grammar text, a single writer on language, a single dictionary. He does not even mention the *Harper Dictionary of Contemporary Usage,* though he is on the "panel of experts" who settle questions for the dictionary, and though he has apparently lifted many of his opinions and prejudices from that book. Newman often demonstrates that he does not know the simple dictionary meaning of words. He invents fanciful histories of the language to prove that phrases he dislikes are illiterate. He denounces as new and corrupt words that are not new at all—that have been in the language for centuries. And Newman is able to gather for his book jackets unconditional praise from such disparate people as Tom Wicker, Joseph Kraft, Kingman Brewster, Kenneth B. Clark, Gene McCarthy, Craig Claiborne, Bob Woodward, Irving Howe, and Richard H. Rovere.

Professional writers are obviously different than professional historians, not because they are necessarily happier about amateur success, but because they never check out the facts in books about language. Some professionals do not know there are facts to check, and would not know where to go to check them; they think *finalize* is a bad word—because everybody says it is a bad word.

For many other writers, the death of English is one of those great ideas—like wildlife preservation, energy conservation, and the danger of television—which are so profoundly and personally important that admitting there are facts to check seems like propaganda for the enemy.

So let's forget the standard objections. Let's start by pretending to concede the need for coercion (without even asking who is entitled to coerce—and how it might be done). Let's simply measure Newman's books by their information: since he sets himself up as an authority on English, let's compare him to other authorities. After all, Newman should at least be familiar with what other writers on language have said. He should have some idea of how words are used historically.

But he doesn't. Here, more or less in the order of their silliness, are instances where Newman shows his ignorance of standard reference works and of simple meanings of ordinary words.

> *The prevalence of Y'know is one of the most far-reaching and depressing developments of our time. . . .*
> *We know less about the origin of Y'know than about the origin of Boola boola, but there is some reason to believe that in*

this country it began among poor blacks who, because of the
disabilities imposed on them, often did not speak well and for
whom Y'know was a request for assurance that they had been
understood. From that sad beginning it spread, among people who
wanted to show themselves sympathetic to blacks, and among
those who saw it as the latest thing and either could not resist or
did not want to be left out.

A few minutes with the OED will demonstrate that whoever is meant by Newman's collective *we*—the reason they know little about the origin of *you know* is that they never bothered to find out. The words first appeared in writing circa 1350. Chaucer used an equivalent in 1386. Addison used it in 1712. *You know* found its way into the excruciatingly polite conversations of Jane Austen's characters in *Northanger Abbey* (1798).

None of those writers knew or especially sympathized with poor Blacks. None were addicted to the latest thing. There is no evidence that *you know* is a significant feature of Black English, and no evidence of any kind to support Newman's fanciful little history.

You know is an old and useful phrase, as important in English as *n'est-ce pas?* is in French. It has never been used as a request for assurance that the speaker has been understood. It is, as Randolph Quirk points out in *The English Language and Images of Matter,* an intimacy signal, a way of drawing the hearer closer to the speaker, making both of them feel more at ease. It may be, says Quirk, that *you know* is not only useful but necessary. If you strike other people as cool, abrupt, dogmatic, or even hostile, part of the reason may be that you are suppressing these expected intimacy signals.

Ironically, the reason that Newman may hear *you know* so much is that he can't stand the phrase. He thinks people are asking him for assurance that they've been understood—what they're really saying is "Hey, come on, loosen up. Show some life."

Newman complains about "the destruction of rhetoric":

Rhetoric does not mean fustian, exaggeration, or grand and empty
phrases. It means—it meant—the effective use of language, and
the study of that use. Suddenly beloved of politicians and
journalists, rhetoric is now used to mean something doubtful and
not quite honest, instead of something desirable. Its
misapplication could hardly tell more than it does.

According to the OED, the word *rhetoric* has been applied to false or empty phrases since 1562. *Rhetoric* is not suddenly beloved of journalists and politicians; it was used to describe fustian and dishonesty by Milton, Cowper, Macaulay, Landor, and Swinburne. It is Newman's misunderstanding of the word, and ignorance of its history, that could hardly be more telling: any dictionary could have told him the real meaning of *rhetoric*.

> *-ize is thought to have a businesslike ring . . . or sound technical. What those who use -ize overlook is that it is usually unnecessary and always dull—it is a leaden syllable—and imposes monotony on the language by making so many words sound the same.*

The objection is, of course, ridiculous to begin with. *-ize* is no more leaden as a syllable than *-ing* or *-ism*—and no more capable of making language dull.

Historically, *-ize* has been used to form verbs since the Elizabethan age; the first use (1591) listed in the OED is by Thomas Nashe, talking back to

> Reprehenders, that complain of my boystrous compound wordes, and ending my Italionate coyned verbes in *-ize.*

If you don't like *-ize* words *(realize, hospitalize, baptize),* don't use them. But just because you bowdlerize your own language doesn't give you the right to tell the rest of us what to do. Who are you to criticize?

It's hard to know what to say about Newman's criticism that *-ize* is unnecessary, has a businesslike ring, and makes all words sound alike. *Capsize* does not sound like *itemize* to me. *Baptize* does not have a businesslike ring. And what word would you use instead of *apologize?*

Newman, of course, picks out special -ize words that he apparently thinks were invented in the last few years, just to annoy him: colonize (first used 1622), popularize (1797), maximize (1802), vitalize (1678). He suggests, with withering sarcasm, that people will soon use optimize to mean "looking on the optimistic side of things." But we don't have to worry about English dying when that happens, because it already has happened. In 1844, the English politician William Gladstone used optimize in just that way. And the language survived—even after he became prime minister.

As is often the case with word haters, Newman imagines *-ize* is a new aberration—and produces an imaginary history as a kind of wish fulfillment. It would be nice for Newman, since he says he dislikes *-ize* words so much, if he could prove they were somehow wrong or bad. But he can't. And there is nothing so pointless, as Lounsbury points out, as arguing about the meaning of a word that was settled long before you were born.

> *The Anglican Digest, reporting on the death of the Bishop of Western North Carolina, noted that he had been consecrated in 1948 and priested in 1936. I wonder when he was postulated and noviced.*

What good fun! And what ignorant fun. *Priested* was first used to mean "ordained or admitted to the priesthood" in 1504, and has continued in use, meaning just that, ever since. Any unabridged dictionary lists the word, no matter how conservative or old-fashioned.

> *The White House transcript did not show it, but the President [Nixon] dropped the g at the end of some ing words, apparently to ensure that his down-to-earthness would be recognized. The g at the end of ing words must be thought by politicians to have class connotations that may offend the masses of voters. . . .*
> *To choose a lower order of speech is, I suppose, antiestablishment in motive and carries a certain scorn for organized, grammatical, and precise expression. Object to it and you are likely to be told that you are a pedant, a crank, an elitist, and behind the times. . . .*

This is an especially interesting objection because Newman sets himself up for us to call him a purist, defending wonderful values like "organized, grammatical, and precise expression."

And because he reveals at the same time that he is totally ignorant of class speech patterns, and of the way that words are ordinarily pronounced in English.

Plus, he uses that *-ize* word *organized,* after he was so insistent that the rest of us should quit. But let that go.

When William Makepeace Thackeray visited America in 1852–53, he was universally acclaimed; but many American journalists (especially in the cheap popular press) were struck by the strangeness of his speech—Thackeray dropped the *-g* at the end of *-ing* words. Not because he was antiestablishment, or full of scorn for organized thought, but because dropping *-g*'s was (and is) a feature of standard British upper-class pronunciation. Mencken mentions that fact in *The American Language* (1938); Randolph Quirk mentions it, again as current, in *The Use of English* (1962).

In fact, all people drop their *-g*'s in *-ing* words. Just as all people sometimes say *duh* and *dem* for *the* and *them*. You do it. I do it. Edwin Newman, no matter how much he denies it, does it himself. We don't hear ourselves, of course—because, as linguists are fond of saying, we don't hear the actual sounds we make, we hear our sonic intention. But you can hear yourself dropping *-g*'s and saying *duhs* if you make a tape of your speech—and you can hear it, if you listen, in everybody else's speech. Those easy pronunciations are more likely to slip in when people are relaxed or when they're highly excited and interested in what they're saying (just like Newman slipped that *-ize* word into his prose when he started kicking Richard Nixon around again—and who can blame him?). Who can blame anyone? People tend to use more careful pronunciations only when they're more conscious of the impression they're creating than the words they're saying.

Newman thinks he has discovered that Nixon is trying to be down-to-earth by altering his natural way of speaking. Actually, Newman has discovered that Nixon, like every other human being, alters his speech artificially in formal situations. You can hear this very clearly in President Carter's news conferences—because Carter's normal speech has very very few final *-g*'s in it. When he is reading the formal statement at the opening of the conference, he frequently makes a conscious effort to stick some in. After he starts answering questions, they slowly disappear.

It is the carefully pronounced *-g* that is the conscious affectation—and it appears from Mencken and Quirk that it is also an Americanism (at least more consciously elitist in America). Carefully making odd little consonant sounds has always been a feature of social climbing in this country—the kind of thing people do when they assume that everything they learned as a child was wrong, and that the purpose of speech is to disguise those shameful origins. It has led to odd American pronunciations of words as they are spelled: saying the *l* in *calm;* the *t* in *often;* the *l* in *salmon;* even in extreme cases, to saying the *t* in *Christmas*.

But that seems a very minor problem. Who would complain about all those extra noises people feel compelled to make (or, more often, imagine that they make) in order to sound like a very educated TV announcer who has eliminated all traces of his native dialect? No one would complain—except a crank, a pedant, an elitist Anglophile who was more than a century behind the times.

Different than rather than different from is wrong.

Short, simple, to the point, and utterly without foundation. The OED defends *different than;* Fowler classes the insistence that only *different from* is correct as a superstition; and the *Harper Dictionary of Contemporary English,* for which Newman works as a member of the panel of usage experts, says:

> *The more common American idiom is* different from *but, as several leading grammarians have pointed out, the use of* different than *is becoming increasingly more popular among careful writers when the object of the preposition is a clause: "Please inform us if your address is* different than *it was in the past."*

The *Harper Dictionary* does not bother to say why *different than* is becoming more popular—that using *from* in a clause requires a lot of clumsy rewording: "Please inform us if your address is different from what it was in the past."

This is one of the clearest examples I have found of people following Lounsbury's rule and preferring "the certainty of dogmatic utterance" expressed by Newman to "the hesitancy that arises from knowledge." And it's useful to remember: suspect all dogmatic statements about language.

Newman especially hates new words he thinks were invented by Ron Ziegler, like nonperformance and inoperative.

Nonperformance is first cited 1509–10; Shakespeare, *Winter's Tale* (1611), I.ii.261: "Fearefull to doe a thing, where I the issue doubted, Whereof the execution did cry out Against the non-performance." Other writers who have used the word include Arbuthnot, Smollett, and Bentham. The word is listed as current by the OED and has been available for anyone to use. The fact that Ziegler may have been lying when he used the word is beside the point. People lie using words like *love,* and *freedom,* and *justice.* But that doesn't make the words themselves into guilty words.

Inoperative was first used around 1631, and by John Donne: "A dead faith, as all faith is that is inoperative." (*Selected Works,* published in 1840, p. 204). The OED lists the word as current, adding that in legal language it means "without standing force, invalid," which is where Ziegler probably came across it—though who knows? Donne may be one of his favorite poets—and at any rate, whatever else Ziegler is guilty of, he is not guilty of bad language when he imitates John Donne.

Newman complains that *guilty culprit* is redundant—*culprit* all by itself means guilty.

Any historical dictionary would have told him different.

At first, *culprit* was formal legal language that meant "the prisoner waiting before the bar for trial." It meant that in 1678, when it was first cited in the OED; and it means exactly that today. Strictly speaking, of course.

But gradually, courts and judges and justice each being what they are, the word began to take on associations of guilt—in uninformed use. The OED finds the first use of *culprit* to mean "guilty person" in 1769.

It's tempting to call that new and uninformed use a corruption because it's tempting to accuse Newman of joining the corruptors—all in the name of organized grammatical thought and precision and the rest of that stuff. But the new meaning isn't a corruption, just an extension—like using *unique* to mean "rare" instead of "single and solitary."

And Newman isn't a corruptor of language—he's just a guy with no legal training who is a little too lazy to be bothered looking up words in dictionaries or finding out their derivation before using them. Nothing wrong with that. The uninformed and lazy have a perfect right to use words in their uninformed and lazy way, and go on convicting all those innocent culprits without trial if it gives them pleasure. This is exactly the kind of ignorance and laziness, frequently disguised as pedantic precision, which makes words change—and keeps our language from stagnating.

Now if only we could convince Newman to go on in his particular lazy and ignorant way, without making lazy and ignorant criticisms of perfectly good words, we would all be happy.

Newman apparently thinks that Nixon invented the word *stonewalling;* it started out in Australia, and was used to describe a strategy in which a cricket batsman did nothing but keep the ball from the wicket—something like fouling off pitch after pitch in baseball. Newman is especially hard on *supportive,* probably

because Rogers Morton used it: "People who are totally supportive of the President." Morton could have said "who support the
President," says Newman, managing to drop the word *totally* as
if it had no meaning—but let that go, he got most of the sentence
right. But, says Newman, Morton preferred *supportive* because:

Supportive is ponderous, a quality much loved in Washington.

But that quality is not much loved only in Washington, or by
politicians, or only by bad writers. *Supportive* is first cited in 1593,
and the user is our old friend of the "boystrous compounds,"
Thomas Nashe, who dedicated a book to a patron and "to the
supportive perpetuating of your canonized reputation. . . ."

Nashe could have written "to spread your fame"—but he
didn't. Because he didn't want to. He wanted to sound grandilo-
quent, polysyllabic, important, and fancy. And there was nobody
to tell him he couldn't do exactly as he pleased (nobody he would
listen to, anyway).

Is it possible that we owe much of the great literature of the
Elizabethan age to that sense of freedom and adventure in language, that delight in invention? And how can we get that delight,
and adventure, and freedom back?

To decimate means to reduce by a tenth.

To decimate did originally mean "to reduce by a tenth"; *noon*
originally meant "three o'clock in the afternoon." But it is perfectly obvious that if we keep *decimate* to its original and mathematically correct meaning, we'll all but exclude it from our
vocabularies. *Decimate* also has an extended meaning, however,
just like *culprit*—and the OED notes that it has been used to mean
"destroy a large part of" since 1663. Charlotte Brontë used the
word that way in 1828.

Newman thinks a president should not *enunciate* a doctrine,
apparently because he thinks *enunciate* means only "to speak
clearly." *Enunciate* has been used to mean "proclaim" since 1864.
Newman objects to *military posture. Posture* has been used to
mean "deployment" since the seventeenth century: "posture of
war" (1642); "ships in sailing posture" (1741).

Newman objects to *equivalency* (1535) and *perpetrators*
(1570). He thinks *capability* (used as a synonym for *ability*) comes
from "the world of business." But *capability* was used by both

Shakespeare and Bunyan without reference to business.

Newman thinks *remind* should be followed by an object, as in *remind us.* Kipling didn't think so:

> It will recall and remind and suggest and tantalise, and in the end drive you mad. (*The Light That Failed,* 1891, p. 249)

Newman apparently thinks *incumbent on me* is a pompous new locution; Bishop Berkeley used it in 1713. Newman thinks *success* means "a happy outcome," so no one should ever say *terrible success.* The OED says that *success* originally meant "that which happens in the sequel . . . (favorable or otherwise)," and says the original meaning is obsolete or archaic. But it lists the use well into the nineteenth century: Southey, *History of the Peninsular War,* I.470: "With so little accuracy do the French relate the circumstances of their ill success." An even later quote (1839) from America indicates that the archaic meaning, like many others, survived in America. Newman thinks we should never, when we are eager for something to happen, say that we are *anxious for it to happen.* That use dates from at least 1742: Robert Blair, *The Grave,* 94: "The gentle heart, anxious to please."

Super as an adjective seems a very bad word to Newman; but he fears the worst is yet to come: *real super.* In fact, worse than both has already been: *extra super* is the way the obsequious tailor describes the quality of cloth to David Copperfield (1850). The word has been in use as "trade colloquial" (i.e., standard in all but the most formal writing) since 1842, short for *superfine.* The extended meaning "of superlative or exceptional quality," as in "We have race meetings here, and super bathing" (*Daily Express,* 1932) is traced by the OED back to 1895. Surely in all that time, *super* has done all the damage it is ever going to do.

It seems pointless to go on: Newman's books are, on the basis of the most cursory kind of examination, a collection of primitive prejudices about language—presented with maximum intolerance and minimum understanding.

Strictly Speaking and *A Civil Tongue* were immensely successful precisely because the attitude of our society to language is just as intolerant, uninformed, prejudiced, and plain dumb.

three

John Simon

> With regard to the question what is to be considered correct and
> not correct in grammar I must repeat what I have said elsewhere
> that it is not, of course, my business to decide such questions for
> Englishmen; the only thing I have had to do is to observe English
> usage as objectively as I could. But psychological and historical
> studies often make one realize that much of what is generally
> considered "bad grammar" is due neither to sheer perversity or
> ignorance on the part of the speaker or writer, but is ultimately
> due to the imperfections of the language as such, i.e., as it has
> been handed down traditionally from generation to generation (or
> rather from older to younger children), or else in general
> tendencies common to all mankind—tendencies which in other
> cases have led to forms or usages which are recognized by
> everybody as perfectly normal and unobjectionable. This is why
> the profoundest students of languages are often more tolerant
> than those who judge everything according to rule-of-thumb logic
> or to the textbooks of grammar that were the fashion in their own
> school days.
>
> Otto Jespersen,
> "The System of Grammar"

John Simon, like Otto Jespersen, is not a native speaker of
English, and still has a trace of a foreign accent. Nothing wrong
with that—a European accent impresses lots of people, and makes
speech more interesting even to those of us who aren't impressed.

And Simon's *writing* is almost always impressive; he has a
superb talent for vituperation and insult, and uses it with a kind
of communicable glee: whether you agree with him or not, you
find yourself enjoying his pleasure in being cruel.

So it's worth pointing out in a book about correct English that
Simon writes with a trace of a foreign accent, too. In *Esquire*
(December 1977), he attacks Paul Owens, a man who dared to
disagree in print with Simon's language strictures:

> *I wonder, furthermore, whether Owens realizes the*
> *implications of a statement like "Except for 'hopefully,' a word I*
> *cheerfully misuse because I like the sound of it, I do not recall*
> *committing any of the four locutions that [Simon] finds definitive*
> *of gibberish." Here's a pretty kettle of fishiness! . . . Even Mr*
> *Owens' arithmetic is off: Once you confess to "hopefully," only*
> *three locutions are left for you to be innocent of.*

What an extraordinary idea that seems to those of us who grew up speaking English! Of course it *is* true—arithmetically—but it's just not the way we talk. Imagine somebody saying:

> Except for Hawaii, I do not recall that any of the forty-nine states is composed entirely of islands.

> Except for Judas, none of the eleven Apostles committed suicide.

Simon's mathematically correct misunderstanding of the way the phrase *except for* is used in English demonstrates that Jespersen's disclaimer printed at the beginning of this chapter was not mere false humility. It is difficult to learn idiom. No one would dream of recommending humility to Simon—he's too much fun without it—but he might study English a little more carefully before he makes certain pronouncements: "[The noun] *chair* sounds, at best, like a fossilized metaphor or metonymy not worth preserving; at worst, like a stick of furniture."

Simon is attacking the use of the word *chair* for *chairman,* a desexed term that is favored by many people who think that the sex of the person who presides over a meeting is as meaningless in that context as the sex of a person who writes a novel. We have *novelist,* a word for both men and women; it does seem that we could get along without the word *chairwoman* or *chairman* as easily as we get along without *noveler* and *noveless. Chair* seems a perfectly reasonable substitute to me—and I suspect that Simon would admire the metonymy (using one object to represent another—as *the crown* for *the king*), if he would only take the trouble to find out a little more about it. The word *chair* has been a metonymy for *chairman* since the seventeenth century. We all remember that it is the usual word for *chairman* in *The Pickwick Papers*—people cry *Chair! Chair!* at meetings because they want the person in the chair, regardless of the person's sex, to recognize them. *Chair* is not, as Simon says, an invention of sympathizers with equality for women; it is the way people talk at meetings. If all the feminists in America were converted tomorrow to docile

helpmeets and mindless little china dolls—horrible and intoler-
able as that would be—the word *chair* would still be used for a
person who chairs a meeting.

Simon is, however, worth more attention than many other
pop grammarians if only because he believes that change can be
stopped. This position has gone out of fashion with his fellows;
they content themselves with announcing that they are fighting
rear guard actions, doomed to failure, outnumbered by the unwashed, and reveling in the glory of the fray: lost causism at its
most elitist and romantic best, the kind of thing that used to be
popular in the movies about the Confederate volunteers, who
were all committed to making a great stand for the Old South. The
movies managed to concentrate on the last stand, and avoid the
fact that it was the last stand of human slavery.

All of which is beside the point, at least at present.

Simon's attitude is that we are now able to rely on nineteenth-century English, because a number of the great minds of
that century settled once and for all every possible question about
language. All we have to do is hold on to what is right:

> . . . *Ignorant, obfuscatory change, unnecessary change,
> producing linguistic leveling and flatness, could be stopped in its
> tracks by concerted effort. The fact that this has not* often
> *[emphasis added] happened in the past is no excuse for the
> present. We have acquired a set of fine, useful, previously
> unavailable tools, culminating in the Oxford English Dictionary
> and a number of excellent treatises and handbooks on grammar.
> While, that is, grammar was still concerned with form, not
> transformation; "transformational grammar," as the new trend
> calls itself, is indeed one of the aberrations of the academic
> bureaucracy. . . .*

It is ironic that Simon should insist that the OED is a weapon
against change. Lounsbury found the OED a weapon against pop
grammarians like Simon. Let's see who is right.

Simon says:

> *My point is that things have at last been sufficiently established—
> classified and codified—and there is neither need nor excuse for
> changes based on mere ignorance. Just because some people are
> too thickheaded to grasp, for example, that "anyone" is singular,
> as the "one" in it plainly denotes, does not mean that the rest of
> us must put up with "anyone can do as they please. . . ." We
> cannot and must not let "one" become plural. That way madness
> lies.*

The OED says of *their:* "Often used in relation to a singular substantive or pronoun denoting a person, after *each, every, either, neither, no one, every one,* etc. Also so used instead of *his* or *her,* when the gender is inclusive or uncertain." Also *they, them,* in the same way.

Among users cited, in a tradition that stretches back to the fourteenth century, are Fielding, Goldsmith, Thackeray, Walter Bagehot, Shaw, Chesterfield, Ruskin, and Richardson.

In no case does the OED call this usage an error (let alone madness). It does say the usage is "not favoured by grammarians." But it refers the reader to grammarian Otto Jespersen and his defense of the usage. Jespersen mentions that the usage can be found in Congreve, Defoe, Shelley, Austen, Scott, George Eliot, Stevenson, Zangwill, and Oliver Wendell Holmes, as well as Swift and Herbert Spencer.

Jespersen points out that if you try to put the sentence *Does anybody prevent you?* into another interrogative formula, beginning *Nobody prevents you,* then "you will perceive that *Nobody prevents you, does he?* is too definite, and you will therefore say (as Thackeray does, *The Story of Pendennis,* II, p. 260), *Nobody prevents you, do they?*"

All this does not matter to Simon—the OED only matters when it agrees with him:

> There are, however, standard excuses adduced by
> well-meaning and misguided liberals or ill-meaning and
> unguidable ignoramuses (some of whom consult and misinterpret
> the Oxford English Dictionary to bolster their benightedness).
> Foremost among them is, "But look at Shakespeare [or Dickens, or
> Hemingway, or any other famous writer] who wrote X instead of
> the supposedly correct Y. If it's good enough for Shakespeare [or
> whomever], why not for you and me?

Simon's answer is extraordinary.

> Well, Shakespeare wrote in an age when what we call modern
> English was still in its formative phase. His grammar was good
> enough for his era; it is not good enough for ours—any more than
> his politics, medicine, or Latin is. As for more recent writers of
> distinction, their forte was not necessarily grammar; or at any
> rate, they could occasionally slip up. . . .

We now begin to see what a useful tool the OED is for Simon: he can leaf through it, find whatever agrees with his own prejudices about language, and claim that he is defending the great nineteenth-century traditionalists. If Simon discovers a writer from the distant past who used *anyone* with *they,* as Shakespeare did, then Shakespeare's language is not good enough for us. If he discovers a modern writer who uses the same construction, then the OED is merely noting "a lapse": "Such lapses were duly noted and set down; sometimes with glee, sometimes dispassionately for the record. Yet merely because we cannot match the excellence of the great writers, we need not duplicate their errors."

It now becomes completely impossible to argue with Simon about grammar—everything he likes is right, everything he dislikes is wrong. *De gustibus non est disputandum:* reviewing language is just like reviewing theater.

Except—the OED did not proceed by noting down errors of famous writers. It proceeded to study the language by studying the actual usage throughout history. There are, in the opinion of the OED editors, grammatical errors, and they are clearly noted: when Thomas Hardy wrote "Who are you speaking of?" (*Far from the Madding Crowd,* p. 70), the OED called it "a grammatical error," and then changed its mind in 1923, when the *Oxford Shorter Dictionary* noted *"Whom* is no longer current in natural colloquial speech."

But the OED does not say that the use of *they* and *their* with singular antecedents is "a grammatical error." The OED does not even say that the use is "considered ungrammatical" (which is the OED's way of warning readers that though there is nothing wrong with a usage, there are lots of uninformed people—the OED does not, of course, use terms Simon is fond of, like ignoramus—who think otherwise).

The OED simply notes the usage as correct.

I add from *The Evolution of the English Language,* by George H. McKnight, still more evidence. McKnight notes that Richard Grant White, in *Every-Day English,* complains about the fact that the British often combine *them* and *their* and *they* with singular antecedents, and adds:

> *The kinds of "misuse" here condemned in American use, in British use are established not only by long tradition but by current practice. The awkward necessity so often met with in American speech of using the double pronoun "his or her," is obviated by the "misuse" of* their. . . .

McKnight then gives a long list of quotes illustrating this point: Jane Austen, Thomas De Quincey, Matthew Arnold, Cardinal Newman, James Stephens, Frank Swinnerton, Lord Dunsany, Samuel Butler in *The Way of All Flesh,* and A. E. (Jane Austen, *Mansfield Park*: "nobody put *themselves* out of the way"; James Stephens, *The Crock of Gold*: "everybody has to take *their* chance.")

I have spent a long time on this single construction, but I want to be very plain about this. If you go away from this book with none of your cherished opinions about good English changed, at least you must recognize that there is *no* justification for attacking the use of plural pronouns with singular antecedents when the sex is uncertain or mixed. For example, says Bergen Evans:

> *Only the word* his *would be used in* every soldier carried his own pack, *but most people would say* their *rather than* his *in* everybody brought their own lunch. *And it would be a violation of English idiom to say* was he? *in* nobody was killed, were they? *The use of* they *in speaking of a single individual is not a modern deviation from classical English. It is found in the works of many great writers including Malory. . . .*

And another list, all of which we have heard before.

Again, from the OED: "The pronoun referring to *every one* [sometimes written as one word] is often plural: the absence of a singular pronoun of common gender rendering this violation of grammatical concord sometimes *necessary* [my italics for *necessary*]."

To Simon, this necessity, this historically correct way of writing and speaking English, is *madness.* But he might as well say using the word *man* instead of *homme* is madness. Plural pronouns with singular antecedents are part of the language, an idiom, as indefensible—and as impossible to justify—as the meaning of words. If Simon prefers to use singular pronouns, and violate this idiom, he is welcome to, of course. Many Europeans who learned English as a second or third language do violate this idiom. We understand what he means. But if he doesn't *like* the idiom—well, nobody asked him to, did they?

Here are other examples of unidiomatic construction:

> *Miss Oates refers to a conversation "between" three people.*
> *Now I realize that in our sadly permissive dictionaries, "between"*

*is becoming acceptable as a synonym for "among." But do not buy
this, good people; the "tween" comes from the Anglo-Saxon "twa"
meaning two, and if we start meddling with such palpable
etymological sense (who cannot hear the "two" in "tween"?) we
become barbarous or trendy, even if we happen to be in the
dictionary business.*

Between is discussed at length on pages 43–47 (the *Harper
Dictionary* chapter), but the OED, that fine and useful tool, insists
that *between* has been "from its earliest appearance, extended to
more than two." And the OED further insists that *between* is the
only word you can use in certain situations where the relationship
is each to each to each: as in a conversation between three people.
You may remember, for example, an old-fashioned way of saying
something was a secret: "Let's just keep this between you, me, and
the fence post." Again, it is okay to violate this rule if you want
to—but criticizing Joyce Carol Oates because she follows it, and
calling the OED barbarous and trendy, is an overstatement which
tends to weaken your standing as an expert, at least a judicious
expert.

In 1977, Simon went to a meeting of the National Council of
Teachers of English, and had a wonderful time criticizing academic jargon: "What would Carlyle and Arnold (to pull two great
names out of a hat) have made of 'Developing Language Arts/
Communication Skills through Interarts Strategies' . . . in the
particular session I audited . . . ?"

Carlyle and Arnold would not, of course, have had an easy
time understanding the title of that session. Ironically, they
would not have had an easy time understanding John Simon
either: it is easy to tell what Carlyle and Arnold would have made
of the verb *audit,* because it is defined in the OED as "1. To make
an official and systematic examination of (accounts), so as to ascer-
tain their accuracy. 2. To examine, 'hear' (a pupil). rare. [one
example listed, in 1805]." And that's all. *Audit* in Simon's sense
—"sit in on a session and listen without participating"—is not
even listed in the OED Supplement (1972), indicating that it is at
the very least an Americanism and, almost certainly, a bit of
academic jargon as arcane as any Simon criticized.

It's kind of fun to think that Simon, if he's lucky, might
eventually be immortalized in the twenty-first-century supplement to the OED as the man who introduced this strange new use

John Simon

of an ancient word to print, and that some equally careless reader of the OED in the future will criticize "ignoramuses" like Simon who can't keep the meaning of simple words straight.

In the January–February issue of Harvard Magazine *... I find one Josh Rubins writing: "What* have *(emphasis Rubins')* surfaced are similes. . . ." *Now it is bad enough not to know that* "What *as subject takes the singular verb, whether the complementary noun be singular or plural" (Eric Partridge,* Usage & Abusage*) but ignorance italicized is considerably worse yet.*

Depends on what it's ignorance of. From the OED:

What are your views? (Austen, Sense and Sensibility, *147). What have often been censured as Shakespeare's conceits are completely justifiable (Coleridge,* Shakespeare Lectures, *90). What I want are details (Wilde,* Lord Arthur Saville's Crime, *20).*

From *A Dictionary of Contemporary American Usage* by Bergen and Cornelia Evans:

The pronoun "what" may be followed by either a singular or a plural verb as in "what appears to be the important points" or "what appear to be the important points."

Maybe Rubins is ignorant of Partridge, but familiar with English literature—and a different grammar book. Taking Partridge at his unsupported word is no worse than taking the Evanses at their unsupported word, of course; but when experts disagree, the rest of us should be allowed to choose what sounds best to us.

I really can't think that Simon, or Partridge, would want that sentence by Coleridge to read:

What has often been censured as Shakespeare's conceits is completely justifiable.

Finally, Simon, who insists that Shakespeare's grammar is not good enough for us, insists that we should all work ceaselessly to prevent "little horrors" from being embedded in the language:

Instead of embedding, let's start uprooting. Wouldn't it be nice if half a millennium from now, people could read today's writers without elaborate footnotes and glossaries such as we require to read Shakespeare?

First, it would not only be nice—it would be amazing.

Second, if Simon is successful in uprooting the word *chair* for "person who chairs a meeting," people will need a glossary to read Dickens—and *Ms.* magazine. If he drives out the ordinary use of *they* with *anyone* and *everyone,* every reader of Shaw and Wilde will have to have help (that way glossaries lie). If he uproots the normal use of *except for,* he will have so changed the way we think in our language that future generations may even need special instruction to understand our mathematics.

And third, our grammar and our politics and medicine have about as much chance of being good enough for the twenty-sixth century as Shakespeare's grammar and politics and medicine had of being good enough for ours.

I repeat that however much I disagree with him, I like to read John Simon. His command of the language, especially for a non-native, is almost unparalleled: the written language, that is.

It's when Simon comes up against an idiom (like "What are your views?") that he feels he has to go to a grammar book for justification, and the justification can only be as good as the book itself. Sometimes, in the case of Partridge, it is just plain mistaken.

It's difficult to talk this way without sounding like a jingoist of the worst kind, but it is a fact that people who learn the language as natives speak it in a different way than people who learn it as students. So—I hope this won't be misunderstood—when Simon begins preaching against the way we talk in English, it would probably be a service to him, and to the integrity of English, if someone would tell him: "Look, Mr. Simon, you're really, like, a good writer, you know? But you're having this trouble understanding when people, like, talk. So, look, why not go back to, like, Berlitz? Or wherever you learned how to write so good? And take a conversational course this time. And get your head straight."

four

Harper Dictionary of Contemporary Usage

Language experts, as this book has constantly pointed out, are different than any other kind of experts. Other experts have to know something about the subject, and language experts only have to know how to write effectively within the confines of standard journalism.

There's no question that this kind of writing is a skill. But asking writers, no matter how skilled, their opinion about word usage is like asking painters their opinion of which colors they prefer on a palette. If you asked Franz Kline (who did lots of paintings in nothing but black and white) and Yves Klein (who painted mostly in a dark rich blue), you'd get different answers. And from Picasso you'd have got a lot of different answers, depending on whether you asked during his rose or blue periods, or when he was painting all those brown cubist paintings.

The different answers would make a fascinating and revealing book about painters. But no one would suggest that it was a reference work where a student could look up, for example, how to paint a guitar.

The *Harper Dictionary of Contemporary Usage* (1975) was produced by William Morris (editor of the *American Heritage Dictionary*) and his wife Mary Morris (coauthor with William of *Dictionary of Word & Phrase Origins* [1977])—with the cooperation of 136 experts "chosen for their demonstrated ability to use the language carefully and effectively."

The Morrises, to start out with, have a little trouble with getting facts straight. They say that the idea for the *Harper Dictionary* was "first suggested to your editors by a monograph of the National Council of Teachers of English—*Facts About Current*

English Usage by Albert H. Marckwardt and Fred G. Walcott
... published in 1938. The authors submitted questions to a group
of judges including linguistic specialists, editors, authors, businessmen and teachers of English and of speech. . . ."

Now that is exactly what Marckwardt and Walcott did *not* do.
Facts About Current English Usage is a monograph that attempts
to complete the work of Sterling A. Leonard, whose monograph,
Current English Usage, was published in 1932. It was Leonard
who submitted questions to a group of judges—and Leonard asked
his judges to "score according to observation of what is actual
usage rather than your opinion of what usage should be."

Marckwardt and Walcott submitted questions to no one; they
took Leonard's results and consulted the literature of the language to find historical precedents for the usages that Leonard
questioned. Their book is, as they point out, a sort of second half
of the Leonard study, one that Leonard himself was almost certainly planning.

But there's a difficulty in taking the Morrises at face value
because of this mistake. Minor as it is, the mistake seems to
demonstrate that they have not even read the book that "first
suggested" the idea. And the Leonard survey is so famous, in
linguistic circles, that the equivalent would be a book on Christian
theology which talked about John Christ and Jesus the Baptist.
It's best to get facts straight, especially basic facts.

There is another problem with the method followed in the
Harper Dictionary. Leonard asked for opinions about current
usage; the Morrises ask panelists for their opinion about whether
the usage is acceptable to them. Many panelists seem to come to
the conclusion that the more usage you rejected, the better your
contribution. Panelists were asked, for example, if they made a
distinction between *admittance* (as in "admittance to a theater")
and *admission* (as in "admission of guilt"). Shana Alexander (one
of the panelists) replied: " 'No, but I will from now on. One function of these ballots is to spruce up the language of your panelists.' "

In *A Dictionary of Contemporary American Usage,* Bergen
and Cornelia Evans answer the question somewhat differently:
"Much ink has been expended to prove that *admittance* refers to
physical entrance and *admission* to entrance into rights and
privileges, but with the exception of the sign NO ADMITTANCE,

admittance is rarely seen or heard. *Admission* serves in all cases."

The answer the Evanses give is a perfect example of the kind that Leonard wanted from his panel. Shana Alexander's is a perfect example of the kind that the Morrises encourage.

In the introduction the Morrises say that the main purpose of the *Harper Dictionary* is to call attention to inaccuracies and correct them, and the secondary purpose is "to show by discussion and example the standards of linguistic usage adhered to by those who use the language well."

And, of course, one of the first things that the Morrises discovered is that there is almost nothing the panelists were unanimous about—people who use language well disagree about how to use the language, which would seem to indicate that, just as there is no one way to paint a guitar, there is no one list of word peeves that will make you a good writer.

But this doesn't seem to bother the Morrises. They print a whole series of burning questions about language, for example:

> *Aggravate originally simply meant to make worse as "The fever aggravated his already weakened condition." It is also widely used in the sense of "to exasperate" or "to vex" as "The loudness of the music aggravated him." Do you accept this second usage?*

Then they print a summary of expert opinion in percentages:

> *In writing Yes 43%; no 57%*
> *In speech Yes 53%; no 47%*

And finally the Morrises print a shorter or longer list of quotes from the panel of experts, justifying their opinion; sometimes, if they accept a word, almost apologizing for it. Here are two quotes from panelists on *aggravate:*

> **Elizabeth Janeway:** *"I don't like it but I think it's too late to stop it."*
> **Lionel Trilling:** *"No, but 'exasperate' once meant what 'aggravate' (in its correct meaning) now means. See OED."*

I did see OED—which is always instructive.

It turns out that the original meaning of *aggravate* (1530) was not "to make worse," but "to make heavy; to load, burden, weigh down." That meaning is now obsolete; it disappeared sometime in the seventeenth century. The Morrises meaning "to make worse" didn't come along until 1597; that may mean that the two meanings were in simultaneous use, but by ignoring the one that was recorded earliest the Morrises, in effect, slant the question.

It's one thing to say that the original meaning of the word is being replaced by a new meaning, and an entirely different thing to say that the earliest use of the word is obsolete—and asking the panel to decide between "make worse" and "exasperate," two meanings that are both, in pop grammarian terms, "corruptions" to begin with.

At any rate, Elizabeth Janeway is right about *aggravate*—it is too late to stop people from using it to mean "exasperate, or provoke," because they've been doing it since 1611 (Cotgrave: *"Aggravanter,* to aggravate, exasperate"). Among writers who have used *aggravate* to mean "exasperate" are Richardson, Thackeray, and Dickens, which should be enough to make the word respectable in any company.

That is, unless the company is a panel of experts who base their opinions on "what sounds good to them." That is, on blind, and sometimes ignorant, prejudice. Lionel Trilling is quoted above because he seems to be an exception: asked about the acceptability of a word he went to the OED to find out about history and etymology. Of course, he looked up *exasperate* when he should have looked up *aggravate,* but at least he made some kind of effort. It is one of the very few efforts by any of the experts to discover anything about any word at all.

The *Harper Dictionary of Contemporary Usage* turns out at times not to be contemporary at all; writers, apparently, do not read much contemporary prose, and refuse to recognize it when they see it in print:

> *In a recent* Newsweek *article, Bob Greene . . . wrote . . . : "We are so cool and so hard and so hip any more. . . ." Anymore [is used in] a new sense, synonymous with "nowadays" or "at this time." Though seldom seen in print, this usage is heard with increasing frequency, especially in the speech of young people. Do you approve?*
> *In speech Yes 9%; no 91%*
> *In writing Yes 4%; no 96%*

Many panelists refused to believe that the expression really exists. But it does. It was first reported in an 1898 *English Dialect*

Dictionary. And it was used in 1920 by D. H. Lawrence: " 'Quite absurd,' he said. 'Suffering bores me any more.' " (*Women in Love,* xiii, p. 159).

Among experts who have not come across the expression are: Isaac Asimov, Stewart Beach, Heywood Hale Broun (" 'I don't much approve the speech of young people,' " says Broun, though Lawrence is his senior by many years), Anthony Burgess, John Ciardi (" 'Barbaric patois!' "), Willard R. Espy, Paul Horgan (" 'Sounds like unsure immigrant speech.' "), Helen Kaufman, Dwight Macdonald (" 'Never heard this—thought it was a typo.' "), Orville Prescott (" 'Illiterate and without meaning.' "), David Schoenbrun, Mark Schorer, and Robert Sherrill.

If none of those experts have read *Women in Love* they should go and do it right now. And think about it.

If they have read *Women in Love,* and did not notice that use of *any more,* they should admit that the use does not bother them. That is, unless they are set up to be bothered by a question which tells them *any more* is part of the vocabulary of "young people." And they should think about that, too.

One of the words that most of the experts agree on—because none of them know anything about its history—is *between.* There are so many "inaccuracies" in the use of *between* that the Morrises list each problem separately:

> *The phrase "between you and I" is often heard, even from*
> *otherwise literate speakers. Do you accept this in casual speech?*
> *In speech Yes 3%; no 97%*
> *In writing Yes 2%; no 98%*

The Morrises are slanting the question again—calling the speakers who use *between you and I* "otherwise literate." But they probably didn't need to slant the question. Experts outdid themselves in objecting—lots of exclamation points and bold-faced caps:

W. H. Auden: *"Horrible!"*
Heywood Hale Broun: *"WHY!" [caps original]*
Anthony Burgess: *". . . Only when 'Give it to I' is also used."*
Paul Horgan: *"Never heard a literate person use it."*
David McCord: *"Flying catfish: NO!!!" [caps and repeated exclamation points original]*
Harrison Salisbury: *"No, no, no!"*

Harold Schonberg: *"No!!!" [repeated exclamation points original]*
Red Smith: *"A thousand times no!"*
Elvis Stahr, Jr.: *"This one, above all, chills me. It signifies an effort to be elegant by one obviously ignorant."*
Herman Wouk: *"Horrors!"*

But *between you and I* is not illiterate, nor an effort to be elegant by the ignorant. It is an idiom. In Early Middle English, says Henry Sweet (*New English Grammar,* Part I, p. 340): "You and I were so frequently joined as nominatives—you and I will go together, etc.—that the three words formed a sort of group-compound, whose last element became invariable."

Shakespeare uses that idiomatic *between you and I (Merchant of Venice,* III.ii.321): "All debts are cleerd betweene you and I."

The OED notes that use of the nominative after a verb or preposition, especially when the pronoun is separated from the governing word by other words, was "very frequent in end of 16th and in 17th c[enturies], but is now *considered* [my emphasis] ungrammatical."

Shakespeare, *As You Like It,* I. ii. 18: "My father hath no childe but I." Shakespeare, *Sonnets,* LXXII: "And hang more praise upon deceased I." Ben Jonson, *Every Man in His Humor,* V. iii: "Brayne-worme ha's been with my cossen Edward and I, all this day." Hughes, *Tom Brown's School Days* (1857): "Let you and I cry quits."

So Anthony Burgess is wrong; the idiom has nothing to do with "Give it to I": it's "Give it to Anthony Burgess and I."

And it's a lesson to all of us, I hope, in favor of tolerance to see W. H. Auden, a great poet then in the twilight of his years, so misled by that phrase "otherwise literate" that he forgot one of the most famous examples of the use of the nominative pronoun in an accusative sense: the famous opening lines of "The Love Song of J. Alfred Prufrock."

Let *us* go then, you and *I,*
When the evening is spread out against the sky
Like a patient etherised upon a table . . .

The OED spends considerable time on the word *between,* trying to point out, in its very prescriptive way, that *between* cannot be restricted to only two things:

> *In all senses,* between *has been, from its earliest appearance,*
> *extended to more than two. . . . It is still the only word available*
> *to express the relation of a thing to many surrounding things*
> *severally and individually,* among *expressing a relation to them*
> *collectively and vaguely: we should not say "the space lying*
> *among the three points," or "a treaty among three powers," or*
> *"the choice lies among the three candidates . . . ," or "to insert a*
> *needle among the closed petals of a flower."*

Among examples of correct usage, the OED gives:

> There were six, who collected between them 15 s. 4d. (*Notes and*
> *Queries,* Ser. VI, xii, 141)

It is not necessary that you agree with the OED about *between.* It's important to recognize, however, that the OED is not
using words like "considered incorrect" or "widely regarded as
ungrammatical." The OED is plainly and simply laying down the
law. And it is just the kind of complicated law, full of nuance and
subtlety, that you would expect conservative language experts to
defend. But the panelists for the *Harper Dictionary of Contemporary Usage* are not conservatives—they can't defend the past because they don't know anything about the past.

The panelists reject: "Pressed for ransom, the three parents
could raise only $5,000 between them."

22% agree (almost certainly without knowing it) with the
OED; 78% insist on *among.*

The panelists reject "negotiations between members of the
European Common Market."

Yes 28%; no 72% (" 'Let's preserve the distinctions we have
and change language only to make it stronger,' " pleads Peter S.
Prescott, voting to abolish this ancient distinction insisted on by
the OED).

As a special bonus the Morrises include the following sentence:

> In the new subdivision there was a driveway between every house.

Bergen and Cornelia Evans, in *A Dictionary of Contemporary
American Usage,* say:

> Between . . . *may be followed by* each *or* every *with a singular*
> *noun, as in* between each house . . . *where the meaning is:*
> *"between each one and the adjoining." Some grammarians object*

to this, but the construction is used by many great writers, including Shakespeare, Pope, Fielding, Goldsmith, Scott, Eliot, Dickens, and is acceptable to most educated people today.

Most educated people do not get on the *Harper Dictionary* panel of experts, however, and 68% of the panel rejected the idiom. Many pretended—for fun—to believe that they thought the sentence meant there must be a driveway right down the middle of every house in the subdivision (Isaac Asimov, Stewart Beach, Hal Borland). But other experts were even funnier. They tried to rewrite the sentence:

John Brooks: *"It would have been OK if it had been 'between each of the houses.'"*
Heywood Hale Broun: *"There's something awry about this—but 'among' is worse."*
Abe Burrows: *"They might try 'a driveway between every two houses.'"*
Walter Cronkite: *"Certainly not 'among' every house, but this whole construction is awkward."*
Alex Faulkner: *"Shouldn't it be 'between each of the houses'?"*
John Hutchens: *"No. Between every two houses?"*
Helen Kaufman: *"No. I suggest 'between every house and its neighbor.'"*
Phyllis McGinley: *"Actually the whole sentence should be recast. It doesn't make much sense with 'among' either."*
Berton Roueché: *"A driveway 'among' every house? My god!"*
Vermont Royster: *"Better: between each house."*
Jean Stafford: *"The only way in which this sentence could be correctly written, I think, is 'There is a driveway between each two houses.'* [You can almost see Stafford look at that sentence after she'd written it, and realize that it means something entirely different. Because after giving us "the only way," she adds another.] *Or 'every two houses.'"*

But Abe Burrows has the best afterthought: " 'Or they could tear down the subdivision.' "

And this is what they'd have to do—if they used this particular dictionary of contemporary usage to write their real estate ads. Here are a few examples of this ordinary idiom:

Between each five paces he looked at an official telegram. (Kipling,
    The Day's Work, *p. 310)*
. . . A row of flower-pots were ranged, with wide intervals between each pot. (Wilkie Collins, The Woman in White, *p. 319)*
She counted the sheets in the linen cupboard, putting a bag of

lavender between each (two). (V. Sackville-West, The Edwardians,
p. 50)
*A certain halting of the breath which made him pause between
almost every word like a drunken man bent on speaking plainly.
(Dickens,* Nicholas Nickleby, *p. 695)*

Asked if they would restrict the word *fulsome* to its "generally accepted meaning" of "disgusting or offensive to good taste,"
69% of the panelists said yes. The question was not entirely fair,
since it was posed by panelist Wright Morris, who does not understand current usage of the word: *"Fulsome* is currently and
chronically assumed to mean flattering—a fulsome talent is one
that is ripe or flowering."

Actually, as Bergen Evans points out in *Comfortable Words,*
the current meaning of *fulsome* is merely "full or copious," with
no implied condemnation. Anyway, here are the objections:

Isaac Asimov: *"One of my favorite criteria of illiteracy!"*
Stewart Beach: *". . . Let's not fiddle with the meaning of
fulsome."*
S. I. Hayakawa: *"Horrors!"*
Orville Prescott: *"Vile."*
Red Smith: *"Let's cling to old established meanings. This 'new'
meaning is the fruit of ignorance."*

Oddly enough, it is the older meaning, "disgusting or offensive to good taste" that is the fruit of ignorance. *Fulsome* is
formed from the words *full* and *some,* and originally had no bad
connotations at all. But, probably because the first syllable was
ignorantly associated with the word *foul*—because both *foul* and
the first syllable of *fulsome* were once pronounced alike—*fulsome*
began to pick up other meanings.

The meaning of "simple abundance" lasted from the first
appearance of the word (c. 1250) till Elizabethan times (last OED
citation is 1583). In the meantime, the word picked up and lost
other meanings: "fat, overgrown" (1340–1678); "overfed" (1642–
1805); "gross and satiating" (1410–1770); "wearisome from excess
or repetition" (1531–1709); "offensive to the sense of smell" (1583–
1725); "morally foul, obscene" (1604–1726); and finally, "gross or excessive, offensive to good taste like flattery" (1663 to the present).

What a spectacular career! What a wonderful word! It should
please all our many purists that after 700 years of wayward use,
and compulsive fiddling, *fulsome* is finally returning to its origi-

nal and etymologically correct meaning, that is, if our purists knew anything about language history or etymology. Instead, they find the correct usage a "favorite criteri[on] of illiteracy," "the fruit of ignorance."

> We usually think of "gift" as a noun, though it has long been recorded in lexicons as a verb. OED records "gift" in the sense of "make a present of" as early as 1619, though noting that it is "chiefly Scottish." In recent years this sense has enjoyed something of a vogue, starting with gossip columnists ("So-and-so gifted her with a twenty-carat diamond.") and has appeared widely in advertising. . . . Do you find this use of "gift" acceptable?

Once more the Morrises, of course, are loading the question: to say *gift* as a verb is chiefly Scottish is somehow to imply that it is less than standard English. And saying that it is found in gossip columns and advertising is really nothing but waving a red flag to madden conservative experts. 95% disapprove of using *gift* as a verb.

Even worse, the Morrises are hopelessly confused about the verb. The chiefly Scottish use of the verb *gift* is constructed with the preposition *to:*

> The Regent Murray gifted all the Church Property to Lord Sempill. (J. C. Lees, Abbey of Paisley, xix, p. 201)

Gift has been a standard verb in English, meaning "to endow or furnish with gifts, chiefly a faculty or power," since the sixteenth century. Here are some examples of the verb constructed with *with:*

> Nothing but the inspiration with which we writers are gifted can possibly enable anyone to make the discovery. (Fielding, Tom Jones, I, v.) The world must love and fear him/Whom I gift with heart and mind. (Elizabeth Barrett Browning, "Swan's Nest")

And of course we are all familiar with the use of the past participle of the verb *gift* as a modifier: "a gifted writer," "a gifted painter." But of course the panel has never considered that *gifted* is a participle, and imagine they have never come across the verb *gift* in normal use:

Irving Kolodin: *"No! No! No!"*
Barry Bingham, Sr: *"Vulgar advertising jargon. NO, NO, NO."*

Harrison Salisbury: *"This is one of the most despicable column-isms. Probably a Winchellism."*

Judith Viorst: *"Horrible!"*

Herman Wouk: *"It disgusts me, and I'm sorry there's an accidental justification in the OED."*

It's worth stopping a minute to consider Wouk's sorrow.

"Wouk's sorrow" is a common complaint among self-appointed guardians of the language. If they don't like a word, they say it is disgusting. Prove that it is an old word, in use for centuries, and recognized by the most conservative dictionaries—and the guardians are filled with sorrow that the history of the language should have taken so little account of their sensibilities. Implicit in "Wouk's sorrow" is the idea that if only Wouk had been around in the past, these disgusting imperfections would have been driven from our native tongue. Slang would die, change would cease, and all invention could go to sleep.

You can induce "Wouk's sorrow" in any of your purist friends by explaining to them what the word *fulsome* really means, if you go back to its roots. Try it and see.

Finalize has figured prominently in the vocabularies of at least two Presidents—Eisenhower and Kennedy. Would you approve "The committee met to finalize plans for the dinner?"
In writing Yes 14%; no 86%
In casual speech Yes 26%; no 74%

Here the Morrises go out of their way to ask the question fairly. Including Kennedy, who is considered an intellectual by many intellectuals, probably helped the cause. All of us associate the word—and not only the word, but the struggle against it—with Dwight Eisenhower.

And, to be fair, Eisenhower has never been considered a particularly intellectual president. In the later stages of his presidency, Ike was afflicted with vocal aphasia, which made him sound even worse than he was. I worked for a newsreel company during the Eisenhower administration, and reporters always tried to ask Ike questions so that the answer would include the word *organization*. Because Eisenhower couldn't say *organization* any more; and every time he tried, he said *orgasm* instead.

Ike could say *finalize,* however, and did—and many people objected to the word for that reason alone.

Isaac Asimov: *"I associate the phrase with administrative gobbledegook, for which I have a hatred. I am far more tolerant of the mistakes of honest ignorance than those of false gentility— and I firmly believe God is, too."*

But *finalize* is not an Eisenhowerism.

Finalize is not even an Americanism.

Finalize first appeared, according to the OED Supplement, in Australia in the 1920s. By 1926, Australians were conscious that there was something new and different in their use of the word: in *Timely Tips for New Australians,* J. Doone wrote:

> The established usage of the word *"finalise"* (to complete) is . . .
> illustrative of the Australian variations of the English language.
> . . . To *"finalise a deal"* is an expression in daily use throughout
> the island-continent.

By 1927, *finalize* had been adopted by the U.S. Navy. In 1945, it reached the West Indies. In 1952, Eisenhower was elected president. And in 1953, the OED records the first complaint:

> When I hear of . . . things being adumbrated, or visualized, or
> finalized . . . I think of that other aim of this [English]
> Association, *"To uphold the standards of English writing and
> speech."* (N. Birkett, The Magic of Words, p. 8)

But that was almost certainly because Birkett, like Asimov, was ignorant of the origins of the word. *Finalize* isn't "administrative gobbledegook." And it is just as regularly formed as *familiarize, brutalize, humanize.* (See pp. 23–24 for more on *-ize* words.) Finally, *finalize* is a product not only of honest experimentation with words, but of that cheery self-reliant barf-in-the-sink vulgarity we all associate with Australians. So the word must now be acceptable—even to Birkett, and Asimov, and God.

> Many stylebooks used to decree that *"over"* should not be used in
> the sense of more than but was to be restricted to use as an
> indication of physical position (a sign *"over"* the door, but not
> priced at *"over"* ten dollars). Do you make this distinction?
> In writing Yes 63%; no 37%

A. B. Whipple: *"This is one still worth preserving."*
Ernest Gann: *"We must have some dignity in the English word."*
Leonard Sanders: *"I have edited copy to conform to the stylebooks cited."*

Hal Borland: *"This use of 'over' is now common and accepted; but I am a stickler."*

But an ignorant stickler. From about 1330, *over* in the sense of "more than" has been standard usage in our language:

> *To a castel . . . thennes over thre miles.* (Arthur and Merlin, anon., line 6648 [c. 1330])
> *His diploma cost him a little over fifty pounds. (Matthew Arnold,* Schools and Universities on the Continent, *p. 50)*

Leonard Sanders is an editor; A. B. Whipple is Assistant Managing Editor of Time-Life Books. It is funny (and a little sad) that they can discard six centuries of linguistic history with the illusion that they are preserving something—and even funnier and sadder that Whipple, a major book publisher, has the power to make other writers conform to his illusion.

> *Panelist Laurence Lafore writes: "I would like to have you ask the panel about 'partially.' It seems to me inelegant jargon. 'Partly' means the same thing and sounds better. 'Partially' is an example of a foolish impulse to add superfluous syllables in the manner of 'administrate' and 'orientate.' "*

The panel mostly agrees with Lafore (62% in speech, 71% in writing).

Richard Edes Harrison: *" 'Partially' is considered obsolete but it has elegant antecedents."*

Russell Lynes: *"I would no more use 'partially' in that sense (i.e., partially completed) than I would use 'impartly' for 'impartially.' "*

Both Harrison and Lynes are wrong.

Partially is not considered obsolete by any current dictionary that I have come across.

Lynes thinks that the only meaning of *partially* is "in a partial manner." That is a meaning, but only one meaning; the OED says it is "now rare."

Partially is from the French *(partiellement)* and has been recorded since 1460. It has been used, in the way that Russell Lynes would never use it, by Sir Thomas Browne and Swinburne.

Partly is a much older word, from the Latin *(pars,* meaning "part"). The OED says that *partly* is "usually repeated in reference to each of the parts considered," because it is used to indicate that an object has actually or can actually be divided into parts:

> This book is partly prose and partly poetry.

Partially is used when the sense is "incompletely":

> The kick was partially blocked.

Two panelists, Walter Lord and Abe Burrows, remembered hearing football announcers using the words *partially blocked.* Lord therefore voted to keep the word *partially.* Burrows, for the same reason, voted to abolish it.

No one is required to follow the OED (or football announcers) guidelines, and change the way they talk or write to conform to this very minor distinction. But a dictionary of contemporary usage ought to try to stop the spread of foolish ideas about the meaning of words. No book should let a contributor accuse Swinburne of "inelegant jargon." A little inelegance now and then by Swinburne would make him a lot easier to read today.

> *Sheridan Baker reports an upsurge in the use of* near-perfect *for "nearly perfect." Would you accept: "The program included a* near-perfect *performance . . . ?"*
> *Yes 52%; no 48%*

Comments with "no" votes:

Hal Borland: *"Sloppy journalese."*
Leon Edel: *"Used, but careless journalese."*
Berton Roueché: *"What's wrong with 'almost'?"*

Nothing wrong with *almost,* but the use of *near* to indicate "close upon, almost at (a state or condition)" is a very old one. It was first recorded in 1635; Horace Walpole, not usually considered a sloppy or careless writer, used it in 1780.

> *On every highway in America one sees signs reading "Go* Slow" *or simply "Slow." However, some people are of the opinion that they should read "Go* Slowly." *Do you agree?*
> *Yes 18%; no 82%*
> *In the following sentence would you use* slow *or* slowly? *"When you reach the dirt road you will have to go* slow/slowly *if you don't want to break an axle."*
> *Slow 37%; Slowly 63%*

Some panelists, to their credit, recognized that *slow* is not only an adjective but also an adverb: Abe Burrows, Willard R. Espy, Vermont Royster, and Harold Schonberg—and also Edwin Newman: "I use 'slow' as I use 'fast'—I would not say 'go fastly.' "

Others invent reasons for preferring *slowly,* at least in their own writing:

Anthony Burgess: *"U.S. English . . . (undoubtedly via Yiddish) . . ."*

Orville Prescott: *"I would use 'slowly' because I am an eccentric conservative in usage."*

David Schonberg: *"Bit of purism here, but what's wrong with being pure, if it is simple and graceful. . . ."*

Charles Silberman: *"I have higher standards for myself than I do for road signs."*

Some writers who do not share Silberman's standards:

But oh, methinks, how slow This old Moon wanes. (Shakespeare,
    Midsummer Night's Dream, *I. i. 3)*
I hear the far-off Curfeu sound, . . . Swinging slow with sullen
    roar. (Milton, "Il Penseroso," 76)
We drove very slow for the last two stages on the road.
    (Thackeray, Vanity Fair, *viii)*

Slow for *slowly* is not "U.S. English," as Burgess says—and of course has nothing to do with Yiddish.

Host *as a transitive verb is relatively new—the creation, perhaps, of radio and TV. However, it has moved into general use. . . . "Miami may, after all,* host *the Republican Convention." Do you approve of this use of* host?
In speech Yes 30%; no 70%
In writing Yes 29%; no 71%

The OED traces *host* as a transitive verb "to receive (any one) into one's house and entertain as a guest" back to 1485, and calls it obsolete in the 1890s. The supplement says "delete obsolete." The first new use the OED traces to 1939—a critical article about W. H. Auden, long before TV got a chance to create words. Isaac Asimov is one of the minority who defend *host* as a "useful new use, inoffensive to my ears." But it is not really that new to Asimov:

Those comments applying to him were read at the celebration dinner hosted (invariably) by Anson himself. (Isaac Asimov, *Whiff of Death,* vi, p. 55 [1958])

Back to the Morrises:

A word much in vogue recently is meaningful, *in such expressions as "a* meaningful *relationship. . . ." Do you use* meaningful *in speech?*
Yes 37%; no 63%
In writing Yes 30%; no 70%

Leo Rosten: *"This is student cant of the 1960s. Baloney."*

And baloney to you, too, Leo Rosten: the OED notes the first use of *meaningful* in 1852 (a very long vogue, if this is a vogue word). The supplement includes among users: *The London Times Education Supplement* (1922); M. V. Quine, *Mathematical Logic* (1940); *The Saturday Review* (1971). Not a sixties' student among them.

Masterful *is usually defined to mean "domineering, imperious."*
Masterly *means "possessing the knowledge or skill of a master." Some reference books indicate that the two words may now be used interchangeably. Do you agree?*

Well, who would ever imagine that a group of language experts would agree that two words—any two words—could be used interchangeably?

Yes 33%; no 67%

Peter Prescott: *"More needless destruction of the language by those who are too lazy to perceive needed differences."*
Berton Roueché: *"This is exactly the sort of shoddiness that erodes a language."*
Harold Schonberg: *"No. And yet I find myself doing it. 'Horowitz gave a* masterful *recital.' I should say* masterly."

The OED says of this use of *masterful:* "Characterized by the skill that constitutes a master; masterly. Now [1890s] only in somewhat rhetorical use, with mixture of sense . . . : Characterized by commanding power."

Variety . . . erects and rouses an auditory, like the masterful *running over many chords and divisions. (Milton,* Animadversions, *II, p. 62) Whether pleasing or displeasing to your taste they are entirely* masterful. *(Ruskin,* The Art of England, *ii, 65)*

The first use of *masterful* in this extended sense was recorded in 1613; long enough ago for any erosion of the language to be beyond our control, and Berton Roueché's too.

> *Thanks to the wide circulation of sex guides incorporating the*
> *word* sensuous *in their titles, the distinction between* sensual
> *(pertaining to the gratification of physical appetites, especially*
> *those of a sexual nature) and* sensuous *(pertaining to the senses,*
> *especially those involved in the appreciation of art, music and*
> *poetry) seems to have been lost, at least temporarily. Do you*
> *regard the distinction between* sensual *and* sensuous *as worth*
> *retaining?*

Yes 82%; no 18%

Sensuous is an interesting word. The OED says it was apparently invented by Milton, because he wanted to avoid the sexual
connotations of the word *sensual* (1641).

The OED cannot find any evidence of the use of the word by
any other writer for 173 years, not until Coleridge:

> *Thus, to express in one word what belongs to the senses, or the*
> *recipient and more passive faculty of the soul, I have reintroduced*
> *the word* sensuous, *used, among many others of our elder writers,*
> *by Milton. (Coleridge, "Principles of General Criticism," in*
> Farley's Bristol Journal, *August 1814)*

Coleridge put the word into ordinary circulation—and almost immediately it began to pick up those old sexual connotations that Milton and Coleridge wanted to avoid. The OED
says:

> *Now often with some notion of self-indulgent yielding to*
> *impressions or of a tendency to the sensual in imagination. . . .*
> *His mouth was cruel and sensuous. (H. Rider Haggard,* Heart of
> the World, *vii, p. 100)*

Whether you like these "new" connotations or not is beside
the point: *Heart of the World* is not a sex guide, and not a recent
book. Once again, the Morrises either pose the question unfairly
—or ignorantly.

Among the small minority (18%), the Morrises got one entirely sensible comment on the distinction between *sensual* and
sensuous:

Norman Hoss: *"It is gone. Who am I to say whether or not it's*
good or bad?"

Norman Hoss was the managing editor of the *American Heri-*
tage Dictionary. Maybe, instead of trusting the Morrises (though
William Morris, as editor-in-chief of the same dictionary, was his
boss), Norman Hoss decided to look the word up.

This is one of the very few times Hoss is quoted in the *Harper Dictionary of Contemporary Usage,* perhaps because, as the quote shows, he calls the whole idea of a dictatorial language expert into question. Who is he—who is anybody—to say whether our language is good or bad?

> Precipitate *[the adjective, not the noun or verb] is defined as "acting hastily, rashly, or impulsively."* Precipitous *is defined as "extremely steep." Yet an expression often heard is "He beat a* precipitous *retreat." Would you use* precipitous *in this context? In speech Yes 12%; no 88% In writing Yes 7%; no 93%*

> A . . . *number of panelists who felt the distinction should be maintained, offer facetious exceptions, including, "Only if he climbed a cliff to get away," . . . Davidson Taylor commented: "This vulgar confusion of time and space annoys me sorely."*

First of all, it is not hard to see why the adjective *precipitate* is disappearing. To anyone who has had a high-school chemistry class, *precipitate* is a noun or a verb, and it means "little flecks" or "form little flecks in liquid." I forget exactly, but it is something that happens if you keep adding salt to a glass of water, right?

But more important, according to the OED, the confusion of time and space is an old one—and it is Davidson Taylor who is voting to continue the confusion.

The problem is that there are two words, both in Latin, that mean different things, and sound almost the same in English.

Precipitous, says the OED, comes from Late Latin *praeceps, praecipit-em,* meaning "headlong." The OED says that the meaning "Rushing headlong onwards; violently hurried or hurrying" is "rare." But it lists among users:

> A course precipitous, of dizzy speed, Suspending thought and breath. (Shelley, The Revolt of Islam, *I. viii) Precipitous, with his reeling Satyr rout about him . . . Bacchus . . . flings himself at the Cretan. (Lamb,* Essays of Elia, Ser. II, *"Barrenness of the Imaginative Faculty") The sweep of some precipitous rivulet to the wave. (Tennyson, "Enoch Arden," 588)*

The phrase *precipitous retreat,* meaning "a headlong retreat," is perfectly correct as far as etymology and use is concerned. It doesn't mean "rash retreat" at all, it turns out—but the Morrises often manage to jumble meanings.

The other Latin word, the one that sounds like *praecipit-em* but isn't, is *praecipiti um,* meaning "a falling headlong, a steep place, precipice." The original English word for "extremely steep" was *precipitious,* which is also etymologically correct. But it is obsolete, because everybody got confused about time and space (actually about precipices and jumping precipices) and started incorrectly using *precipitous* instead.

So, now you have the whole story about those three odd words —it's sort of fun that all of us are using a word derived from "headlong" to mean "steep," one of those odd little facts you can amuse your friends with, if you have friends who are amused by that kind of trivia. But it does not seem like something that language experts, or even users of language, should worry about. What's done is done—who are we to say whether or not it's good or bad?

Most of the questions in the *Harper Dictionary of Contemporary Usage* seem stunningly unimportant. Many of the majority opinions turn out to be ignorant of any kind of usage, contemporary or historical. Much of the individual opinion seems senseless, uninformed, silly, and/or downright useless for anyone who wants to know how to write clearly and well. And yet the panel of experts includes writers such as W. H. Auden, Anthony Burgess, Saul Bellow, Art Buchwald, John Ciardi, Justice William O. Douglas, Maxwell Geismar, Jessica Mitford, Jean Stafford, Judith Viorst. . . .

Long ago, George Bernard Shaw said, "Those who can, do; those who can't, teach."

Maybe it works the other way around too: Those who can do —can't teach.

five

Theodore Bernstein

Mind Your (Native) Tongue—A
Word from Mr. Thistlebottom

From the Greek, hoi polloi *means the masses;* hoi *means the* and polloi *means many. For that reason it is improper to speak of* the hoi polloi; *the article* the *should be omitted. However, that makes for clumsy speaking and writing, so the best thing to do is avoid the expression altogether.*

This quote, from Theodore Bernstein's *Dos, Don'ts & Maybes of English Usage* (1977), shows journalistic pop grammar at its silly prissiest, which is kind of sad, because Bernstein himself was a distinguished and obviously humane newspaperman, a long-time editor of *The New York Times,* a man who liked to think of himself as a tolerant liberal among all the bitter reactionary language watchers.

But like many liberals, like many many newspapermen, and like almost all pop grammarians, Bernstein had trouble getting the facts straight.

First, the phrase *hoi polloi* has been in the English language for at least three centuries—first cited in the OED for 1668 (John Dryden)—long enough for it to be understood and treated like an English word. It is not necessary to learn Greek in order to speak and write English correctly, and English words take the article.

As a sample of this unvarying rule that borrowings become English, take the phrase *double entendre,* which means "double meaning" in French—many of us think until we learn French.

Theodore Bernstein

Actually, *double entendre,* which many people like to pronounce with a rich academic French accent, the kind you learn in college, is an English botch of a French phrase. Should it be changed? Should it be avoided? I quote from one of the most revered of pop grammarians, H. W. Fowler, in *Modern English Usage* (2nd ed., 1965):

> **double entendre** *is the established English form, and has been in common use from the 17th c[entury]; the modern attempt to correct it into* double entente *suggests ignorance of English rather than knowledge of French. . . .*

Second, with the single exception of a quote from 1932, every citation of *hoi polloi* in the OED shows it used with *the.* Dryden and Byron used it that way, incidentally, because both were Greek scholars printing it as οι πολλοι. James Fenimore Cooper printed it in English (1837), and it wound up in Brewer's *Dictionary of Phrase and Fable* (1895) listed with *the.* Do we really believe that Bernstein knew more Greek than Dryden and Byron? Sadly, we do not. We suspect that Bernstein has found out this fascinating little bit of information about *hoi* and cannot wait to show it off. It is a harmless way to show off, of course, since it is so transparent.

And oddly enough, it is easy to find out where Bernstein got that prescription against *hoi polloi*—from Fowler's *Modern English Usage*:

> **hoi polloi.** *These Greek words for the majority, ordinary people, the man in the street, the common herd, etc., meaning literally "the many" are equally uncomfortable in English whether the (=hoi) is prefixed to them or not. The best solution is to eschew the phrase altogether.*

Fowler did know Greek, of course, and took it a lot more seriously than French. Remember that he attacked words like *neolithic* and *paleolithic* as "barbarisms" because they combined the Greek and Latin languages in prefix and root. So he naturally complained bitterly about Greek words that were made into English words, and forgot his good advice about *double entendre.* His stricture may have influenced the quote in 1932, where *the* is not used with *hoi polloi.* It obviously influenced Bernstein—Bernstein's paragraph is hardly more than a paraphrase of Fowler. Wouldn't we all feel more comfortable if Bernstein had mentioned

59

he got this idea from Fowler, instead of giving us the impression that he got it from his intimate knowledge of Greek?

In *Watch Your Language* (1958), Bernstein's first work as a pop grammarian, he writes:

> The helicopter was about 500 feet over the field when trouble developed, and it began to sink toward the ground.

Bernstein says that *toward the ground* is redundant—where else could the helicopter sink? So we rewrite the sentence:

> The helicopter was about 500 feet over the field when trouble developed and it began to sink.

And the connotations of the word *sink,* even though we know the helicopter is over a field, are so strong that we get a mental picture of the helicopter sinking in water. It won't do to change *sink* to *fall*—obviously the helicopter is not in enough trouble to fall to the field, it is just having trouble maintaining its altitude. We understand all that, clearly, from the first sentence. We do not understand all that—at least I have trouble understanding it— from the second. And I believe that *The New York Times* and other newspapers ought to be willing to make things plain even to me, especially if it's only at the cost of an extra three words.

Bernstein sometimes does tell us where his knowledge comes from—but he never lost the habit of picking up little bits of fact and retailing them as knowledge.

A story in *The New York Times* mentions a mortgage burning ceremony. "A member of the bar" informs Bernstein that the original mortgage is actually filed, and what is burned is "a copy of the mortgage release." So, says Bernstein, in future stories "it might be well to point out what document is really destroyed, to alert prospective mortgage-burners to the peril of too literal a ceremony."

This warning supposes that (a) people with mortgages will be too stupid to follow instructions of the bank when they pay them off, (b) that people read *The New York Times* the way lawyers read Brandeis and Douglas, and (c) that this is a brand-new ceremony, not one that has been performed certainly for a hundred years in this country without any mortgagee coming to a too literal-minded grief. None of these suppositions have any foundation in fact—the warning is just publicity for Bernstein's legal "knowledge."

Sometimes this kind of knowledge is worse than ignorance. Bernstein was one of the few American pop grammarians to discover the OED, but he got many of his strictures from that book —again without credit—oddly skewed. Here's an example:

> Between *essentially does apply to only two, but sometimes the two relationship is present when more than two elements are involved. For example, it would be proper to say that* The president was trying to start negotiations between Israel, Egypt, Syria and Jordan *if what was contemplated was not a round-table conference but separate talks involving Israel and each of the other three nations.* Among *would not be improper in that context but would be vaguer and less exact. Likewise it would be proper to say that a triangle lies* between *points A, B, and C, and less proper to say that it lies* among *them.*

The OED has this to say about *between:*

> *In all senses* between *has been, from its earliest appearance, extended to more than two. . . . It is still* the only word available *[my emphasis] to express the relations of a thing to many surrounding things severally and individually,* among *expressing a relation to them collectively and vaguely: we should not say "the space lying among the three points," or "a treaty among the three powers," or "the choice lies among the three candidates in the select list," or "to insert a needle among the closed petals of a flower."*

It's probably necessary to point out here for American readers that the *should* in *we should not say* is British standard: that is, it does not mean "we ought not to say"; it means "we would never say." I give several other examples of my own based upon definitions in the OED:

> *A coalition was formed between the communists, socialists, and social democrats.*
> *Friendly communications are opened between the United States, China, and the Soviet Union.*
> *Only the three of us know this—let's just keep it between ourselves.*
> *The estate was divided between her and her three grandsons.*
> *Between the three of them, they killed the courier.*

Now it is alright for Bernstein to disagree with the OED, but he should have gotten his disagreements straight. Any talks between nations at a round table have to be talks "severally and individually"—because that's what negotiations are—everybody participates. Similarly, we have a conversation *between* friends—everybody participates. And the school teacher, finally as tired and bored as the students themselves, sometimes gives up by saying, "You may talk quietly *among* yourselves," because not everyone participates in the same conversations *between* two or three or four friends.

Bernstein's confusion came from the fact that he was unable to get the *two* of *tween* out of his mind—which is like insisting that a *matinée* performance cannot be in the afternoon, since *matinée* means "morning"; or that *noon* cannot possibly mean twelve o'clock, since *noon* comes from the Latin word *nōna, nōnus* —meaning "ninth." Etymology is fascinating, but you do not need to study it to speak English. You need to listen to English to speak English.

Bernstein did make two important contributions to pop grammar: one an improvement, and one not at all an improvement.

As an improvement, Bernstein introduced a tone of quiet geniality into pop grammar. Not for him the Simon or Follett habit of calling people who disagree with him "ignoramuses" or even "illiterate"; Bernstein always wrote against the word, not the user:

> **Aggravate:** *A widespread but inept use. . . . A person can be irritated but not* aggravated. *. . . It is true that its application to a person has become quite common, but that does not make it proper. . . .*

Jane Austen, as we know, thought otherwise, so did Richardson and Thackeray, but that's not the point here. Although Bernstein is wrong, he is politely wrong. And that's an indication of his humanity; not a bad quality in someone who sets himself up to judge and correct human language.

The second contribution demonstrates that Bernstein's humanity had limits—he invented, in his role of liberal prescriptive grammarian, a straw man who represented everything old-fashioned and nit-picking about illiberal prescriptive grammar. Only it was a straw woman—Miss Thistlebottom, a grade-school teacher who insists on pointless points of grammar. First of all, it is a liberal gambit to set up extremes and find a mean between them; Bernstein could hardly attack "permissiveness" without also attacking "senseless rules." But it is also true that women are rarely pop grammarians. It is men of a certain age who are most likely to take the English language under their protection. I do not know why this should be so. Maybe it is because, as Jespersen points out, women teach children to talk (almost all of us learned to talk from women); and their method is one of congratulation and understanding rather than prescription and punishment. Maybe, on the other hand, the reason for the relatively few women in pop grammar can be found in Thorstein Veblen's insistence in *The Theory of the Leisure Class* that "a punctilious use of ancient and accredited locutions" is conspicuous consumption —exactly because it is evidence of idleness and "argues waste of time and exemption from the use and the need of direct and forcible speech." Maybe working women journalists simply have to work too hard to sit around with the boys working up a style sheet for the English language. If you are a purist, and if you need a symbol for the kind of ultra-purist who is as archaic and unenlightened and vituperative as possible, then at least write with Swift and Walter Savage Landor and Fowler and John Simon and Wilson Follett in mind—if you need a symbol, it's *Mr.* Thistlebottom to you.

One more habit of Bernstein's is not new with him—he sometimes argues with the dictionary:

> **Intrigue** *as in* He has always been intrigued by big problems. *Dictionary or no, this is a use that is best avoided. . . . [First citation in the OED, 1894; H. G. Wells and Sir Arthur Quiller-Couch among users]*

> **Officer** *as in* "But that story about an onion odor on his breath," the officer said, "that's hooey." *Despite the dictionary . . . it is worthwhile to preserve the distinction between ordinary cops and officers, i.e., those of higher grade. A story about a police lieutenant properly bore the head POLICE OFFICER'S TRIAL DELAYED. [I was unable to find a single pop grammarian who ever proposed this fussy distinction—though I did find a quote from E. H. Marshall, in the scholarly journal* Notes and Queries, *1888, insisting that* officer *for* police *was good standard usage. So some Mr. Thistlebottom, now unknown, must have thought of it before Bernstein.]*

> **Verbal** . . . *It is true that dictionaries sanction the use of* verbal *to denote both spoken and written communication.* Oral, *however,*

can apply to spoken language only. Confronted with a choice between a word that can mean two things and another that can mean only one, are we not making better use of the tools of the language if we select the precise word? [Verbal meant precisely "oral" to Pepys, Swift, Marryat, and Froude, among others; the OED traces it to 1591.]

Now it does not seem to me to make much sense for purists to quarrel with "the dictionary"; many of them contradict dictionaries, of course, but usually without realizing it. Either the language, English, is the language we speak, and there is no sense arguing about new words and new constructions, or the language is the language written down, the language in "the dictionary." The purists can't really have it both ways, and try to make all of us believe that correct English, that great international language native to the citizens of several different countries in Europe, Africa, Australia, and North America, English with its centuries of history and its wide variety of usage, comes down to being nothing more than whatever the purist happens to say himself.

Other than these differences of manner, however, Bernstein was very much like his fellow pop grammarians. He differed in style (for the better) but not in content. He was capable of New-manesque blunders:

Critique *. . . The article read, . . .* "he visited Miss Dottin's classroom and invited several of us to write poems which he promised to critique." *Other such uses of critique make one wonder if writers are trying to change the part of speech of the word from its usual noun function to that of a verb. Critique appears as a verb in a couple of new dictionaries. . . .*

And in at least one old dictionary: the OED, which traces the use of *critique* as a verb back to 1751, indicating that writers are not trying to change the word to a verb; they have tried, and to try is to succeed.

It is considered substandard usage to say, Let's have a couple *(rather than a couple of) drinks.*

This also appeared in *Dos, Don'ts & Maybes of English Usage,* which was published in 1977—five years after the appearance of the 1972 Supplement to the *Oxford English Dictionary* which labeled this usage American colloquial—that is, standard in ordinary American usage.

Bernstein advises us that we should say *a drunken driver*

caused the accident, rather than *a drunk driver.* Chaucer thought otherwise: "A dronke man woot wel that he hath an hous" [c. 1386]. And the OED says that *drunken* in its "more common current" use means "given to drink, habitually intemperate." That's the difference between a *drunk driver,* who commits a crime though he is drunk for the first time in his life, and a *drunken bum.* The Evanses, in *A Dictionary of Contemporary American Usage,* published in 1957, twenty years before Bernstein's incorrect advice, add a little more careful observation of actual usage:

> *When applied to persons,* drunk *is now the commonest form in America* . . . a drunk soldier. . . . *As applied to persons,* drunken *now sounds a little archaic and poetic* (What shall we do with a drunken sailor?), *though it is still used to describe states and actions that pertain to, proceed from, or are marked by, intoxication* (This drunken babbling . . . drunken disregard of all regulations).

"To speak of a dark-*complected* man is to use what amounts to a non-word," says Bernstein. The OED lists writers who have used that nonword: Meriwether Lewis of Lewis and Clark fame (1806), Mark Twain in *Life on the Mississippi* (1883), O. Henry (before 1906), and William Faulkner in *Light in August* (1932). There is of course no such thing as a nonword in language. Bergen Evans, in *Comfortable Words* (1962), writes:

> *I am sent an advertisement of a phonograph that boasts of the machine's "custom componentry" and asked if "there is such a word as* componentry."
> *Plainly there is such a word. There it is, black and white, boldly blazoned to sock us in the eye. . . . It is not listed in any dictionary. That, however, doesn't mean it's bad English. Our language would never have become the wonderful thing it is if people had not felt free to make up words whenever they wanted to.*

Evans does not think that *componentry* is a good word—but good or not, a word's a word for all that.

Despite what Mr. Thistlebottom might think.

six

Safire

William the Few

Because I enjoy thin beer and even like simplified spelling, I was prepared to let the "lite" guys get away with it [advertising their beer had less, *rather than* fewer, *calories].... Now comes American Airlines ... doing what it does worst ... with "One less line [to stand in.]" [If this keeps up, we'll have one fewer airline.]*

This quote shows William Safire at his best and at his worst: withholding his hand because he happens to like those insipid and watery lo-cal beers (a very good reason to withhold your hand if you can think of no other) and then striking out with all the prescriptive force of a Simon or a Follett at a perfectly established idiom.

Let's take the idiom first. It is a fiction of pop grammar that in English *less* is always used with quantity and *fewer* with number. The OED, noting that the usage is "now regarded as incorrect," traces the use of *less* with numbers in every sense back to the ninth century—as far back as the OED goes. The current supplement (1975) says *less* with numbers (*less flowers* rather than *fewer flowers*) is "more frequently found, though still regarded as incorrect." Here are a couple examples:

There might have been less barbed wire, less *flaring flowers.* (American Journal of Philology *[1904]) The 47 page prospectus shows that there are* less *restrictions than is generally supposed.* (Manchester Guardian *[1971])*

This use is growing, and this use is the one Safire does not mind in "lite" beers with *less* calories. However, there is another use of *less* with numbers. We would never say:

Write *I love grammar* on the blackboard 100 times—and not one time fewer.
Complete this sentence in twenty-five words or fewer.
My coat cost sixty dollars—much fewer than I expected.
Dinner will run you around fifty dollars—more or fewer.
The baby is fewer than six months old.
America now has fewer than 40,000 troops in Southeast Asia.
This building is eight stories high, one fewer than the New York City average.
Six is one fewer than seven.

In every instance, because a number is considered as a limit and a new number is offered as a lesser quantity, we all use *less,* even Safire, except when he is led astray by analogy. The correct idiom is *one less line* to stand in, and *one less airline* to correct in the Sunday papers.

However, Safire as a prescriptive grammarian is Safire at his worst; at his best he is the wittiest and the most *likable* of all the pop grammar writers. Even when he is worrying about permissive dictionaries (Webster's Third) and "language slobs" (people who say things like: "Yesterday I left a fifty-cent tip—today I'm leaving five cents less"), Safire writes with genuine good humor, and without any parade of make-believe "learning."

Safire is even more unique: alone among pop grammarians he does not equate textbook good usage and political integrity. He has never written us a bitter little sermon indicating that if we'd only paid attention to our fourth-grade grammar teachers we could have seen through the corrupt rhetoric which described Watergate as "excess of zeal," and the invasion of Cambodia as a mere "incursion," and the secret bombing of Hanoi as "a measured response to Communist aggression."

Of course, Safire is not really in a position to do that; as a former Nixon speech writer he must have been responsible for at least some of that rhetoric, mustn't he? But that is a cheap jibe—because I doubt that those other guardians of the language saw through Nixon and Johnson (and Kennedy, lest we forget who sent the first "advisors") any quicker than Safire, and because Safire, again almost alone among pop grammarians, actually did wind up getting his phone tapped as a potential danger to the police (or at least the plumber) state.

So I only mention Safire's political past to point out that most pop grammarians are liberals, the kind of liberal who voted for Hubert Humphrey, very big on public welfare and also on the cold war. So it seems a little odd that they're so angry about language. Liberals in general would never dream of discriminating against Blacks because of the color of their skin—so why insist on distinctions that are just as racially or culturally determined? It's like claiming you love the Irish—but can't stand people with brogues. We do not usually think of liberals as defenders of inherited wealth and the life values that can be acquired only by people who have never had to work their way up in the world, but here is a sample liberal describing his liberal attitudes for the *Harper Dictionary of Contemporary Usage:*

> *I am anything but a snob in my social relationships. But I'm a terrible snob regarding language. I can't abide words that through debased usage by adolescents, commentators or careless authors appear overnight in our literature and, like nouveau riche Southern rednecks who have found oil on their property, try to make ugliness and ignorance fashionable.*
>
> Ben Lucien Burman

How much better, more humane, and even politically more liberal (after all, what are the Rockefellers but Northern rednecks whose granddaddy happened to find oil on other people's property, and take it for himself?), how much more sensible is this, from William Safire, former speech writer for Nixon:

> *The guardians of the language (John Simon, Edwin Newman, assorted usage panels, assorted writers of letters to the editor), all grimly determined to preserve the chastity of English from her would-be violators . . . are guarding not the language but their vision of an ideal and logical structure that does not exist and never did. And the lady, friends, is no virgin.*

How much more interesting than all that screed about adolescents and novelists and rednecks and politicians, is Safire's defiance of every pop language piety when he asks:

> *What, after all, was so terrible about* finalize?

But Safire is not always at his best, and not always up to that confident, educated, Tory tolerance which permits him to accept the language of Dwight Eisenhower (and Kennedy, lest we forget that he also liked using *finalize*). Trying to decide if it is alright to say *anxious* when you mean *eager* ("I am anxious to go to the ball game tonight"), he quotes Sir Ernest Gowers (yes) and William and Mary Morris of the *Harper Dictionary* (no). Then he adds his own opinion:

> *We cannot say that the use of "anxious" minus its* Angst *is incorrect—in the end, usage calls the tune—but we can say that people who know the difference and use the word precisely are more expressive of their meaning. . . .*
>
> *A little group of wilful men, representing no opinion but their own and anxious about the fuzzying-up of English, are eager to make an issue out of "anxious–eager." Hats off to them; the fight may be a loser, but it is the good fight to call attention to the beauty of precision in speech.*

Alas, not even Wilson Follett in all his romantic ignorance of the history of the English language could be so apparently sensible, so eloquent, and so totally wrong. The OED shows *anxious* as "full of anxiety" but also as "anxious *for* a desired event" (Macaulay is cited in 1849). The meaning of "solicitude, anxious to do something" goes back at least to 1742: Robert Blair, *"The gentle heart, anxious to please."* (Nelson and Carlyle are also cited.) The precision of the precise is once again the fuzzied-up maunderings of the unread and invincibly ignorant—and Safire's hat would be better off on his head.

Safire defends the word *hopefully* used as an adverb and then manages to attack an even more innocuous word:

> *Now that "hopefully"—replacing "it is to be hoped"—has won the usage battle, another adverb is making its bid. "Clearly" —to replace "it is clear that"—. . . .*
>
> *"Clearly," however, is a transparent cop-out: It is the equivalent of the Soviet propagandist's "as is well-known. . . ."*
>
> *The vogue use of "clearly" . . . [debases] the precision of "it is clear to me."*

As is clear from the history of the language, *clearly* has been used parenthetically to mean "it is clear" since at least 1867. Jowett used it in his translation of Plato (1875), long before there were any Soviets or Soviet propagandists. Clearly, Safire needs to watch out for prejudices connected with the word *precision*—and with politics. Disliking a word just because it sounds like the *equivalent* of Soviet propaganda is carrying guilt by association to extremes—probably the very sort of thinking that led Nixon to tap Safire's phone.

Safire has enough trouble without guilt by association. Because his column appears in *The New York Times Sunday Magazine,* he gets more reader mail than most other pop grammarians —and more bad-tempered mail than many other men would bear cheerfully. Safire spends an awful lot of time kissing the rod (needlessly, if he would only stick to his insistence that English is already so screwed around with that nothing can hurt it) and then getting in even more trouble because he has an ear for ordinary idiom:

> *. . . I wrote "centers around". . . . A reader circled "centers around" and wrote, "neat trick."*
> *When you stop to think about it, nothing can center "around" anything. The center is the middle, the focal point, the place around which all else circles. If the metaphor is to mean anything, it should be expressed, "centers on."*
> *The confusion stems from the alternate phrase, "revolves around."*

A few months later, Safire writes:

> *A reader in England makes this correction, "to use alternate as a synonym for* alternative *is considered to be a sign of semi-literacy outside the United States. Unfortunately Webster's Third allows this misuse. . . ."*

Well, we wait for Safire to answer that he is writing in the United States. After all, what the British call a *reel of cotton* we call a *spool of thread.* It seems pointless to argue about which is better—and pointless in the extreme to call one literate and the other semiliterate. Instead, Safire surrenders meekly and advises all of us to use *alternative* for *alternate.* It will make you feel better, he says, just by saying the word *alternative.*

> *You have now struck a blow for precision. Lexicographers will call you elitist—a "self-appointed protector of the language"—but a worthy distinction deserves all the protection it can get.*

There's that word *precision* again—and there's Safire joining up with the guardians of the easy virtue of our language. This time, though, he does have sort of an excuse.

The Supplement to the OED published in 1933 lists: *"To centre or to be centred round, around, about:* an illogical phrase, now very frequent." That is good enough for Safire, and will be good enough for many people besides—provided they have not checked an older or a new edition of the OED. However, the original OED, the great nineteenth-century masterpiece, used the phrase *centre round* itself, in defining the verb *centre:* "to gather or collect as *round* a centre."

And the 1972 edition of the Supplement, possibly embarrassed by the prescription that crept into the 1933 edition—which seemed directed at the dictionary itself—altered that entry from 1933 to read:

"To centre (or *to be centred) about, around* or *round:* to have (something) as one's or its centre or focus; to move or revolve round (something) as a centre; to be concentrated on, to turn on . . . to be mainly concerned with."

The word *illogical* has disappeared—tidied up without leaving a trace. It is easy to see how Safire could go wrong here —checking words through the OED until he finds a rare prescription, and accepting it as eternal truth. But as Safire himself sometimes points out, language truths are not eternal—one year's illogical construction is another year's standard. And it is always best to check the latest editions of any dictionary. I add that the construction *center on* (we might as well drop back into American standard spelling) is a perfectly good one—but that it would sound extremely odd in some uses where *center around* is used. For example, this cite, from *The London Times Literary Supplement,* October 3, 1929:

The group of gifted men and women who centred round Henry Adams.

Centred on (or *centered on*) would be too specific here—as if the writer meant that in some way Henry Adams was the mathematical center of a specific circle.

Now for *alternate*—the use of *alternate* to mean *alternative* is in fact an Americanism—provided we are talking about the word as an adjective. This sense is traced only to Webster's Third by the newest Supplement of the OED, though of course the word must have been in use before publication date (1961) for it to be included in that dictionary.

But there is also a noun *alternate*—"a delegate who goes to a national party convention as a possible substitute for another who gets too sick or too drunk to vote." This is an extremely old Americanism, dating back to 1848, and it is almost certain that this meaning influenced the use of the word by people who are very familiar with major-party politics in America.

Back in the sixties, for example, people talked of "alternative newspapers" and "alternative lifestyles" because the people doing the talking were unlikely to have spent much time covering the Democratic or Republican conventions. There were no "alternate" papers—because to workers on those papers *alternative* meant not merely "something that can be substituted easily" but "something that is completely opposite."

Safire's use of the word—"an alternate phrase"—does not involve any sense of contradiction; so it is of course not only correct because it is an Americanism, but delightful because it is obviously part of his personal history. And *alternate* is always likely to be used by people like Safire—people whose experience and whose practice almost always seem to be better than their opinions, which may be the best way of describing the Tory humanism that Safire typifies in his columns. If only he could get rid of that goose-stepping word *precision* and think about language as charmingly, idiomatically, and *nicely* as he writes it.

Two

The

Joys

of

Watergate

How to Stop
Worrying and Love the Language

one

The Joys
of Watergate

One of the most sacred of all the sacred cows of pop grammar
is its insistence that there is a connection between clear thinking
and good grammar—that bad thinking, and especially bad political thinking, produces bad writing. This proposition was stated
with much pop certitude in George Orwell's essay "Politics and
the English Language." But it goes back even further, at least as
far as 1927, when Ezra Pound wrote:

> *The individual cannot think and communicate his thought,
> the governor cannot act effectively or frame his laws, without
> words, and the solidity and validity of these words is in the care
> of the damned and despised* literati. *When their work goes rotten
> —by that I do not mean when they express indecorous thoughts—
> but when their very medium, the very essence of their work, the
> application of the word to thing goes rotten, i. e., becomes slushy
> or inexact, or excessive or bloated, the whole machinery of social
> and of individual thought and order goes to pot.*

This is brilliant pop grammar writing—the simple declaration of the connection is itself so well written that we believe it
immediately. But it's not true.

And I can demonstrate that it's not true with a simple list of
writers who never let their work go rotten, who were never slushy
or inexact, or excessive or bloated: Ezra Pound, William Butler
Yeats, T. S. Eliot, Wyndham Lewis . . . all of these writers had
more or less open flirtations with fascism, which is arguably the
most indecent form of social organization ever proposed. If good
writing makes good politics, and bad politics makes bad language,
how come the *Cantos* is such a great poem?

It is possible, buyers of language books being what they are,
that some readers are unduly sympathetic to fascism. In that case

I have another list of great writers: W. H. Auden, Stephen Spender, Hugh MacDiarmid, Richard Wright, who have had more or less open flirtations with communism.

George Bernard Shaw went to the end of his life insisting that the careers of Stalin, Mussolini, and Hitler—who he defended indiscriminately—demonstrated the failure of democracy as a viable form of government. So whether you are pro-left or pro-right in your personal politics, you have in Shaw a man who never wrote an inexact sentence—and never escaped a reputation for outrageous paradox.

If good thought made good writing, and good writing made good thought, then Immanuel Kant, Hegel, and Ludwig Wittgenstein are not worth reading.

If good prose made great art, then Theodore Dreiser would be a worse novelist than either Arthur Machen or Thorne Smith.

If it were not possible to lie in English, and to disguise your thoughts, and put bad meanings in a better light, then we would have to have another language, because one of the functions of language is deceit. English does not belong to people with virtue, or people with talent, or people who can remember very clearly the difference between a gerund and a gerundive, or people who have succeeded in imitating the affected unregional accents and measured sentences of television announcers. English belongs to everybody—the liars, the fuzzy thinkers, the dishonest ad writer, the crooks, the presidents of the United States. . . .

The Joys of Watergate—How You Can Learn to Stop Worrying and Love the Language

The refusal to recognize that reprehensible people can and do make good speakers and writers is in fact the most ignorant kind of sentimental humanism: it is just not true that people we agree with are more likely to be talented or intelligent than people we disagree with.

One of the best examples of the sentimental humanist style of pop grammar criticism is Edwin Newman, who in *Strictly Speaking* goes on like this:

> *One of the things the Watergate hearings revealed was a poverty of expression, an inability to say anything in a striking way, an addiction to language that was almost denatured. . . .*

> *Watergate, in the course of revealing so much else about*
> *American life, also revealed the sad state of the language;*
> *apparently form and substance are related. In Washington, as we*
> *learned from the White House transcripts, a president may speak*
> *of kicking butts, call a problem a can of worms, decide not to be*
> *in the position of basically hunkering down, anticipate something*
> *hitting the fan, propose to tough it through, sight minefields*
> *down the road, see somebody playing hard ball, claim political*
> *savvy, and wonder what stroke some of his associates have with*
> *others. He may be told by members of his staff what is the bottom*
> *line, that a situation has cycled somewhat while another*
> *situation is a bullet biter, that a lawyer has done some*
> *dove-tailing for him, that a lot of people have to pull oars, and*
> *that another man was a ballplayer who carried tremendous water*
> *for the President's cause.*

It seems extraordinary that Newman can, on the same page, complain about denatured language, and at the same time provide so much compelling evidence that linguistic vitality is not limited to the good guys, or to the friends of American freedom. What a wonderful range of metaphor in that second paragraph! From carpentry *(dove-tailing)* to Western novels *(bite the bullet)* to accounting *(bottom line)* to massage parlor *(?have stroke with someone)*, to sports *(play hardball, pull oars)* to laundromats *(?cycled* = a washer cycling into rinse) to medical examinations *(?carry tremendous water for* = be prepared to help out even in urinalysis) to war *(minefields)* to superb American inventions like *Let's kick ass, Don't open that can of worms* (=don't open a new line of inquiry, because once the can is open the worms can never be put back inside), and *when the shit hits the fan.*

Newman is not alone in his conviction that somehow the people he dislikes talk worse than the people he likes. In the *Harper Dictionary,* the Morrises reprint a letter from panelist Barry Bingham, Sr., a man they call "one of the country's most literate journalists." (Bingham, not to be outdone, calls the Morrises, "our most valued watchdogs of the English language.") In his letter, Bingham complains about the "lame and degenerate language" of the hearings. The Morrises agree that the testimony and the tapes are "fraught with solecisms and sheer illiteracies," and they provide translations of expressions they doubt will survive "except as horrible examples of language torn asunder":

Stroke *(translation: soothe or cajole a potential troublemaker).*
[Alas, the masturbatory metaphorical sense of stroke *is lost on
the Morrises.]*
Go the hangout road *(translation: tell the truth). [Once again,
this is a faulty perception of this fascinating metaphor.* Let it all
hang out *was popularized by football players, and to them it
means roughly,* act like an animal. *Of course,* let it all hang out
also means expose yourself—*possibly from an old joke of a guy in
a factory walking around with his penis hanging out of his pants.
Asked by the foreman why he doesn't button up, he replies, "You
work me like a horse, I might as well walk around looking like
one."]*
Launder the money *(translation: pass illegal campaign
contributions through foreign banks so that the donor's identity is
hidden). [The Morrises at least understand what this metaphor
means, but they seem unable to appreciate its aptness: to clean
money would mean that something was done to it, to launder is to
use a laundry: drop it off, and pick it up later when it has been
cleaned for you. Neatly put.]*
Plumber *(translation: undercover political espionage agent).
[Really, this is rewriting history. The Plumbers may have been
espionage agents from the beginning, but they were formed to stop
leaks. (Get it, William and Mary Morris? See, a leak is like a leak
in a pipe.)]*

But William and Mary Morris do not, of course, get it. They
simply know that the Watergate and presidential tapes were
"revelations of corruption both political and linguistic."

Now it is a curiosity of pop grammarians that they are always
discovering the close connection between political and linguistic
corruption—but it is always after the fact. Even Edwin Newman,
determined to prove that bad language makes bad thought, suddenly comes to himself with a start, and writes:

"The argument for preciseness of language has limits, of
course. I don't know whether grammarians were less taken in by,
for example, the Gulf of Tonkin affair than other groups in the
population."

Come to think of it, as a longtime antiwar marcher, I never
remember seeing a contingent calling itself Copy Editors Against
Genocide, or Proofreaders Demand an End to Linguistic Evasions
like Body Count and Pacification Program.

I like to think about what those copy editors would have
done to an old friend of mine who I will call M. J. Weed. I returned to Temple University, a large innercity school in Phila-

delphia, in 1965. There was so little antiwar activity on campus that the administration (whose stupidity was actually astounding) decided to let the United States Army, as part of its recruiting program, put up an exhibit of captured Vietnamese weapons in the middle of the student union. The ten or fifteen people who were part of the antiwar groups on campus decided we had to do something—and what we did was set up a vigil in front of this display. A vigil was technically different than a sit-in—at least in a Quaker city—but there was a problem about whether we would let other students see the display. There was much talk about censorship, and then M. J. to the rescue. I see him now: hair just beginning to reach his collar, Indian temple bells sewn along the seams of his jeans, a leather thong tied around his forehead, and an expression of laid-back innocence:

"Hey, man, everybody like listen to me a minute because we shouldn't stop anybody from seeing this like stuff, man. I been looking at it and looking—you know what I see? I see rifles. I see pistols. I see little sticks with the ends sharpened. I don't see, like tanks, like helicopters, machine guns, and B-52s. So they must not have them. I mean if they had them and since we're winning, we would show them, right? But you mean this is all that they got? And we keep on winning, but we never win? This is like . . . like the army and the air force fights the ghetto. And we still can't win? We should ask everybody who sees this, how come with all our like guns we're still having so much trouble with these little mothers? Could it be, man, that the whole country is on their side? Could it be, man, we are the invaders? War is a bummer anyway, you know? But this kind of war, where we got all the bombs and big guns and they got all the sticks . . . like wow . . . unfair, man, unfair. And this whole country, if we keep letting this go on, we're just building up the karma. . . ."

I remember that I winced at M. J.'s language at the time, and I suspect that I have cleaned it up—certainly dropped a couple *man*'s and *you know*'s; but as political analysis, it beat a lot of the editorials in papers like *The New York Times* and *The Washington Post*.

There is a possibility, of course, that I am wrong, and that it is only nostalgia for the sixties that makes me think that the thinking of M. J. Weed was superior to that of the high-paid, hardworking, highly educated, and articulate men and women who write editorials for our major papers.

But I do not think so.

two

Detestable Words

... No one who has once taken the language under his care can ever again be really happy. That way misery lies.
Thomas Lounsbury, *The Standard of Usage In English*

Lounsbury did actually seem to feel a kind of amused concern for the feelings of the language purifiers of his day, and he even proposed an antidote: the experience of the past. He described the purifiers as people "who look upon the indifference [of] . . . the public to their warnings and to the awful examples they furnish as infallible proof of the increasing degeneracy of speech." For therapy, Lounsbury prescribed a sampling of identical sentiments from their long-vanished predecessors. "It would save [purists] hours of unnecessary misery were they to make themselves acquainted with the views of prominent men of former times, who felt as did they and talked as foolishly."

In the spirit of scholarly fun, Lounsbury provided some of the views of these earlier Cassandras. I print some of them here, along with a few that I've gathered myself—it's hard not to join in spreading joy and hope.

Jonathan Swift attacked the word *mob* in *The Tatler* (September 28, 1710), with forlorn fury: "I have done my utmost for some years past to stop the progress of *mobb* and *banter,* but have been plainly borne down by numbers and betrayed by those who promised to assist me."

Swift's hatred of the word continued until his death. As Lounsbury relates:

> *Walter Scott tells us of an old lady who died in 1788, and who was on terms of intimacy with the dean. She used to say that the greatest scrape she ever got into with him was owing to her*

*employment of this particular word [mob]. "Why do you say
that?" he exclaimed, in a passion: "never let me hear you say that
again." "Why, sir," she asked, "what am I to say?" "The rabble,
to be sure," answered he.*

Swift was, of course, right: there was no need for the word
mob because English already had a perfectly good word, *rabble*,
that meant the same thing. However, one perfectly good word
does not necessarily banish another; a fact we can all try to remember when someone tells us that *hopefully* or *input* is unnecessary. Actually, I have always been a trifle sorry that the old
lady and the rest of us did not follow Swift's advice; we would be
able to write things like:

> The president appeared at a rally and was rabbled by his
> supporters.

In 1712, Swift addressed a public letter to the Earl of Oxford,
the Lord High Treasurer of England, complaining about the state
of the language and urging that something be done to stamp out
horrible new practices like pronouncing *drudged, disturbed,
rebuked,* and *fledged* as if they were spelt *drudg'd, disturb'd,
rebuk't,* and *fledg'd:* "Where by leaving out a vowel to save a
syllable, we form so jarring a sound and so difficult to utter that
I have often wondered how it could ever obtain."

Is there a single reader who has ever thought the word *disturbed* hard to say? Or *rebuked* ugly? Remember Swift when
somebody tells you *finalize* is not beautiful enough to be added to
the vocabulary of English.

Swift urged that something be done immediately to stop the
language from changing—or in a few years no one would be able
to read with pleasure at all, or to speak to one another without
interpreters. Even if something were done, Swift said, all he could
promise the earl is that in 200 years "some painful compiler" who
had studied the language of Queen Anne's time would be just able
to decipher the name Earl of Oxford, and write in his history that
he was a wise and excellent man who had saved his country.
Everything else from the period, including the writings of Swift
himself, would be dropped because their antiquated vocabulary
and grammar would make them unintelligible. Lounsbury continues: "Every word of Swift's Letter can be understood now as easily
as it was on the day it was published." Swift died in 1745, thirty-

three years after the letter to the Earl of Oxford was written, and long enough to see that his prediction about the need for interpreters in a few years was exaggerated. "But this failure to note ... any sign of the realization of his dismal forebodings never once shook his faith in their correctness," writes Lounsbury.

Swift's unshakable conviction—in defiance of all linguistic experience—has been passed on, unshaken, to the pop grammarians of today.

For example, on the dust jacket of Richard Mitchell's *Less Than Words Can Say,* Clifton Fadiman, who ought to know better, calls the book: "The wittiest, the most brilliant and probably the most penetrating discussion now available of our growing American illiteracy. This book must be read *at once,* in the short time that remains before all of us become incapable of reading and writing." The italics are Fadiman's own; the anxiety is perennial.

Like many writers, Coleridge had his word peeves:

> *I regret to see that vile and barbarous vocable* talented, *stealing out of the newspapers into the leading reviews and most respectable publications of the day. Why not* shillinged, farthinged, tenpenced, *etc.? The formation of a participle passive from a noun, is a license that nothing but a very peculiar felicity can excuse. If mere convenience is to justify such attempts upon the idiom, you cannot stop till the language becomes, in the proper sense of the word, corrupt. Most of these pieces of slang come from America.*

Coleridge was wrong—the word *talented* does not seem to be originally American (first OED cite is 1827, and English). Richardson had used *untalented* in 1753, without causing any trouble, and of course nowadays we do say *moneyed;* in fact the OED traces *moneyed* back to the fifteenth century. But at least Coleridge was right about one thing—the word *talented* was relatively new. The OED's first cite is 1827, and he is complaining about the word in *Table Talk* in 1832, an almost unheard-of degree of accuracy about the history of usage in a purist.

Coleridge was himself attacked for coining the word *reliable* —a word that first appeared in print in 1569. The word was supposed to be formed badly: De Quincey in his essay on style spoke of Alcibiades as being "too unsteady and (according to Mr. Coleridge's coinage) 'unreliable,' or perhaps in more correct English, too *'unrelyuponable.'* " Mercifully, no one took De Quincey's advice, and, as the OED points out, *reliable* is as regularly formed as *dependable* (able to be depended upon) and *dispensable* (able to be dispensed with). Still, the struggle over *reliable* was a bitter one; Lounsbury writes:

> *[Frederick] Locker-Lampson tells us that Dean Stanley complained that much as he had associated with Gladstone, he had never influenced him in anything. "Yes," he said, recollecting himself, "I influenced him in one matter. I told him he ought never to use the word* reliable, *and I gave him my reasons. Some time afterwards I met Mr. Gladstone in the street, and he said as we parted, 'I have never used that wretched word* reliable *since you spoke to me about it.'"*

The OED cites Gladstone's use of *reliable* in *Oxford Essays* (1857). I am unable to discover if this was before his conversion, or a bit of backsliding, or just evidence that Gladstone never really was influenced by Dean Stanley in anything at all.

Some words seemed to have developed many purist enemies who were unable to provide any reason at all for their abhorrence. The word *influential* is an example. Here is Thomas Babington Macaulay writing to his sister (May 31, 1831), describing his visit to the home of Lady Holland,

> *a woman of considerable talents and great literary acquirements . . . yet there is a haughtiness in her courtesy. . . . The Centurion did not keep his soldiers in better order than she keeps her guests. It is to one "Go," and he goeth, and to another "Do this" and it is done. "Ring the bell, Mr. Macaulay." "Lay down that screen, Lord Russell;—you will spoil it. . . ."*
>
> *In the drawing-room I had a long talk with Lady Holland about the antiquities of the House and about the purity of the English language—wherein she thinks herself a most exquisite critic. I happened in speaking about the Reform bill to say, that I wished that it had been possible to form a few commercial constituencies, if the word* constituency *were admissible. [This is the first OED citation for* constituency.] *"I am glad you put that in," said her Ladyship, "I was just going to give it you. It is an odious word. Then there is* talented, *and* influential, *and* gentlemanly. *I never could break Sheridan of* gentlemanly, *though he allowed it to be wrong." I joined in abusing* talented *and* influential; *but* gentlemanly, *I said, had analogy in its favour, as we say* manly *and* womanly. *But her ladyship was perverse. She said truly enough that analogy was not a safe guide. "As to the word* womanly," *said she, "I hate it. You men never use it but as a term of reproach."—It is a reproach, thought I, which I shall scarcely bring against your ladyship.*

This ought to demonstrate to purists that they may win the argument but lose the last word. *Gentlemanly,* by the way, did not have only analogy on its side—it had been used in English since 1454. *Influential* had been in use since before 1734, in other words, at least a century, when Macaulay and Lady Holland joined in attacking it.

Walter Savage Landor was, to Lounsbury, "one distinguished exception" to Lounsbury's rule that worry about debasement of the language and anxiety about the future of English "came rarely from writers of ability or learning." For example, Landor was, Lounsbury said sadly, "in his remarks on words and their uses . . . almost invariably wrong whenever it was possible so to be."

Landor wanted to drop the letter *s* out of the word *island:*

> *"We write island with an* s *. . . as if we feared to be thought ignorant of its derivation." The truth is, [says Lounsbury,] we write island with an* s, *because we are ignorant of its derivation. It was not till the sixteenth century that men, under the fancied belief that the word was connected with* isle, *inserted the* s, *which hides from us its real origin. [*Iland *is the Old English; and has nothing to do with* isle, *which is from the French* ile.*]*

Landor objected to the word *execute,* when it was used to mean "hanging, beheading, or . . . putting a man to death." Lounsbury points out that "from the fifteenth century on, [*execute*] is to be found in the works of every writer of English, good or bad, who has had occasion to describe the act denoted by it."

Landor joined with many other purists in insisting that *I had better* was not good English, but a mispronunciation of *I'd better,* which in turn was a contraction of *I would better.* Browning, who used the phrase *I had better not,* in *Pippa Passes,* changed it in later editions to *I would better not,* defending the change by saying that Landor had asked him to make it, and citing Landor's "magisterial authority."

One change that Landor did not ask him to make is in Browning's curious use of the word *twat*—a use that has made *Pippa Passes* (iv, "Night," 292–295) a favorite with graduate English students:

> *Then, owls and bats,*
> *Cowls and twats,*
> *Monks and nuns, in a cloister's mood,*
> *Adjourn to the talk-stump pantry!*

The OED lists *twat* (erroneously or disingenuously) as "low obsolete," and says that Browning erroneously used the word "under the impression that it denoted some part of nun's attire" apparently because of *Vanity of Vanities* (1660), where Browning read:

> They talk't of his having a Cardinalls Hat,
> They'd send him as soon an Old Nuns Twat.

It is difficult, for anyone who has not sat through a seminar in Victorian poetry, to appreciate the vindictive glee that students find in discovering that line in such a respectable and thoroughly married poet as Browning: a glee, and a vindictiveness, that the long-dead author of *Vanity of Vanities* would have shared, I think.

Edgar Allan Poe, in an essay on the poetry of Margaret Fuller, objected to her use of *mutual friends* and a "multitude of *wilful* murders" committed not on the Queen's English but

> on the American of President Polk. She uses . . . the word
> *"ignore,"* a vulgarity adopted only of late days (and to no good
> purpose, since there is no necessity for it) from the barbarisms of
> the law, and makes no scruple of giving the Yankee [that is, New
> England] interpretation to the verbs *"witness"* and *"realise,"* to
> say nothing of *"use,"* as in the sentence, *"I used to read a short
> time at night."*

Used to has been good English since the fourteenth century; the OED cites Chaucer, Spenser, Webster, Milton, and Gay. *Witness* has meant "to see or be actually present at an event" since 1582—the word is not an American or Yankee invention; Chapman, Milton, Cowper, and Macaulay are among the users. *Realize* in the modern sense does seem to be an Americanism (the OED's first cite is Abigail Adams, 1775), though of course firmly established before Poe was born in 1809.

Ignore was in fact taken over from legal language. A grand jury which refused an indictment was supposed to return it with the word *ignoramus* (Latin for "we do not know," or "we take no notice of [it]"). The word *ignoramus* was used that way in the sixteenth century. By the early seventeenth century the word was already being used to mean "an ignorant person." The word *ignore,* said Samuel Johnson, was one that "[Robert] Boyle endeavoured to introduce, but it has not been received." In the sense of "refuse to take notice of" the OED traces it only to 1801—new enough to make Poe right, at least about history. But it is hard to think what substitute he had in mind when he called the word unnecessary. *Overlook?* That seems to imply mere inattention, not deliberately refusing to recognize something. Some people merely overlook evidence that contradicts their language peeves. Purists, Poe among them, seem to delight in ignoring evidence; as he said of Margaret Fuller's poetry: "It will not do to say, in defence of such words, that in such senses they may be found in certain dictionaries—in that of Bolles, for instance;—*some* kind of 'authority' may be found for *any* kind of vulgarity under the sun." The italics, and the quotes around *authority,* are Poe's; the argument is still a popular one with purists: invincible in its ignoring.

Benjamin Franklin returned from France and found lots of new words to displease him in the language of Americans. In 1789, he wrote to Noah Webster, whose work he knew and admired, saying, "If you happen to be of my opinion with respect to these innovations, you will use your authority in reprobating them." The innovations included:

> *a verb formed from the substantive* notice: I should not have noticed this. . . . *Another verb from the substantive* advocate: the gentleman who advocates . . . that motion. . . . *Another from the substantive* progress, *the most awkward and abominable of the three:* The committee, having progressed, resolved to adjourn. *The word* opposed, *though not a new word, I find used in a new manner, as:* The gentlemen who are opposed to this measure. . . .

For the figurative meaning of *to progress,* "to make progress," the OED cites Ben Jonson in 1610 and George Washington in 1791. For *to advocate,* it cites Edmund Burke, circa 1767. For *to oppose* (a measure), "Adverse to a measure, practice, system, etc.," this letter is the first citation in the OED. The next two cites, from 1844 and 1874, are both from Englishmen—one of them John Henry Newman. I do not know why that should be, but it is obvious that Franklin had as much trouble defending the American of President Washington as Poe had defending that of President Polk—maybe because Polk, like Washington, was one of the offenders.

Franklin was not alone in attacking Americanisms. A reviewer in *The British Critic* (1793) writes: "We shall, at all times, with pleasure, receive from our transatlantic brethren real im-

provements of our common mother-tongue: but we shall hardly be
induced to admit such phrases as . . . 'more lengthy,' for longer,
or more diffuse." Unlike many so-called Americanisms, *lengthy*
really did come from this country, and the OED provides a little
history of usage. It quotes Southey, who uses the word in 1812,
with a little apology "that, to borrow a trans-atlantic term, may
truly be called a lengthy work." Bentham uses it without apology
in 1816. Scott, in 1827, writes: "The style of my grandsire . . . was
rather lengthy, as our American friends say." Dickens, in 1837,
uses it also with no apology. Southey, in 1834–1843, apologizes
again: ". . . what in America would be called a lengthy poem
. . . ." The OED then cites uses in 1844, 1871, and finally one by
George Eliot in 1879, for whom *lengthy* is obviously a standard
word in English vocabulary. The first user listed is John Adams
(1759)—apparently he and Abigail both liked writing nice new
words. The second user cited is Benjamin Franklin in 1773;
twenty years before the word was even attacked as an Americanism, an American enemy of Americanisms included it in his corre-
spondence. Many of our current purists seem unable to resist
using the words they pretend to hate. Sometimes they do it with
a little apology ("as the youngsters say," is very popular today).
Sometimes they do it with quotation marks (to show that, though
they are forced to use the word, it does not meet with their august
approval, says Lounsbury). Sometimes, like Franklin, they do it
without realizing it.

Lindley Murray, in *Grammar of the English Language*
(1795), attacks the use of a passive verb with a direct object.
Lounsbury points out that this usage has a long history in English, and that it can be found in both Latin and Greek, but to the
rationalist grammarian there was only one way to make a passive: take the object of the active verb and turn it into the subject
of a passive verb:

> The boy gave the book to the girl (Active)
> The book was given to the girl by the boy (Passive)
> The girl was given the book by the boy (False Passive—The
> subject of the sentence is the indirect object of the active
> sentence, and the object in both the active and false passive
> remains the same.)

Many readers will have never heard of the false passive, and
will find it hard to imagine that someone could be upset by it. Yet

Noah Webster, in *Philosophical Grammar,* said "The idiom is outrageously anomalous," then added, sadly, "but perhaps incorrigible."

Lindley Murray thought the idiom could, and should, be stamped out, but as Lounsbury points out: "It requires, indeed, painful and protracted vigilance on the part of the most scrupulous pedantry to avoid falling inadvertently into the use of an idiom so common, so convenient, and supported by authority so abundant and so great." Among writers Lounsbury cites are: Shakespeare, Bacon, Jonson, Milton, Dryden, Swift, Pope, Fielding, Burke, Goldsmith, Johnson, Wordsworth, Byron, Austen, Coleridge, Washington Irving, Dickens, Tennyson, Ruskin, Browning, Emerson, . . . and Lindley Murray: "We too," wrote Murray, "must be allowed the privilege of forming our own laws."

Goold Brown, in his *Grammar of English Grammars* (1851), used this quotation as an example of Murray's "betrayal of his principles." Lounsbury, of course, is more gracious, and more interesting: "In this sentence, which Brown cited as a specimen of false syntax, his predecessor had uttered a great truth about his own language without being aware of the extent of its application."

The progressive form of the passive ("The house is being built") was new in the eighteenth century, and so of course was attacked in the nineteenth. Richard Grant White, in *Words and Their Uses* (1870), writes:

> *"The full absurdity of this phrase, the essence of its nonsense, seems not hitherto to have been pointed out . . . a new phrase which has nothing of force or of accuracy in its favor . . . [not] consistent with reason . . . [not] conformed to the normal development of the language . . . a monstrosity, the illogical, confusing, inaccurate, unidiomatic character of which I have, at some length, but yet imperfectly, set forth."*

George H. McKnight, in *The Evolution of the English Language* (1928), says that when White attacked it, the usage could already be found in "Southey, Lamb, Coleridge and even Landor." He quotes De Quincey as an example of the obligatory early apology: "not done, not even (according to modern purism) *being done."* McKnight thought that by *purism* De Quincey must have meant "exactness." But it is hard to tell, among purists, what is meant with anything like exactness.

Noah Webster was full of odd opinions about language. Lounsbury writes:

> *There are those who will recall what grief the second* r *in* bridegroom *caused Noah Webster. In consequence of its insertion, he said that the word really meant a bride's hostler. Thereupon he wanted us all to go back to the original [Old English]* bridguma—*in which* guma *means "man"—and use* bridegoom. *So he printed the word in the edition of his Dictionary which came out in 1828. The insertion of the* r *lay heavy on his heart. "Such a gross corruption or blunder," he wrote, "ought not to remain a reproach to philology." He could not be consoled by the fact that though the form* bridegroom *did not make its appearance until the sixteenth century—the final word of the original compound [*guma*] having died out—no one ever attached to the personage so designated any debasing associations connected with the stable.*

But consoled or not, the word was printed as *bridegroom* in later editions of the dictionary. Webster may have had an impulse to correct ordinary speech—but he also realized when an idiom was "incorrigible."

Landor was one of the first to complain that speakers of English sometimes combined prefixes and roots from different languages: "It disturbs me to find in Southey . . . the word *rewrite*. I had thought it, and *reread,* the spawn infecting a muddier and shallower water. Properly *re* should precede none but words of Latin origin, though there are a few exceptions of some date and authority." The OED gives two: *rewrite,* since 1730 (Young, in a letter to Pope); *re-read,* since 1782 (Fanny Burney; Thackeray [1848] is also cited). Lounsbury calls this delusion of Landor's "the demon of derivation," and it has not disappeared.

This combining of prefixes and roots from different languages also disturbed H. W. Fowler. His list of barbarisms is a long one: *bureaucrat, coastal, cablegram, climactic, electrocute, pleistocene, speedometer* (should be *speed-meter,* says Fowler), *gullible, pacifist.* Of *electrocution,* he writes:

> *This barbarism jars the unhappy Latinists' nerves much more cruelly than the operation denoted jars those of its victim. . . . He is horrified by the dawning suspicion that the word-maker took -cut (from* quatere*) instead of the indivisible* secut- *(from* sequi*) for the stem of execution, and derived it from* excutere. *The best that can be made of a bad business is to pretend that* electrocute *comes from* electrocutere *(to strike electrically) and to change* electrocution *(impossible on that assumption) into* electrocussion.

No one that I know of has followed Fowler's advice—very few speakers of English even seem to know enough Latin to follow his argument. But Fowler's Latin seems to have been extraordinarily good. Attacking the word *coastal,* he says: "[it is] a barbarism, the *-oa-* showing at once that *-al* has been added to an English and not a Latin word. If an adjective had been really needed, it should have been *costal;* but the attributive function can be performed perfectly by *coast* (the coast trade, the coast towns) and the predicative by *coastwise. . . ."*

To show the changes in shibboleths of purism, Fowler's two solutions to the problem of that barbarism *coastal* would now be condemned by today's pop grammarians as barbarisms in themselves. Using a noun like *coast* to modify another is condemned not only as language but as thought by Richard Mitchell in *Less Than Words Can Say:* "It is no coincidence that many of our problems come from the fact that we can combine nouns together with abandon."

The following pop grammar story, from the *Harper Dictionary,* is one of my very favorites, since it ends not in misery but in mutual congratulation. Experts were asked about the word *graduate.* Formerly, say the editors, purists insisted on the formation "She *was graduated from* Vassar." Today, the simpler "She *graduated* from Vassar," is considered entirely acceptable. But what about the new construction: "She *graduated* Vassar"?

Heywood Hale Broun rejected even the sentence that the editors called entirely acceptable, and in doing so told this story:

> " 'She graduated from' is not acceptable to me. . . . Years ago, Herbert Bayard Swope, one-time editor of the World, asked me when I had left college.
> 'Sir,' I replied, beginning as most people did in addressing Swope, 'I was graduated in 1940.'
> Although he was elderly and heavy, he dragged himself up from an easy chair and lumbered across the room with outstretched hand.
> 'I haven't heard it correctly used in years,' he rumbled in a voice agrowl with emotion. It was, for me, a ribbon on my diploma."

Southey is cited by the OED as using *graduate* in the active voice in 1807—so there really had been quite a few years of misuse —but at least Swope and Broun got some fun out of being more pure in their English than the English poet who used to apologize for Americanisms. *Was graduated from,* a construction even the editors of the *Harper Dictionary* thought old-fashioned, has some-how got into several newspaper stylebooks, and many articles—especially in the more disreputable and fun-to-read tabloids; they used to say something like *Heywood Hale Broun (Swarthmore, '40),* but now they do the whole rounded period: *Heywood Hale Broun, who was graduated from Swarthmore College in 1940,* which probably does no harm, except making it hard for new purists to get the same ribbon on their diplomas.

Wilson Follett liked to attack words not merely as barbarisms or unidiomatic, but as philosophically dangerous. Of the word *controversial,* he wrote:

> *Twentieth-century politics in the democracies has so shifted the meaning of this word that it now seldom refers to actual controversy but more often to some latent quality in a person or an object that may provoke unfavorable comment. . . .* [A controversial book used to be a book that engaged in controversy; now it seems to mean a book that somebody might disapprove of.]
>
> *. . . A controversial temperament is one thing; a quiet worker who has controversy explode around his ears is another. The only suggestions are to continue to use* controversial *in its former sense and to describe in as many words as necessary the pegs on which controversy hangs. This course has other merits than the linguistic, for* controversial *in the new sense may well degenerate in a tag for discrediting everybody who is not colorless, to the detriment of both democracy and the individual.*

The original meaning of the word *controversial* was "subject to controversy; open to discussion; debatable, questionable; disputed." It has been used that way since 1583. The meaning that Follett thought was the original one appeared first in 1659, and the OED has no citation for all of the eighteenth century. Not until Crabbe in 1807 was *controversial* again used to mean "of, pertaining to, or of the nature of controversy; polemical." Follett's notions of the history of the English language were, of course, always controversial (in both senses of the word).

Sometimes, words do become dangerous—because of the bad uses they are put to. Consider the word *occupy:* the OED traces the word to the fourteenth century but says:

> *The disuse of this verb in the 17th and most of the 18th c[enturies] is notable. Against 104 quot[e]s for 16th c[entury], we*

have for 17th only 8, outside the Bible of 1611 (where it occurs 10 times), and for the 18th c[entury] only 10. . . . The verb occurs only twice (equivocally) in Shakes[peare], is entirely absent from the Concordances to Milton and Pope, is not used by Gray; all Johnson's quot[e]s, exc[ept] 2, are from the Bible of 1611. It was again freely used by Cowper (13 instances in the Concordance). This avoidance appears to have been due to its vulgar employment. . . .

From the late fifteenth century until the beginning of the eighteenth, *occupy* was a euphemism: to occupy someone meant to have sex with them. This is kind of a nice euphemism, as a metaphor for the way troops *occupy a town* sometimes after a battle, sometimes without a struggle. When the word stopped being used to mean sex, it came back into use again—its meaning unchanged, and the language unharmed. Remember to tell your friends about the verb *occupy* when they complain about *gay* being ruined forever because it is now used to mean "homosexual."

Lounsbury says that there was a great controversy over the word *tireless.* Some people insisted that *-less* was a suffix that could only be applied to nouns, "and we must all take pains to say *untiring.*"

George H. McKnight, in *The Evolution of the English Language,* says that there was a similar struggle over the word *environment*—but he does not say what it was, and I have not been able to find any evidence of the struggle, or what it was about. Maybe people thought we should use *environs* instead? But to the OED *environs* means "the outskirts . . . of a town." *Environment* seems to have been used a lot of times by Carlyle, and that fact was enough for many people to attack a word as non-English. Lounsbury mentions new back-formations "of a class frequently used in newspapers"—*to burgle, to enthuse,* and *to resurrect* (to rob the grave of a dead body for the purposes of dissection), and assumes that all three will remain colloquial, "stigmatized as *low* in the dictionaries." He was right about *burgle.* New laws have made *resurrect* obsolete in the sense of graverobbing—but of course it is a very respectable word with purists, who are always trying to "resurrect old meanings of words." *Enthuse,* which Lounsbury called "the worst of the three," seems perfectly standard to me, but only 14% of the experts in the *Harper Dictionary* agree. The OED originally called the word *enthuse* "an ignorant back-formation from Enthusiasm," and labeled it an Americanism. The Supplement calls it originally an Americanism, and cites recent use by *The London Times* and *The Manchester Guardian.*

Lounsbury lists several more prescriptions of the nineteenth century: never say *Tomorrow is Sunday;* it should be *Tomorrow will be Sunday.* Since *none* is a contraction of the Old English words for *no one,* it must take a singular verb: *None is left,* not *none are left.* Lounsbury, though he does make distinctions among words (and thinks *enthuse* is worse than *resurrect,* for example), is very hard on both these prescriptions—because they are attempts to change very old idioms. *None is* seems to have bothered him especially: "There is no harm in a man's limiting his employment of *none* to the singular verb in his own usage, if he derives any pleasure from that form of linguistic martyrdom. But why should he go about seeking to inflict upon others the misery which owes its origin to his own ignorance?" Possibly because the misery of the word worrier is the kind that not only loves, but creates, its own company.

One way of dealing with this misery is the way of Sir Walter Scott, who was often criticized for Scotticisms and solecisms. In his diary, April 22, 1826, he says that his son-in-law has joined the critics and

> points out . . . *some solecisms in my style, as* amid *for* amidst, scarce *for* scarcely. Whose, *he says, is the proper genitive of* which *only at such times as* which *retains its quality of impersonification. Well! I will try to remember all this, but after all I write grammar as I speak, to make my meaning known, and a solecism in point of composition, like a Scotch word in speaking, is indifferent to me. . . . I believe the Bailiff in the Good-natured Man is not far wrong when he says, "One man has one way of expressing himself, and another another, and that is all the difference between them."*

three

Your Welcome to Using My Idiom

(If You're Careful Not to Breaking It)

The preference for the infinitive over the participle also inter-
feres with idiom. Ear and mind insist that we say I look forward to
going away, not I look forward to go away. But less common paral-
lels to this construction are repeatedly mangled; e.g., You're welcome to use my typewriter. . . .

That's what Wilson Follett says in *Modern American Usage,*
and he goes on to provide us with an example of the unmangled
idiom:

You're welcome to using my typewriter.

This is an extraordinary sentence, which becomes even more
extraordinary when you consider the history of the book it appears in. Follett began *Modern American Usage* in 1958. He was
in his seventies, a distinguished teacher, editor, and critic. Edward Weeks, former editor of *The Atlantic,* called him "a tart and
vigorous defender of the English language," and ranked him with
Fowler as a champion of good usage. Follett saw the book as his
greatest achievement—but died in 1963, before he had a chance
to finish it. Jacques Barzun, himself a distinguished academic,
critic, and writer on usage, then gathered together a group of
almost equally distinguished scholars and poets to help him complete Follett's work: Carlos Baker, Frederick W. Dupee, James D.
Hart, Lionel Trilling, Dudley Fitts, and Phyllis McGinley. "Each
of them," says the publisher's note in the beginning of the book,

"gave *Modern American Usage* the benefit of his literary skill and educated judgment."

But all these distinguished writers—many of whom we read with pleasure—turn out to be wrong.

First, *You're welcome to using my typewriter* is not good English. The OED traces the idiom *welcome to* back to the fifteenth century. In every citation, the OED shows *welcome to* used with the infinitive. No one, anywhere that I can find, has ever written *welcome to using,* except Wilson Follett.

Second, and more important, *You're welcome to using my typewriter* is just simply not what our ear and mind demand when we're speaking normal idiomatic English. If we heard a foreigner say that sentence, our impulse would be to correct him, as gently as possible, because "that's not the way we say it in English."

What does *idiom* mean, then, in fullprofessorese? Well, it seems to mean whatever we don't say:

"Americans, who practically never say *different to,* an extremely common locution in British English, are addicted to *identical to,* which is probably almost as unidiomatic everywhere as *different to* seems in the United States."

Well, if we're addicted to it—doesn't that make it our idiom? Even the *Harper Dictionary,* no model of permissiveness, says that after *identical,* either *with* or *to* are acceptable. But in fullprofessorese, when there is a choice, one is always wrong and must be struggled against: as Follett says in the introduction:

"In writing as in morals, negative and positive merits are complementary; resistance to the wrong and weak is, *ipso facto,* cultivation of the right and the strong. . . . Prose is not necessarily good because it obeys the rules of syntax, but it is fairly certain to be bad if it ignores them."

This belief of Follett's leads him to give us little examples of "right and strong prose" throughout the book, examples that demonstrate in themselves how foolish his belief is. Here, for example, is a "wrong and weak" sentence:

> While I may not have realized it as a student, the education I received was the basis for whatever success I have achieved.

Those readers who are not fluent in fullprofessorese will need a guide to all the errors in that sentence. And luckily for us Follett provides one: Here is what makes that sentence "wrong and weak":

(a) The pronoun *it* comes before the word *it* refers to—its *antecedent*. And *antecedent* means, according to the Latin roots of the word, "what comes before." Therefore, an antecedent must always come before the pronoun. This is both logical and irrefutable. So we must never say, "I can't help it, I just don't like English teachers."

(b) The pronoun *it* refers to the entire clause that follows; as in "I can't help it, I just don't like English teachers." But an antecedent must be single word, not a clause—because that's the way antecedents worked in Latin, and that's the way they ought to work in English, and in *Modern American Usage*.

(c) The sentence *really* means:

> The undergraduate did not know what produced the success he achieved later.

This is the most difficult part of the Follett argument—as always, it is hard for an ordinary native speaker of the language to figure out what a sentence *really* means in fullprofessorese. But read the sentence again. We think it more or less means:

> While I was a student, I did not realize that education would be the basis for my success in life.

Follett thinks it *really* means:

> While I was a student, I did not realize that education was the basis of my success in later life. And of course how could I? I didn't even know I would be a success in later life.

Follett therefore rewrites the sentence to avoid all those terrible problems:

> Though as a student I may not have realized the importance of education, my education has been the basis of whatever success I achieved in later life.

Now, read those two sentences again—Follett's correction and the original. If you agree that the second sentence is better, maybe you'll agree with all the following improvements:

"The car was given five coats of primer paint and hand-rubbed between each coat." It should be: "after each coat." That sounds sensible, but it's because the example is an odd one. Try using that form of improvement for a sentence like this: "Each car is given five coats of paint, and hand-sanded between each coat." You'll wind up with a sandy car.

Bergen Evans, in *Comfortable Words,* adds this little bit of wisdom about *between each:*

> *There's a great to-do about the expression* between each. . . . *But actually, each is what is called a "distributive." That is, it refers to an individual but only in its quality as a member of a group. There is always a plural in mind when we say* each. *We can't use* each *where there is only one; we can't say "each Europe. . . ."*
>
> *When we say "between each" (as in between each coat), we are saying by elision, (between each coat and the next one). And the language permits elision.*

As an added argument, Evans merely notes that the expression has been used "by almost every distinguished writer of English" from Shakespeare on.

Follett writes:

"Like another Philadelphian, Benjamin Franklin, Dr. Squibb's interests were catholic." Faulty parallelism. Should be: "Dr. Squibb's interests, like Franklin's, were catholic." That sounds sensible—until you realize that the fact that Franklin was "another Philadelphian" was left out of the sentence. Try putting it back in:

> Dr. Squibb's interests, like Franklin's, another Philadelphian, were catholic.
> Dr. Squibb's interests, like Franklin, another Philadelphian's, were catholic.

The improvement starts to look a little confused. It's almost as if the author, by concentrating so hard on logical and grammatical rules, lost sight of what is being said.

There is a tendency to use *each other* for two, and *one another* for more than two, says Follett, "but it creates no obligation." Still, "it is sensible to preserve the distinction." First, there never has been such a distinction, and pretending that there is, "is an attempt to improve on the language and not a report of how the words are used or have been used in the past" (Bergen and Cornelia Evans). But Follett is not content with calling the distinction sensible, he must show us how sensible the attempt to preserve it becomes:

The whole circle took each others' hands. *But they will have to take* one another's hands *and be held fast in a logical clinch, for each takes a hand of each of two others—two hands—and yet* another's *cannot be anything but grammatically singular. It would be* simpler *[my emphasis] to start again and say:* They formed a circle by holding hands.

Phyllis McGinley was a Pulitzer Prize–winning poet; Dudley Fitts a translator of Homer and the editor of the Yale Series of Younger Poets; Carlos Baker is a distinguished biographer of Hemingway; Jacques Barzun a famous writer on education—a former dean of faculties at Columbia University—a translator of Beaumarchais and Flaubert. Didn't any of them—couldn't one of them—have looked at that passage and realized what nonsense it is?

Here is more nonsense:

"Most readers will feel the ineptitude of: *The three explosions were touched off one after the other.*" The sentence full of eptitude will read: *one after another.*

"When describing the material of which an object is made, *of,* not *in,* is idiomatic. . . . The temptation to substitute *in* arises from the shopper's natural query, *Have you the same model in green? . . .* But this variation does not authorize *He treated himself to a tomb in marble.*" This idiomatic use of *in* is traced by the OED back to 1663. In 1710, Addison uses it: "The Statue of an Horse in Brass." Defoe and Dickens are also cited.

". . . The Latin plural *insignia* is easily mistaken for a singular. . . . The legitimate singular . . . *insignee* . . . occurs in print so rarely that many are unaware of its existence . . . [an error] amounting to a retroactive alteration of Latin, as if the Romans needed us to straighten out their language." Among other retroactive alterations of Latin is the use of *stamina,* the plural of *stamen,* as a singular. Among retroactive alterers of Latin—that is, among those who use *insignia* as if it was an English word and singular—are Washington Irving: "In his hand he bore a slender white wand, the dreaded insignia of his office"; and the United States of America, which officially uses *insignia* as a singular when referring to Army insignia, and officially uses a plural: *insignias.*

Jargon is one of those words which seems to make professors forget about meaning and concentrate on form. Under the heading *Jargon,* Follett lists a number of examples and offers his own improvements. Like all scholarly improvements, they are worth examining carefully. Here is Column A *(Jargon)* and Column B *(The Right and Strong)*

Column A

After trying a variety of methods of operations, this year the seminar operated against the framework of an outline the chairman prepared and presented at the opening meeting. While the various presentations did not follow, or indeed in many cases tie into, this outline, yet it definitely provided a greater coherence to the seminar as a total operation and I am grateful for the distinct contributions which were made to my thinking.

Column B

After trying various ways of conducting it, this year the seminar used an outline I presented at the outset. Although some of the reports diverged from the outline, yet the outline helped, and I am grateful for what I learned from the discussions.

First, the opening phrase in both Column A and B is what Follett elsewhere calls *a dangler*—that is, what normal pop grammarians call *a dangling modifier.* It seems to modify *seminar* or even *year,* but actually it is *I* who have been trying the various ways. Second—oddly enough—Column B starts with the pronoun *it* placed before its antecedent, something that Follett himself complains about elsewhere in his own book.

Third, the two columns mean different things.

The speaker in Column A is congratulating the other members of the seminar and being rather humble about his own work as chairman. He provided an outline. Some people ignored it. Still, the outline provided "greater coherence," and he is grateful for all the contributions made by the various speakers. They have changed his own thinking.

The speaker in Column B seems to be congratulating himself. It's true that he leaves out that he prepared the outline as well as presented it—but it appears that he has been trying all these various ways of conducting the seminar all by himself. He notes that some reports diverged from the outline (a touch of asperity there?) but insists that the outline helped (because the rest of the reports followed it? that seems to be the implication). And this speaker is grateful "for what I learned from the discussions" (not the reports? especially not the reports that diverged?).

Thanking participants to a seminar who may have disagreed entirely with the speaker's idea of what was important is one thing (Column A). Congratulating yourself on what you learned is another (Column B). The reader can choose whichever way of talking he likes—but he should recognize that if he talks jargon he will probably get people to return; if he talks fullprofessorese they will probably stay away.

"One thing is preferable to another," says Follett. "There is no defense for *A cold war is more preferable than peace on dishonorable terms.*"

First, the defense: *preferable* has never been considered an absolute in the English language. Samuel Johnson used "far preferable" in 1751; Nathaniel Hawthorne "infinitely preferable" in 1850 (in *The Scarlet Letter).*

Next, the solution: "Nothing but a certain awkwardness" prevents Follett from proposing this solution: *Cold war is more preferable to abandoning allies than nominal peace would be at that price.* At least here, *more preferable* refers to two *preferences,* says Follett; but there are better ways: *"If the choice is peace at the price of betraying one's allies or a cold war, then a cold war is more to be preferred";* or else: *"Better cold war than nominal peace at the price of abandoning allies."*

Once again, Follett proposes solutions that seem much more awkward than the problem. Once again, he not only rewrites the sentence but tampers with the thought—those allies, which keep recurring in all his proposals for improvement—are not in the original sentence at all.

Let's go back to Follett's Column A and Column B for more improvements:

Column A
The prediction of the existence of antiparticles was made by P. A. M. Dirac in 1927 and its confirmation was an important reason for the construction of the Bevatron at Berkeley in 1954.

Column B
Dirac predicted in 1927 that antiparticles exist. Once this statement was confirmed, the Bevatron was built at Berkeley in 1954.

Column A sounds funny because we are not used to a prediction about the present, and a prediction that something already exists is a contradiction. Column B sounds different because it says the confirmation of the prediction was the *only* reason for the construction of the Bevatron, and because Column A implies that the confirmation came in 1954, and Column B that the builders of the Bevatron waited twenty-seven years for no reason at all.

Column A	Column B
Now they would suffer the proximity they had always avoided.	Now they would be together as they had never wanted to be.

Column A sounds like they don't like being near each other; Column B seems to mean they might like to try another position.

Column A	Column B
A waitress in a restaurant at a missile base can tell by who is not there what missile—or missiles— is going up.	A waitress in a restaurant at a missile base can tell what missile is—or missiles are— going up or: what missile is going up—or what missiles.

Neither suggestion in Column B is attractive, says Follett himself, because the construction that joins a singular and a plural "always poses a choice of evils." And if there is a choice—and it's between a sentence that sounds fine and a sentence that violates Follett's idea of grammar—then it's better to be unattractive and correct.

> *American English has lately developed, largely under the influence of advertisers and packagers, a construction deeply at variance with the genius of the language. We now have* easy-to-read books *and* ready-to-bake foods. *This agglutination . . . goes against the normal articulation of thought, which is* books easy to read, food ready to bake. . . . *One may surmise that our minds have been prepared by reading the algebra of headlines . . .* NEW STEEL PEACE HOPE. . . . *The reader must unscramble the ideas for himself. In the headline it is only the* hope *that is* new, *though the adjective stands before* steel *and* peace. . . . *In a certain sense all these locutions can be uttered; but when in publicity for a directory we are promised* 4,000 hard-to-find biographies *and in a dictionary we are asked to note its concern for* hard-to-say words, *we have reached a point where agglutination resembles baby talk. . . . If we wish to protect ourselves from this new assault on our wits, we must begin by*

avoiding every form of easy compounding—*e.g.,* accident-prone, action-oriented *and* air-conditioned.

Follett does not bother to tell us how to avoid *air-conditioned* —which is a distinct loss to modern American usage. I imagine that *air-conditioned apartment* would turn out to be something like *apartment with air cooled*—though that sounds like it just has a fan in it. *Apartment with air cooled by machine?* Well, a fan is a machine. All that seems left is *apartment with air cooled by that machine which the vulgar call an air conditioner,* which has the ring of the Follett style to it.

It's odd that Follett should find compounding so difficult on the one hand that "the reader must unscramble the ideas for himself," and so easy on the other that it "resembles baby talk." It is even odder that he should believe that compounding has lately developed, only in America, and under the influence of advertisers and packagers:

> Your inns-of-court man (Ben Jonson, *The Alchemist*)
> She stopped his halfpenny a week pocket money (Charles Dickens, *Nicholas Nickleby*)
> The hand-to-hand nature of the battle (Rudyard Kipling, *The Light That Failed*)
> She did not make her calculations in this debtor-and-creditor fashion (W. M. Thackeray, *The Newcomes*)
> The Walter Scott Middle-Age sham civilization (Mark Twain, *Life on the Mississippi*)

Among other users of what Otto Jespersen calls *string compounds* are Brontë, Swinburne, Dickinson, Tennyson, and Hardy. It seems extremely odd that all these writers use a construction "deeply at variance with the genius of the language."

But oddest of all is the fact that Follett should use a string compound himself as a correction of normal idiom. Yet that's what he does.

> *Florida's governor, . . . the town's high school, . . . the*
> *nation's capital . . . [:] The truth is that these possessives in the 's*
> *form are newfangled and false. . . . The of in these phrases is not*
> *a true possessive but a defining and partitive of, as in* loss of
> breath. . . . *We must stick to the ancestral rule which, with a few*
> *exceptions, reserves possessives in 's for ownership by a person . . . [:]*
> The governor of Florida, . . . the national capital, . . . the town
> high school. . . .

The *town high school* seems to me to be very much like NEW STEEL PEACE HOPE: it is the school that belongs to the town, even though *town* stands before *high*—and *town* isn't even an adjective, it's a noun made up of other nouns, exactly like a *Steel Peace Hope.*

And of course Follett is wrong again in his "ancestral rule" that *'s* indicates ownership by a person "with a few exceptions."

The problem with all these possessives, says Follett, is that they do not "stick to the ancestral rule which, with a few exceptions, reserves possessives in *'s* for ownership by a person."

In five minutes, with a copy of a dictionary of quotations, I found examples of the *'s* used without indicating ownership by a person, by Tennyson, Prior, Shakespeare, Gilbert (of Gilbert and Sullivan), Emerson, Marvell, Milton, Lamb, Byron, Kipling, Shelley, and Marlowe. The rule is not ancestral, and the exceptions are not few.

Bergen and Cornelia Evans point out: "No ownership is intended in *one's elders, a man's murderer, our son's school,* and no personification in *tomorrow's breakfast, the play's success, the earth's surface, the nation's economy.*" It's easy enough to add other examples: *a good day's work, a good night's sleep, New Year's Eve.*

In fact, in 1940, Charles Fries, working on a study commissioned by the National Council of Teachers of English, discovered that in a representative sample of prose by college graduates, only 40 percent of the *'s* constructions implied ownership (and even this was a "liberal" interpretation—it allowed *man's wife* and *boy's parents* as ownership).

Here are some other examples of the use of *'s* as classified by Fries:

Subjective genitive: since the soldier's enlistment (= since the soldier enlisted).

Genitive of origin: the mother's affidavit (= the affidavit made by the mother).

Objective genitive: he contributed toward the family's support (= he contributed money to support the family).

Descriptive genitive: a women's college (= a college for women).

Genitive of measure: a month's time (telling us how much time).

Bergen and Cornelia Evans point out that there was a time in the development of the English language when the genitive form of certain words could be used as an adverb.

> *Most of our adverbs that end in an* s *(or* z*) sound, such as* nowadays, since, sometimes, upwards, *are survivals from this period. The final* s *in* on all fours, at sixes and sevens, *and in* needs *in* he needs must *is also a sign of the adverbial genitive. Today there is no feeling that this is a genitive relationship and an apostrophe is never used in words of this kind.*
>
> *Although the construction is no longer understood, the habit of forming adverbs on the old genitive pattern is not entirely dead. It shows itself in certain final* s*'s and substitute* of *phrases, such as* I work evenings *and* I work of an evening . . . I like to read of a rainy afternoon *[Rainy afternoons, I like to read] and* Wednesdays I work in the garden.

"It is a serious mistake to dismiss the genitive as the 'possessive' case, because more than half the time it represents some other relation," say the Evanses. "Unless these relations are understood a speaker does not know when he can substitute a phrase for the genitive or the genitive for a phrase and is tied to stereotyped forms of expression."

I hardly ever disagree with the Evanses—here they seem guilty of overstatement. Probably few of us are aware of all the uses of the genitive 's in English—but all of us have been using it, and substituting phrases for it, at will. It's only by reading Wilson Follett, and believing him, that we become tied to stereotyped forms of expression.

Still more nonsense:

"The user of the word [*human* instead of *human being*] can plead historical precedent as well as logical parallel and the support of some dictionaries, but not without convicting himself of a stylistic blind spot and a defective sense of present usage." I have the feeling that if Follett had seen that sentence in someone else's prose he would have been busy telling us that the sentence really means it is the *pleading* of historical precedent which convicts the user of a stylistic blind spot— but let that go. The important thing is that dictionaries are based on present usage—and not on a defective sense of pre-

sent usage. What is defective in that sentence is the use of
plead. We don't have to plead. We use words. And if not all
the dictionaries have caught up with us, sooner or later they
must, and will.

Column A	Column B
There is a growing conviction that "neither party is worth a damn" on civil rights on the national level—and, in some cases, on the local level.	. . . in the nation at large or in the towns and counties.

Follett's intention here is to get rid of the word *level* which
he thinks is jargon. And he has done it—and, of course, changed
the meaning. Column A means that in some cases one party *is*
worth a damn on the local level. Column B forgets this—and also
forgets there are other local levels, for example, neighborhoods
and cities; it seems to mean that neither party is worth a damn
in rural areas.

Unpractical (rather than *impractical*) is the word generally
used "by careful writers," says Follett. Among the careless, according to the OED, is John Stuart Mill. Bergen and Cornelia
Evans say that *impractical* is the normal American use; *unpractical* what the British "generally" use (the Evanses admire the
British use, and even urge its adoption—but do not presume to tell
us what "careful writers" do).

Finally, I give one more Column A and B, which I do not
present side by side because Follett spends so much time explaining what's wrong with Column A, and the explanation, and the
results, are so indicative of full-blown fullprofessorese.

Under the heading of *verbiage,* Follett says:

> Getting rid of superfluous words has an advantage commonly
> overlooked: the automatic suppression of weaknesses that flourish
> in diffuse writing but are starved out by economy. . . .
> . . . Take a passage from a book about life within the Arctic
> Circle—. . . a book that has everything one could ask for except
> good, tight writing. Here is a representative paragraph about one
> of the ways of catching seals:

> Column A
> Another way of luring the seal—although not so profitable as
> the first—is to fool him while he is under the water. Two men

> *walk behind each other, keeping step with one another, so that the seal down below hears them. To the seal it sounds as if only one man were walking. When they reach the blowhole, the location of which must be known first, the first man continues on, while the other takes a stand by the hole without moving at all. The seal thinks that the man has passed by without noticing the blowhole, and after a while he confidently comes to the hole, only to find out too late that he has been fooled.*

Now Follett lists the defects: two men can't walk behind each other. It's clumsy to use *each other* and *one another* in the same sentence. *Seal* occurs four times. And more: "Why write *continues on,* and mention *luring the seal* since that is the subject of the whole chapter? Why point out that the seal is under the water? *Blowhole* is enough" to indicate that the seal is under water, and

> *it is obvious that the two men could not approach if its location were not known. Further waste . . . the seal listens twice to their footsteps* (hears them; it sounds as if). *And a good reader will not care what the author thinks a seal thinks about what the hunter thinks. The writer talks as if to feeble minds. By the right kind of effort he could have had his say in a paragraph as short as this:*

> *Column B*
> *Another, less profitable way is this: Two men approach a blowhole, keeping step, so that the seal hears them as one. The leader walks on past the blowhole; the harpooner stops by it, motionless. Soon the deluded seal confidently comes to the hole and is caught.*

It's hard to know what to say about those two paragraphs. Follett really seems to be pleased with his improvements, and really does not seem to understand that something has been squeezed out of Column A: not verbiage, or weakness, but strength —an almost indescribable kind of strength. Reading Column A, you *know* that the writer was there, and you see the scene he describes. Reading Column B, you *know* just as certainly that you are reading a summary of somebody else's experience: less words, less language, less meaning, less realism.

But even that doesn't seem to begin to explain what's wrong with Column B. It's just . . . it's just that there is such a thing as a tin ear, for language as well as for music; the writer of Column B has a tin ear, or at least had a tin ear in this one particular sentence.

It's hard for me to believe that any small group will ever be a threat to the English language. But it does seem that the professor of English, the teacher of writing, if he sets out to force students to turn Column A writing into Column B writing—and succeeds—is the carrier of appalling ideas about language.

Worst
Words Defended

Thunderbore
and the Instinct for Poetry

"Use words correctly to mean what they mean and half the difficulties of life will be solved," roars Thunderbore Absolute. But, alas, how do you do it? Words have many meanings, often contradictory meanings, and their meanings change. The most one can say is, "This is what these particular people thought this word meant in that context at that time." And, of course, some of them disagreed; or the question would never have been raised.

Bergen Evans, *Comfortable Words*

Comfortable Words was published in 1959, more than twenty years ago. It predates *Strictly Speaking* by fifteen years, the *Harper Dictionary of Contemporary Usage* by sixteen, Wilson Follett's *Modern American Usage* by seven—and it answers most of the objections to plain modern talk raised in all those books. *Comfortable Words* is out of print, but it turns up from time to time on the dusty shelves of the used bookstores, where the Fowler and the Pei and the old-time imitation Webster's are stored. It is a shame the book is not better known—especially by pop grammarians and ignorant purists: Evans is a real conservative, a defender of good diction who complains about the use of the word *fun* as an adjective, but manages to do it with style, wit, and a sense of language that all writers on language might envy:

> *Can* fun *be used as an adjective ("We had a fun time") or an adverb ("Fun drive the Lark today")? Not in my hearing without*

inducing nausea. However, it is only fair to add that hundreds of nouns have become adjectives and hundreds of words from all parts of speech have become adverbs and there is no reason why fun *should not be so used if the people who speak the language want to so use it. For centuries* fun *was used as a verb (*"Do you think to fun me out of it?"*) and the participle was used as a noun (*"Cease your funning"*) and while both of these now strike our ears as offensive, they didn't bother the distinguished writers who used them. As often with what is posed as a grammatical problem, the real question is one of taste or style. One reason, perhaps, that* fun *as an adjective is offensive is that its use in this way doesn't seem natural. It is so used almost entirely by affected, shrill young people striving a little too hard to be gay and breezy.*

This passage seems to me to be a model of linguistic prescription: it reveals that the prescription itself is a personal opinion, shows how the opinion is based on observation of people, and points out that there is no linguistic reason to avoid using *fun* as an adjective—and certainly no "danger to the language" from the rather inconsequential people Evans heard using it.

More often, Evans is convinced by actual usage:

Rebecca West in one of her novels has an unpleasant, affected American woman say, "I'm just awful, amn't I?" On first reading this I assumed that Miss West assumed that amn't I *was an American locution, and I rashly said in print that it had never been heard on land or sea or in the air. But I was soon informed by a host of correspondents, mostly Irish, that* Amn't I *is not only in wide general use but is definitely preferable to the vulgar* Ain't I? *or the genteel* Aren't I?*

Justly reproved, I have been more alert and have been rewarded by finding Amn't I *in the writings of Honor Tracy, Rumer Godden and James Joyce. That will do for me.* Amn't I *is in the language and unimpeachable.*

Still more often, Evans delights in twitting unreasonable and silly prescription:

A determined mother writes that whenever her wayward children had used lit *instead of* lighted, *she had "corrected" them. Her fourteen-year-old son, however, plainly a lad of mettle, had shown her* lit *where she would have insisted on* lighted *in the magazine* Life. *Broken and bewildered, she stretches lame hands and gropes for guidance: "Is* lit *now acceptable in place of* lighted?"

Let her drain the bitter chalice to the last drop: it is not only

> *now acceptable, but always has been. From the beginnings of the*
> *language, ages before Henry Luce said, "Let there be* Life!" *the*
> *two forms* lit *and* lighted *have been interchangeable.*
>
> *About two hundred years ago some self-appointed oracle*
> *decided that* lit *was "low and vulgar" and millions, of whom this*
> *poor mother is one, have become afraid of it.*

Evans has a knack for picking out quotes. He reports that Theodore Bernstein objects to *and* in the sentence from *The New York Times*: "Mr. Smart decided to try and get Ernest Hemingway to write for the publication," and then quotes, without comment, from *The Sun Also Rises:* "Don't look at the horses, after the bull hits them. . . . Watch the charge and see the picador try and keep the bull off." One example is worth a thousand arguments—if it's exactly the right example.

Comfortable Words is slightly out-of-date—there are a few new additions to the pop grammarian's hit list that it does not mention. But it is still useful, and delightful, and full of counterarguments and counterexamples. Here are a few of the current worst words—the kind that every purist hates—as defended by Evans, or by extrapolation from arguments presented by Evans.

All Right

". . . There are no such forms as *all-right* or *allright,* and *alright* . . . is still regarded as a vulgarism . . . ," says Fowler in *Modern English Usage,* "though even the last, if seldom allowed by the compositors to appear in print, is often seen (through confusion with already and altogether) in MS." Pop grammarians are almost unanimous in condemning *alright*—and there is probably no word more often edited out of contemporary prose.

Evans notes that no dictionary lists *alright* as acceptable (that is no longer true—*Webster's Third New International Dictionary* cites the word without any indication that it is substandard, and uses Gertrude Stein as an example of its use; the Supplement to the OED simply calls *alright* "a frequent spelling of *all right*"). He then goes on to defend the word in an eminently sensible way: we can hear the distinction between *all right* and *alright* in speech; the words mean different things:

His answers were all right does not mean the same thing as *His answers were alright.* Evans says that the people who write *alright* are not slovenly—"they are simply asking for the privilege of making a distinction in writing which is accepted in speech. And since the tendency of writing for more than a century has been toward approximating speech, the chances are that *alright* will soon be regarded as standard."

As we see from Webster's and the OED—the reward of good sense is being able to make sensible predictions: *alright* is now regarded as standard by some lexicographers. Of the others, Evans writes:

> *Those who feel that in insisting on* all right *they are manning the bastions of purity and defending our language from the corruption of the vulgar may be a little startled to learn that their counterparts across the Atlantic insist with equal firmness on* near by *and regard our defenders as vulgar illiterates because they write* forever *instead of* for ever.

Once more, Evans presents us with an elegant argument by example.

Dangling Participles

But, lying in my bed, everything seemed so different.

Galsworthy, *On Forsyte 'Change*

We all learned about the dangers of dangling participles, usually in grade school, and from made-up sentences like this, quoted by the Evanses in *A Dictionary of Contemporary American Usage:*

Having eaten our lunch, the bus went on to Chicago.

Evans calls this a "pernicious rule" and insists that in this sentence, the trouble is not that *having eaten our lunch* is "dangling"—on the contrary, *having eaten our lunch* is firmly attached to *bus.* The blunder, says Evans, lies in connecting a participial phrase which has force of time, manner, or circumstance to a noun. He adds that this is likely to happen only when one is using *having* followed by a past participle—and that otherwise it is extremely rare, except in made-up examples.

This seems to be true:

Our lunches being eaten, the bus went on to Chicago.

This does not have the same comic effect of the first sentence.

The Morrises, in the *Harper Dictionary,* give this example of dangling participle:

Coming out of the subway, the sun blinded me.

This is exactly the kind of supposedly dangling participle that the Evanses are defending—and exactly the kind that is defended by Otto Jespersen as *loose participles,* "generally blamed as slipshod language by grammarians . . . but found even in some accurate writers. In some cases the participle relates to the *I* implied in *my,* etc." Just like the *coming* in *coming out of the subway* clearly relates to *my eyes.*

Among the writers using this construction and cited by Jespersen are Marlowe, Shakespeare, Milton, Defoe, Fielding, Goldsmith, Franklin, Keats, Shelley, Austen, Brontë, Dickens, Rossetti, Huxley, Shaw, and Galsworthy.

Besides these, Jespersen gives examples of loose participles that are "firmly established in the language." *Talking* ("talking of chasms," Keats; "talking of war, there'll be trouble in the Balkans," Kipling). *Speaking* ("Speaking of daughters, I have seen Miss Dombey," Dickens). *Judging,* as in "Judging by the time she spent over it, the letter must have been a long one," Collins) (Jespersen adds that this is a common phrase). *Counting,* as in "There were three or four of us, *counting* me" (Dickens).

Strictly speaking, as Jespersen notes, *strictly speaking* is always a loose participle—perhaps if Newman had known anything at all about grammar he would have avoided that "dangler" for the title of his first book. *Begging your pardon, generally speaking,* and even *considering*—"That's very good of you, considering" (Galsworthy)—are all loose participles.

It rained hard coming back is a loose participle, used by Thomas Huxley. George Bernard Shaw habitually used this idiom to set the scene when his plays were printed in book form: *Looking up the hill, the cottage is seen in a left-hand corner of the garden, etc.*

So, looking at the subject objectively, there is nothing wrong with the loose participle. Even granting that it is attacked by pop grammarians, people will continue to use the loose participle—without even being conscious of it, as those last two sentences demonstrate.

Between Every/Between Each

Between each is dealt with elsewhere. There are only two reasons to bring it up here:

One, Bergen Evans, in *Comfortable Words,* demonstrates that *between* is a distributive. It refers to an individual but only as a member of a group—there always has to be another individual or some kind of plural in mind when we use *each.* "We can't use *each* where there is only one; we can't say *each Europe* or *each China.*" (Of course, politics being somewhat different than geography we now can say *each China,* if we believe in the two Chinas theory).

"When we say *between each* as in *He rested between each stroke,* we are saying by elision *He rested between each stroke and the next.* And the language permits elision."

The second reason to mention *between each* again is *A Dictionary of American-English Usage* (1957), an adaptation of Fowler's *Modern English Usage,* by Margaret Nicholson. Nicholson disagrees with Evans—we must not say *"A pitcher who tried to gain time by blowing his nose between every ball."* Among several alternatives proposed by Nicholson is this one: *"A pitcher who tried to gain time by blowing his nose between the balls."* Must have been interesting to watch his contortions on television; and I, for one, would have given him all the time in the world.

I Could Care Less

William and Mary Morris, editors of the *Harper Dictionary of Contemporary Usage,* report that they have been dumfounded by the increasing use of *I could care less* to mean *I couldn't care less.* It seems, they say, "an ignorant debasement of the language."

I could care less has moved into the forefront of fad language prescription. Unlike the word *hopefully* it has no defenders worth mentioning—since it is a sentence, not a word, it cannot turn up in dictionaries to confound the precisionist. Many people who talk about language to me bring up this neat little rejoinder: "What you say may be true—but surely you don't accept abominations, like *I could care less.*"

In the beginning I tried to defend *I could care less* by pointing out there is such a thing as irony—and ironical rejoinders are very common in English: *Big deal* means *small potatoes; oh sure* means *I don't believe a word you say; very funny* means *that isn't funny in the slightest.* So, *I could care less* is an ignorant debasement of the language? I'm really worried.

But appreciation of irony, or even cheap sarcasm, is not a strong point with pop grammarians when they are in one of their lemming rushes to defend the language. At least all my attempts have been both unsuccessful and unsatisfactory. I should have looked through *Comfortable Words.* Without mentioning *I could care less* (which apparently only began appearing in the sixties), Evans gives several examples of opposite idioms:

I'm afraid I can't come.

This is exaggerated courtesy that implies the person who invited us is so important we are frightened of offending him or her: "Amusingly, it would be unthinkable to use the expression to anyone of whom we might have a genuine fear."

I'll see if I can't take you along means *I'll see if I can take you along.*

Can't I go, too means *Can I go, too?*—the negative only makes it more wheedling, and useful to children (as every parent knows).

Don't be surprised if he doesn't visit you one of these days means *don't be surprised if he does.*

"One would think that *yes* and *no* were the clearest words in the language," says Evans. "But they are the most confusing. . . . *Don't be surprised if he doesn't* must be accepted as an idiom, a construction peculiar to the language that defies grammar and logic and yet is in daily use and is fully understood. We are not the only ones who have this difficulty. The French say *n'est-ce pas?* and the Germans *nicht wahr?* And in each case they, as we, expect the answer to the unnecessarily negative question to be *Yes.*"

So language often proceeds by opposites, and *I could care less* is a perfectly understandable development. Isn't it?

Presently

"The primary meaning of presently is soon," says Edwin Newman, "giving way and allowing it to mean *now*—over which, for some people, it has the great advantage of being two syllables longer—creates confusion."

The confusion, of course, has already been created. In fact, the confusion is one of the oldest traditions of our language. In *Words and Their Ways in English Speech* (1916), James Greenough and George Lyman Kittredge are amused by a group of words that

> should mean *"instantly,"* but to which the procrastinating habit of mankind has attached an implication of delay. Soon *is the Anglo-Saxon word for "immediately."* . . . By and by *was originally an adverb of place, meaning "side by side" [which is the way Chaucer used it]. From adjacent place it was transferred to time immediately future.*

Kittredge and Greenough set up a sort of scale of delay:

> . . . By and by *has become the proverbial motto of the determined procrastinator. . . . "I will attend to your business* soon" *is cold comfort to the waiting petitioner.* Presently *and* directly *are better, especially the latter, for they are newer words and have not had time to break down utterly. . . . Even* immediately *is backsliding a little.* Instantly *stands firm, but will doubtless go the way of all the rest.*

As usual, Newman demands the "utter breakdown" of the word *presently,* while at the same time believing he is stopping the spread of confusion. He is not alone. Here is an extract from the *Harper Dictionary:*

> **Anthony Burgess:** *"This is a bad Americanism. It kills a word."*
> **Stewart Beach:** *"It is utterly unnecessary to use 'presently' under any circumstances. It's pretentious. I can't imagine anyone except a sociology professor using it."*
> **Herman Wouk:** *"This is a barbarism."*

The OED says that the meaning of *presently* (at this time, at present) is *"obs*[olete] (since the 17th c[entury]) in lit[erary]

Eng[lish]. (No certain instance in Shak[e]s[peare]). But in regular use in most Eng[lish] dialects, and common in Sc[ottish] writers." The OED then cites Sir Walter Scott (Scottish), and also John Ruskin (born in London): "Our presently disputed claims" (1849). Edna St. Vincent Millay also used *presently:*

> *Death devours all lovely things:*
> *Lesbia with her sparrow*
> *Shares the darkness,—presently*
> *Every bed is narrow.*

It seems worth pointing out that Stewart Beach, in the *Harper Dictionary,* is attempting to kill the word much more thoroughly than anyone who follows Millay in attempting to revive this good old meaning of this good old word. In *Comfortable Words,* Evans says that the draft (the peacetime draft back in the fifties when the old soldiers called it "The Paper Army") may have helped the revival:

> *In military affairs, however, where language is conservative and where no procrastination is allowed in trifles, the old meaning has been retained. Orders beginning "You will proceed presently" do not mean that you are to proceed some vague time after lunch or the day after tomorrow.*

One more procrastination word is worth mentioning, though not included by Greenough and Kittredge. *Anon* once meant "instantly." That meaning became obsolete in the fourteenth century; however, as the OED notes, it was revived by later writers who attempted to restore the old meaning (for example, the scholars who produced the King James Version of the Bible—perhaps the last learned linguistic reactionaries we have had in the English language). But that attempt did not stop the progress of *anon* which was "a response by a servant . . . [meaning] 'Immediately! presently! coming!' "—and then extended to an expression of attention and general readiness: "At your service! awaiting your orders!" and then finally "implying that the auditor has failed to catch the speaker's words or meaning, and asks him to repeat [—equal to] . . . 'Beg your pardon? what did you say? eh?' " All of which you can find, with its attendant confusion, in *Henry the Fourth,* Part 1, Act 2, Scene 4, if you will put this book down and go look it up *directly. Right now! Drop Everything! . . .* Aw come on, can't you hurry, just a little?

Ain't That a Shame?

> *The aura of horror that surrounds this word (ain't) is a classic*
> *instance of the damage done by genteelism. For centuries,* ain't *for*
> am not *was perfectly good English, as any pre-1850 novel shows,*
> *but the Victorian schoolmarms, worried by its use for* is *not* and
> are not *as well, proscribed it so effectively that it became a mark*
> *of ignorance and vulgarity to use* ain't *at all. Yet there is no*
> *other workable contraction, for* amn't *is unpronounceable and*
> aren't *is ungrammatical.*
>
> Dwight Macdonald, *"Sweet Are the Uses of Usage"*

This is an interesting, and classic, example of the kind of
linguistic liberalism that is directed at supposedly dead issues.
Dwight Macdonald, insisting that the campaign against *ain't* was
wrong-headed, does not conclude by saying that *I ain't going to be
pushed around by Victorians,* ain't *is now part of my vocabulary.*
He assumes that the "schoolmarm" victory was complete,
and possibly only points out the elegance of *ain't* because he
believes it is no danger to standard Northeastern United States
American.

But by 1977, in *Dos, Don'ts & Maybes of English Usage,* Theodore Bernstein was warning us all over again against *ain't:*

> *There can be no doubt that* ain't I *is easier to say than* aren't
> I *and* amn't I, *and sounds less stilted than* am I not.
> *Nevertheless, what should be not always is. Incidentally,*
> *Webster's New International Dictionary, Third Edition, says that*
> ain't *is "used orally in most parts of the U.S. by many cultivated*
> *speakers esp. in the phrase* ain't I," *a statement that is open to*
> *serious doubt.*

Now we see the reason for the warning. Idiom raises its lovely
head again, and the guardians of genteelism rush in to crush it.

The *American Heritage Dictionary,* which came out in 1969,
eight years after Webster's Third, put the matter to its (mostly
old, mostly white, and mostly male) usage panel and reported:

> Ain't, *with few exceptions, is strongly condemned by the*
> *Usage Panel when it occurs in writing and speech that is not*
> *deliberately colloquial or that does not employ the contraction to*
> *provide humor, shock, or other special effect.*

The *Random House Dictionary* (1970), another of the books
produced after Webster's Third in an attempt to resubmit English

to the canons of good taste and genteel thought, rather than the vulgar tongue, says this:

> Ain't. *Nonstandard in U.S. except in some dialects; informal in Britain.* . . .
> *Usage.* AIN'T *is so traditionally and widely regarded as a nonstandard form that it should be shunned by all who prefer to avoid being considered illiterate.* AIN'T *occurs occasionally in the informal speech of some educated users, especially in self-consciously or folksy or humorous contexts* . . . , *but it is completely unacceptable in formal writing and speech. Although the expression* ain't I? *is perhaps defensible—and it is considered more logical than* aren't I? *and more euphonious than* amn't I?— *the well-advised person will avoid any use of* AIN'T.

I add one more dictionary definition, from the *Concise Oxford Dictionary* (1976):

> Ain't (colloq.)=am not, (vulgar) = is not, are not.
> Aren't (interrogative) = am not.

The simple fact is that *ain't* is in current cultivated usage, a statement that is not at all open to doubt. That is what the word *colloquial* means in the *Concise Oxford Dictionary:* "not used in formal discourse, but widely used and entirely acceptable in informal circumstances." That is what the word *colloquial* meant in Webster's Second—and the conviction that colloquial is somehow lower-class or substandard, a widespread misconception—led Webster's Third to drop the label "colloquial" and substitute the rather long-winded but very accurate sentence. The reaction of Bernstein, and the horrified gasps of the genteel usage writers in the American Heritage and Random House dictionaries, is a demonstration that the editors of Webster's Third were right—no pop grammarian attacked the Concise Oxford for calling *ain't* colloquial, because they thought the word was being condemned by that description.

Ain't is of course used by many, perhaps the majority, of educated speakers in the South and West, and educated Blacks in all sections of the country. It sounds a little funny in the big cities of the Northeast—and to graduates of Eastern colleges—I certainly have had it driven out of my own speech. But to say that *"ain't* . . . should be shunned by all who prefer to avoid being considered illiterate," as Random House does, after defining the word as informal in England, is the worst kind of linguistic jingoism. Surely the English are literate? And a word defined as colloquial in the Oxford dictionary is one that anyone has a right to use without being called names.

A Thousand Times No

Geoffrey Chaucer, describing the Knight in *The Canterbury Tales,* emphasized his courtesy this way:

> He *never* yet *no* vileinye *ne* sayde
> In al his lyf, un-to *no* maner wight.

Four negatives in two lines. The double negative, attacked by eighteenth-century grammarians as an illogical construction except when used to equal a positive, has a long history in English. And in other languages, it is still considered standard. The French, for example, *require* two negative words: *Je ne sais rien* means, literally, *I do not know nothing.* And nobody says that there is a positive meaning in:

> I'll never never go there again.
> No, no, a thousand times no.
> Not only was she not paying attention, she was not even
>   pretending to.

The Evanses, in *A Dictionary of Contemporary American Usage,* point out that a double negative is "the normal way of strengthening a negative in all Teutonic languages, of which ours is one."

They add a few more examples of the sneaky way we have managed to keep the double negative alive despite all grammar books:

> He couldn't sleep, not even with a sedative.

means the same as

> He couldn't sleep, even with a sedative.

except that it's more emphatic. Sometimes a single negative is just plain wrong.

We don't say, *No one thought so, even you;* we do say, *No one thought so, not even you.*

The writer who used even *when he meant* not even *undoubtedly dropped the* not *because he thought it was a double negative. In attempting to show that his English is "purer" than it really is, he has succeeded in showing how worried he is about it. Mistakes of this kind are inevitable when one tries to apply a rule that runs counter to one's speech habits. It is much safer to trust one's ear, and to be satisfied to speak and write the language used by the great majority of educated people.*

Here are two more examples of the hidden double negative: Jane Austen: "There was none too poor or too remote not to feel an interest"; Charles Darwin: "It never occurred to me to doubt that your work would not advance our common object."

As the Evanses point out, a double negative never does quite equal a positive: *"I am not unhappy* . . . the words do not completely cancel each other. This double negative expresses rather, the weakest possible positive attitude."

Hopefully, The Special Badness

Hopefully, the war will soon be over.

This use of *hopefully* is a new one—much too new to be defended, or even mentioned, by Bergen Evans in either *Comfortable Words* (1959) or *A Dictionary of Contemporary American Usage* (1957). In fact, the honor of being the first to discover the danger in this new use of *hopefully* to mean "it is to be hoped" seems to belong to Wilson Follett, in *Modern American Usage* (1966):

> *The German language is blessed with an adverb,* hoffentlich, *that affirms the desirability of an occurrence that may or may not come to pass. It is generally to be translated by some such periphrasis as* it is to be hoped that; *but hack translators and persons more at home in German than in English persistently render it as* hopefully. *Now,* hopefully *and* hopeful *can indeed apply to either persons or affairs. A man in difficulty is hopeful of the outcome, or a situation looks hopeful; we face the future hopefully, or events develop hopefully. What* hopefully *refuses to convey in idiomatic English is the desirability of the hoped-for event. . . .*
> *The special badness of* hopefully *is not alone that it strains -ly to the breaking point, but that it appeals to speakers and writers who do not think about what they are saying and pick up* VOGUE WORDS *by reflex action. . . .*

This ringing call to arms has had its effect. By 1975, Jean Stafford, a Pulitzer Prize winner, was declaring, as a sample of her language attitudes, in the *Harper Dictionary of Contemporary Usage:*

> *On my back door there is a sign with large lettering which reads: THE WORD "HOPEFULLY" MUST NOT BE MISUSED ON THESE PREMISES. VIOLATORS WILL BE HUMILIATED. My friend and neighbor Berton Rouerché and I several times a week on the telephone mourn the infusion of hogwash into the bloodstream of the American language. . . .*

And by 1978, John Simon was declaring, in *Esquire,* that there are basically two kinds of people in the world—those who speak language and those who are incapable of language and who demonstrate the fact by saying *oh wow* and *like, I mean* and *mind-blowing*—and by using *hopefully* for "it is to be hoped." Two of the expressions on that list—*oh, wow* and *mind-blowing* had a nostalgic, sixties flavor even in 1978—but pop grammarians frequently complain about faults of contemporary speech long after they have ceased to be contemporary. The point is that the use of *hopefully* to mean "it is to be hoped" had moved in twelve short years from an almost desirable new word (Follett points out that German is "blessed with" an equivalent—indicating that German is pretty lucky to have one), to the most hideous of linguistic crimes (talking like a druggy teenager).

How did this happen?

Well, apparently it happened because the use of *hopefully* to mean "it is to be hoped" was increasingly accepted by highly educated and cultivated writers. If that seems a paradox—it is a common paradox in the world of pop grammar, where, after a word is accepted, the greatest fuss is made about it. We can trace the progress of *hopefully* through the writing of Theodore Bernstein because he produced so many books, each one influenced by different stages of fad prescription. In *Watch Your Language* (1958), *hopefully* is not mentioned. In *The Careful Writer* (1965), he repeats Follett's idea that "the Germans have a word that covers the intended meaning—*hoffentlich.* And in English we can take care of a somewhat similar situation with *regrettably....* But regrettably *hopefully* is not equal to the burden sometimes placed on it. What is needed is a word like *hopably,* which is not here being nominated for the job."

Wilson Follett had also suggested an alternative to *hopefully,* but his nomination was quite serious: "Writers who feel the insistent need of an English equivalent for *hoffentlich* might try to popularize *hopingly,* but must attach it to a subject capable of hoping." This, however, seems to miss the point of what *hopefully* is good for—but back to Bernstein and the progress of *hopefully.* In *Miss Thistlebottom's Hobgoblins* (1971), he writes:

> . . . More and more the word is being used—and no doubt overused—to mean it is to be hoped. . . . There are plenty of precedents in English for the acceptance of "distorted" meanings of words. . . . The newer dictionaries are beginning to open their arms to the "incorrect" meaning of hopefully *(with the strange exception of the permissive Webster's Third, which ducks the issue altogether). The American Heritage Dictionary says in its first edition that the new meaning is acceptable to "only 44 per cent of its usage panel," but there are indications that figure will rise in the next edition. Webster's New World . . . says of the latter-day meaning, "regarded by some as loose usage, but widely current." And the Random House accepts it without question.*

The reason that Webster's Third was silent on the new meaning of *hopefully* was not, of course, that it was ducking the issue: the usage was simply too new for a dictionary published in 1962. The supplement to the OED finds one instance in the 1930s, but every other citation is dated after 1965. (Where Follett got his horrible examples—and he cites several—is unknown to me.) This is also a side issue in the sad story of the fad for condemning *hopefully.* In *Dos, Don'ts & Maybes of English Usage* (1977), Bernstein wrote:

> To be quite honest, a decade ago I was on the side of objectors, but in recent years additional thought about the matter has changed my mind. . . . To use [hopefully *to mean "it is to be hoped"] in no way distorts or corrupts the first meaning of the word. But strangely, the opposition continues to grow. Bruce Bohle, usage editor of the American Heritage Dictionary, tells me that the approval of the secondary sense among the dictionary's usage panel was 44 per cent in 1968, 42 per cent in 1970 and 37 per cent in 1975. But he adds this personal opinion about the secondary meaning, "Realistically, I suppose it is* here."

One of the keenest of all the delights of researching this book was the discovery of that sentence quoted by Bernstein, in which the usage editor of the *American Heritage Dictionary* reveals not only that he thinks his own usage panel is unrealistic, but also that it has grown increasingly unrealistic over the years. His usage panel is not alone. The *Harper Dictionary* found that only

24 percent of its panel would accept the use of *hopefully* to mean "it is to be hoped" in writing. Asked to comment on the sentence, *"Hopefully,* the war will soon be ended," expert response was among the most intemperate of any in the whole intemperate *Harper Dictionary:*

> **Hal Borland:** *"I have fought this for some years, will fight it till I die. It is barbaric, illiterate, offensive, damnable and inexcusable."*
>
> **A. B. Guthrie, Jr.:** *"I have sworn eternal war on this bastard adverb."*
>
> **Charles Kuralt:** *"Chalk squeaking on a blackboard is to be preferred to this usage."*
>
> **Orville Prescott:** *"Popular jargon at its most illiterate level."*
>
> **Leo Rosten:** *"This is simply barbarism. What does 'hopefully' modify? Does a war hope?"*
>
> **Harold Taylor:** *"This is one that makes me physically ill."*
>
> **Judith Viorst:** *"I want to correct everyone who makes this mistake."*
>
> **T. Harry Williams:** *"The most horrible usage of our time."*

By 1976, one year after the publication of the *Harper Dictionary, Webster's New Collegiate Dictionary* caught up with the new usage of *hopefully* and, as usual, cited an example of the use: Dr. Nathan Pusey, president emeritus of Harvard University.

The OED Supplement (1976) says that this new use of *hopefully* was originally American and adds that this use is avoided by many writers. Then it cites as examples *The New York Times Book Review* (1932), scholarly books like *Political Behavioralism and Modern Jurisprudence* (1965), and *A Word Count of Spoken Russian* (1966), scholarly journals like *Language* (1969) and *Science Journal,* plus *The New Yorker* (1965), *The Daily Telegraph* (1970), and *The Manchester Guardian* (1971).

The OED Supplement was not available to the Harper usage panel, of course. But if it had been, would it have made a difference? It made no difference to John Simon. Jean Stafford did not take down the sign from her back door. And the campaign against *hopefully* continues:

Andrew Knight, editor of the *Economist* magazine (England), writing in *The New York Times,* indicates that he has done a considerable amount of new research on the word: "German is wrongly blamed for the odious use of *hopefully*, which is not derived from *hoffentlich* (meaning *it is to be hoped*). *Hopefully* (in a hopeful manner) in German is *hoffnungsvoll*, which the Germans use adverbially. They do not confuse the two."

By 1976, the *Concise Oxford Dictionary* was listing the use of *hopefully* to mean "it is to be hoped" without any warning at all, as the standard and *only* use of the word.

The use of *hopefully* to mean "it is to be hoped" is current among people who *are* in fact polite and educated. The *Concise Oxford Dictionary* does not think any other use worth mentioning. Every other contemporary dictionary of any standing also accepts the word as standard (except, of course, the one cursed with a usage panel). Andrew Knight calls the usage "odious." Orville Prescott finds it characteristic of "the most illiterate level" of contemporary speech—perhaps at the very moment when it is being used by Nathan Pusey, one of the most literate of his contemporaries. Jean Stafford promises to "humiliate" Dr. Pusey if he dares to enter her house through the front door (unwarned, because the sign is on the back) and speak naturally and correctly.

Is there any better evidence that the pop grammarians' objection to new words is not based on their being introduced by vile admen or viler politicians (first use, *New York Times Book Review*), not based on the word's popularity among the ignorant or faddish or writers who do not think what they are saying (among the users, Nathan Pusey, and many respected scholars), not based on any concern about language at all? The resistance is simply a blind resistance to any new word under any circumstances—and words like *illiterate* and *odious* are thrown around with abandon, without any regard to their precise meanings, or to the meanings of words in general. The intention is to intimidate by intemperate language, and the basic rule seems to be that intimidation grows more severe as it increasingly becomes a substitute for argument of any kind.

Mindless, arrogant, eager to humiliate anyone not in on the latest secret of good usage—which is not discoverable from any dictionary, and only passed around privately in conversations like the joyful mourning of Stafford and Roueché—the pop grammarians are themselves the creators of fads and vogue words. Rather than fads of usage and slang, which at least sometimes enrich the language, they create fads of anti-usage, with no purpose but allowing the faddist to look down on the standard speech of his neighbors, his country, even of the whole English-speaking world.

Despite that dreary snobbery, however, isn't there some purpose in the vogue peeves of the pop grammarians? Don't these little snits about usage essentially help language by at least slowing down the rate of change, and keep us all from simply blithering away our heritage?

That interesting argument was actually proposed by Paul Robinson in *The New Republic:*

> *[The use of* hopefully *to mean "it is to be hoped"] is precisely the sort of issue that separates linguistic conservatives from linguistic liberals. It arouses enormous polemical passions. And rightly so: for the way one thinks about the propriety of this utterance reveals the essence of one's linguistic sensibilities. Hopefully is a classic example of a lost cause. Its incorrect usage is now so common that only a fool would expect to recover its original meaning.*

We expect that Robinson will therefore declare that conservatives should not be fools. Not so.

Robinson believes that

> *language exists in a kind of tension, and if there are no forces to resist the inevitable process of evolution, the result will be linguistic incoherence. . . . Conservatives therefore, should think of themselves as performing an essential role in an historical drama. They know that certain causes are lost, but they must fight them nonetheless because that is their part in the play. "Hopefully" is just such a cause, and the linguistic conservative realizes his historical function by contesting it to the bitter end. If nothing else, he distracts the forces of change from launching a premature assault on some other hapless word or phrase.*

This seems to say that the inevitable evolution of language is toward incoherence, as if there were some inner force directing people to use words in a way that cannot be understood at all. This is, of course, a paraphrase of the old pop grammarian's fear that in a few short years we will have forgotten or debased words altogether and be reduced to communicating in grunts.

Humph, says a true conservative—grunts are often very expressive—can Robinson, or any other pop grammarian, point out a single example of a language degenerating into incoherence? In Elizabethan England there were no schools for the study of English, no grammar books, and no significant resistors of language change. Invention was riotous—new words came from everywhere and apparently from nearly everybody. Did the language of Shakespeare degenerate into incoherence? Chinese is a language very far along the road of linguistic evolution: it has no articles, no way of distinguishing singular or plural in nouns or verbs, no verb *to be,* no real distinction between parts of speech (the same word can be adjective, noun, adverb, verb, depending on its place in the sentence). The Chinese language is still coherent, still used for and adequate for any and every human purpose.

Robinson believes that a doomed struggle against *hopefully* will stop other assaults, ignoring the fact that *hopefully* to mean "it is to be hoped" is used exactly like other adverbs that modify the whole sentence rather than the verb. *Mercifully,* for example, can be used to mean "in a merciful manner" and "it is a mercy." No one objects to

Mercifully, the war was soon over.

though there is nothing in that sentence capable of mercy.

Does a war have mercy? We can say

Clearly, [apparently, evidently, fortunately, happily, presumably, or luckily,] the war will soon be over.

A war does not have luck, or happiness, or presumption—a war is not in any sense modified by any of those words, which is not so very odd because—despite Leo Rosten—we do not *very* often use an adverb to modify a noun in English.

The idea that Jean Stafford and Orville Prescott, by adding their unthinking voices to the chorus of unthinking protest against *hopefully,* might serve to distract Nathan Pusey from committing assaults on other hapless words is of course laughable in itself.

Hopefully is used in its new sense in a way exactly parallel to all those other adverbs that modify a whole sentence in our language. Invention seems to follow tradition in language—a comforting thought for true conservatives.

Hopefully is not used primarily by druggy teenagers, admen, or corrupt politicians. Almost all the citations in the OED Supplement are scholarly and literary.

Hopefully to mean "it is to be hoped" is accepted in the Concise Oxford, the OED Supplement, Random House, Webster's New World, and by American Heritage's unfortunately helpless usage editor, though not by its panel.

Hopefully, that settles the matter. Reasonably, it should. Obviously, it will not. Mere reason is defenseless against pop grammar.

Modern American Word Chain Usage Defended
A Newly Spoken Speak

> *[Linguists] cannot wash their dainty hands and pretend that anyone who uses the term* language deterioration *displays "ignorance of the facts of language change." Well, there may actually be some ignorance at work in that, though not as [the linguist] perceives it:* deterioration of language *would be better than* language deterioration.
>
> *John Simon, "The Corruption of English"*

Simon has discovered, and of course disapproved, a new way of using language. The term *language deterioration* is "worse" than *deterioration of language,* I assume, because it does not show its grammatical bones through the skin of usage. There is no indication of the relationship between *language* and *deterioration,* both nouns, except that of word order. We assume from word order that the one that comes first is an adjective. *Language deterioration* is a very short example of this new kind of usage. There are several longer kinds of "word chains." Here is a favorite of mine, a caption to a photograph of a gesticulating general in *The Philadelphia Daily News* (February 6, 1980):

> *Former NATO commander Alexander M. Haig Jr. gestures to the crowd yesterday at the Chapel of the Four Chaplains Annual Awards Banquet. Haig, a Philadelphia native, received the Rabbi Louis Paris Hall of Heroes Gold Medallion for providing the nation with leadership and integrity.*

Here we have all sorts of words—nouns, adjectives, articles, prepositions—strung together in long snaky units that remind you of certain kinds of compounds common in German. The odd thing is that we are able to follow them so easily. We know, for example, that *Chapel of the Four Chaplains Annual Awards Banquet* is the equivalent of *the Annual Banquet held to give Awards by the Chapel of the Four Chaplains,* and not of other discoverable meanings, like *The Chapel in which Four Chaplains give annual awards at a banquet.*

I admit that we have a little trouble—at least I have a little trouble—with *the Rabbi Louis Paris Hall of Heroes Gold Medallion.* At first reading, I thought there was a rabbi named Louis Paris Hall, and an organization called Heroes Gold Medallion that Rabbi Hall somehow represented: something like *Salesman Louis Paris Hall of General Motors Acceptance Corporation.* But even that confusion was momentary, and, though the sentence still makes me laugh, with that long mouthful of words on a string of nothing, I do understand now that there is a gold medallion named for a hall of heroes which is in turn named for Rabbi Louis Paris, who was, I assume, one of the four heroic chaplains who went down with a ship (I do not remember which) in the Second World War.

Fifty or a hundred years ago, many people would have had just as much trouble accepting *language deterioration* as I had with the Rabbi Paris Medallion. English used to insist, in standard usage, on connecting nouns with words that indicated relationships.

There is also, in that brief *Daily News* quote, an example of a word string and an adjective especially despised by pop grammarians—provided they notice it. *Former NATO Commander Alexander M. Haig* instead of *Alexander M. Haig, formerly Commander of NATO.* Edwin Newman, in *Strictly Speaking,* notices this use of *former* in *The New York Times* and pretends to believe it means that *former commander of NATO* is an office you can be appointed to. That is an odd way of reading English, and worthy of the general level of understanding in the book. This use of *former* was originally an Americanism (1905 is the first cite in OED), but spread rapidly to England. The 1970 cite is from *Encyclopaedia Britannica,* which ought to establish the word as educated standard. Putting the man's title before his name is a form of premodification that is also noticed and deplored. In a bad-tempered book with a very bad-tempered title, *A Dictionary of Diseased English* (1977), English writer Kenneth Hudson says the phrase

Pianist George Shearing

comes about from "the immigrant's literal, but illiterate, translation from his own language, which strikes roots in the country of his adoption." Dr. John Baker, in the English magazine *Nature* (November 1955), also insists that premodification comes from the United States, where it was introduced by the many German-born scientists working in American laboratories.

This is an extremely odd argument—one that is made only by Englishmen, and one that is worth spending a little time on. Yet another English writer, Philip Howard, of *The London Times,* puts it this way:

> *Ethnic minorities in the United States tend to preserve the languages, accents and idiosyncratic uses of the lands that their migrant forefathers came from, and to campaign vigorously for these immigrant dialects to be brought into the educational system and officially recognized in other ways. Having their language accepted means jobs and money. As a consequence the central core of American English is breaking up into dialects, and becoming an increasingly unattractive model for speakers at a distance. Even within the United States different communities and regions are finding it more and more difficult to understand each other.*

This delightfully innocent passage seems to mean that people from Chicago with Polish names have trouble understanding people from the same city with Irish or Jewish names—and that all Chicagoans have difficulty understanding the arcane ethnic dialects of New York and Southern California. There is no real answer to that—except laughter. And the other main idea of the quote—that somehow Polish Americans lobby for Polish-accented English teachers, and Irish Americans demand the schools teach their children a rich Dublin brogue—is equally silly.

But the English are always worried that somehow their language has got out of their control—and into the hands of the dread foreigner who doesn't understand its ancient spirit. There is a little hint, it seems to me, of the traditional British anti-Semitism in all that—because the German scientists working in America were mostly German Jews who had fled from Hitler. Maybe I'm making too much of a mere hint, however.

And that hint has little to do with answering the objections to word chains. There is a much better way. English is a Germanic language—and formerly, like German, made new words by building them up from smaller elements. In Anglo-Saxon days, *carpenter* could be *treow-wyrhta*—tree-wright; *library* was *bochus*—book-house; *butcher* was *flaesc-mangere*—fleshmonger. In *History of the English Language,* Thomas Lounsbury, my old favorite, mourns the passing of this ability in English to form "self-explaining compounds." He points out that even later speakers of English once used *sun-stead,* that is, "the sun's stopping-place," for "that part of the ecliptic in which the sun is farthest from the equator." This was replaced by a word derived from the Latin *solstitium*—which means "the sun's stopping-place"—and we now talk of the *solstice.* "By this we certainly lose something in picturesqueness and force of expression. . . ." Instead of calling a substance that oozes from a rock, *rock-oil,* which is a very easy word to understand, we call it *petroleum* (which comes from the Latin *petra,* "rock," and *oleum,* "oil"), the meaning of which has to be learned from a dictionary. However, says Lounsbury, "This power of forming self-explaining compounds can . . . hardly be said to be lost: it is rather a power held in abeyance, dwarfed by disuse, but by no means destroyed."

And, in fact, we find lots of compounds in traditional nineteenth-century English. Randolph Quirk, in *The Use of English,* points out that we (that is, the English) not only have *refreshment room* and *railway station* but also *railway station refreshment room,* "which few would prefer to see broken down into *room for refreshments at the station of that special kind of way which consists of rails.*"

In fact, English has always kept this habit of making word strings, or self-explaining compounds, alive—but it has usually only been used to form names for people or things: *pickpocket, tattletale, breakwater, go-between, out-of-work carpenter, undergraduate student, has-been, village green,* and even more complicated strings.

Jespersen cites, in the second volume of his *Modern English Grammar,* such complicated strings as *bread and water punishment, a life and death struggle, pepper and salt tweed, an easy man-of-the-world air, five o-clock shadow,* and *flash in the pan success;* and there are many other examples provided. Jespersen talks about the loss of compound-making ability in English this way:

> *Those English philologists who speak with regret of the loss*
> *of the power to form compound substantives in English as in*
> *German, generally overlook the fact that it is only in the free*
> *formation of technical compounds that English is inferior to*
> *German—an inferiority which is intimately connected with the*
> *predilection for classical or pseudo-classical formations—and that*
> *there is in English a facility unknown even to German of forming*
> *free combinations of substantives, each retaining its own natural*
> *stress and pronunciation as well as its proper signification, while*
> *one is made subordinate to the other.*

In other words, string compounds have always been with us,
except in cases where knowledge of Latin and Greek led inventors
to translate the compound into either or both languages—usually
keeping the words uninflected and free of any grammatical relationship. *Petroleum* does not mean "oil of rock," it means "rock"
plus "oil"—a noun chain in disguise. The fact that fewer scientists, technicians, and writers are now learning Latin and Greek
has naturally led to the appearance of this supposedly new kind
of English—actually, as we have seen, the oldest kind of English
there is. And it should cheer up those worriers about "the central
core of English" (which seems to mean "the way we talk in my
neighborhood") that the mongrelized Americans, foreigners all,
children of immigrants, are responsible for just the kind of invention that men like Lounsbury thought was lost forever back
around the time of the Norman Conquest.

This is not a mystic book, but it does seem to me that there
is something extraordinary in this recapturing of a power that lay
dormant in the language for centuries: as if the language itself,
passed along mostly by illiterates, then fussed over by schoolteachers who knew nothing of its powers, was a system almost
independent of time. Free compounds pass out of English—centuries later, free compounds return. There is something inexplica-
ble in this—as if the great vowel shift would suddenly reverse
itself and we should all go back to saying *ee* for *I*. Maybe that will
happen; it is possible to believe anything after realizing what the
return of string compounds means to English. All that we can be
certain of is this: whatever recovery there is of ancient language
habits, the Edwin Newmans and John Simons and Philip How-
ards of the world will worry that this is finally the end of English
as we know it—and especially of its central core.

Does Anything Go?

one

A Democratic
Approach to Grammar

Back in 1959, Professor Bertrand Evans (who should not be confused with the blessed Bergen Evans) wrote an article called "Grammar and Writing" (*Educational Forum,* no. 23, pp. 215–228). It began like many articles by teachers of college composition, bitterly complaining about "the utter disregard of discipline" and the "grammatical incompetence" of freshman themes. But then, Bertrand Evans went on to do something that may have been entirely new. He blamed the freshmen's problems on:

> *"Linguisticists" . . . with . . . high-sounding jargon . . .*
> *flushed with victories over old-fashioned philologists in colleges*
> *and universities, and affecting the dispassion that more*
> *conspicuously marks true scientism than true science, are*
> *urgently, even fanatically storming the classroom in order to*
> *persuade the old-fashioned grammar teacher that she, too, should*
> *be dispassionate in her attitude toward language . . . let her just*
> *accept the view that there are merely "different" levels of usage—*
> *not "good" and "bad," "acceptable" and "unacceptable,"—and all*
> *will be well.*

Bertrand Evans may be the first writer in our language to blame the language scholars for destroying language standards and the ability of college freshmen to measure up to those standards. The "linguisticists" quickly became "linguists," and the linguists became "permissive linguists" (the average reader will never have heard of any other kind of linguist), but the idea has remained intact.

Somewhere there is a body of men and women who spend their lives studying language—and destroying it. Somehow, they are so lost to ordinary human feeling that words like *finalize* and sentences like *It be's that way* sound perfectly fine to them. And though they all defend every possible mistake in English, they will, of course, write grammatically standard English themselves (somewhat marred by "high-sounding jargon").

Theodore Bernstein warned us about them in *The Careful Writer:* ". . . The twisting of our language . . . is being encouraged by linguists and teachers who find it easier to follow their sometimes benighted charges than to lead them."

"Antigrammarians and homogenizers," grumbled Wilson Follett, in *Modern American Usage,* can't even be consistent. First, they defend *who* for *whom* in sentences like *Who do you mean?* And then they "perversely permit *whom* for *who* in its fairly frequent misuses": *I got the news from somebody whom I thought was in the know.*

Otto Jespersen, a particularly hard case to Follett,

> *rationalizes this false* whom *as the natural outcome of a rather involved speech instinct; he does not recoil even from such a monstrosity as Disraeli's* individuals whom, *if you do not meet, you become restless. But,* [and here is the final irony] *you can read a thousand pages of Jespersen's own prose without encountering any such aberration.*

This is one of Follett's favorite arguments against writers who do not share his opinions about right language: they preach "unbuttoned grammar" in books like Jespersen's *Modern English Grammar* or Mencken's *American Language,* but they write in "the fastidious syntax of a precisian. If we go by what these men do, instead of what they say, we conclude that they all believe in conventional grammar, practice it against their own preaching, and continue to cultivate the elegance they despise in theory."

That last charge almost seems to mean that linguists write too well—but we know what Follett really means:

Linguists give in to the ignorant (either from laziness or from some cowardly desire to be popular).

Linguists defend every contradictory, illogical, and illiterate mistake imaginable.

Linguists themselves would never dream of using the kind of language they permit and even encourage in others.

That more or less sums up the pop grammarian's case against linguists. Of course, there are a few additional minor charges: linguists refuse to make value judgments about the use of language; they think talking is more important than writing; they reject the need for clarity and logic, thought and culture; they do not even recognize the need for our traditional grammatical structures (linguists do not even recognize that the word *you* has a nominative and an objective case, grouses Follett—just because the word is identical in the nominative and objective case!).

Who are these linguists? And why are they doing such terrible things to the English language?

In order to answer that, we have to start with the fact that there are demonstrable problems with English grammar. The native speaker of English doesn't seem to be able to follow the few simple rules of this language. People who grow up speaking a highly inflected language—Finnish, for example—are able to manipulate all the verb forms without effort and without conscious thought. Finns who have never learned the names of all those verb forms, who have never seen a grammar book, are able to speak Finnish clearly and well. But most people who grow up in England or America can never be taught to pay attention to things like dangling modifiers or pronoun reference; no matter how long they go to school, no matter how much practice they get in writing, they are certain to make mistakes.

To some people—to the kind of people who believe that rules are rules and books are always right—that means that the English, and especially the Americans, are uniquely incapable of good grammar, or even of coherent and logical thought. Of all the peoples in the world, and with the least rules to follow, we make the most mistakes. And oddly enough, if you take children born in Finland—where language learning is effortless—and bring them to the United States where they grow up speaking English as natives . . . they will make just as many mistakes as any other native speaker. We are not only incapable of grammar, we infect our immigrants.

There is an alternative conclusion: scholars of the language, in a tradition that goes back at least a hundred years, have insisted that there is something wrong with the rules.

While we're in grade school, we think that all our textbooks are infallible. We learn the rules of English—a noun refers to a person, place, or thing. We learn the rules of mathematics—two plus two is four. We learn the facts of history: the Civil War was fought to free the slaves, the First World War was fought to make the world safe for democracy; George Washington could not tell a lie.

Later on, we discover there is some dispute about those last facts: the Civil War was fought for economic reasons, the First World War was a struggle for colonial empires, and George Washington padded his expense account.

We never learn there is a problem about the rules of mathematics: two plus two always equals four.

But the kids who like history enough to become history buffs like the fact that there is so much dispute about the facts of history, and so many motives and causes to sort out. That's exactly what gives history its fascination—and its intellectual respectability. If someone told us that he loved history so much he had memorized all the birthdates and all the addresses of all the presidents of the United States, we would suspect that he didn't love history—he loved memorizing. That's like trying to be a mathematician by memorizing all the multiplication tables up to seventy-seven times twelve is . . . whatever seventy-seven times twelve is. It doesn't matter. It isn't an idea.

Many of us imagine that the rules of English are like the rules of mathematics—and you can find people who insist that they are "lovers of the language" because they know how to diagram a sentence, what the difference between a gerund and a gerundive is (there is none in English, by the way), and the difference between a limiting and an unlimiting clause. Luckily, there are less and less of them—the body of "rules" has shrunk in the past few decades from a concentration on points of actual grammatical construction to a concentration on diction.

Still, the attitude of the memorizer has remained the same—a shocked sorrow that we don't care enough to learn the seventy-seven times table, and a reliance for all truth on textbooks that do not differ from our fourth-grade grammar books except in complexity, books that still do not matter because they do not contain ideas.

There is another way to study language—equivalent to the way we learn to study history in college: we abandon our preconceived notions, our patriotic and chauvinist prejudices; we forget what the textbooks said; we do our best to find out the facts. We learn to question.

Here is an example of what happens if you hold up the received rules of grammar school textbooks to any kind of reasonable scrutiny. It is taken from an article by Paul Roberts, printed in *College English* in 1960 (twenty years ago): "The Relation of Linguistics to the Teaching of English" (vol. 22, no. 1, October 1960, pp. 1–9):

A sentence is not a complete thought. If *that* were true every sentence would be completely independent of every other sentence, no pronouns would exist, and this sentence would be unintelligible.

A noun is not a person, place, or thing. A verb is not a word that expresses action.

Arrival is a noun, but it is certainly not a person, place, or thing. *Action* is a noun, but there must be some sense in which the word *action* expresses action. *Cage* can be a verb, though it is a thing. *Arrival* cannot be a verb, though it is an action. He can cage the bird, but he cannot arrival at the airport.

"The traditional definition of adjective—anything that modifies a noun—simply buries and conceals a large and important part of English expression, throwing together such quite different structures as:

> our sink, dirty sink, kitchen sink, leaking sink, scrubbing sink,
> repaired sink, sink upstairs . . .

To ask in the traditional framework whether *kitchen* in *kitchen sink* is a noun or an adjective is like asking whether John Jones is a man or a commuter."

Upstairs in *sink upstairs* is surely an adverb, since it tells where. *Upstairs* in *upstairs sink* is just as surely an adverb, though the meaning might seem slightly different to some people: *There's a sink upstairs,* simply tells us where the sink is. *There's an upstairs sink,* implies that there is also a downstairs sink; it seems completely different information than *there's a sink upstairs.* We never think about that difference—but we constantly make use of it.

I include just one more of these rules of English that we never think about, but that almost all of us follow:

"In the third person singular present of English regular verbs, (iz) is used after stems ending in a sibilant, (z) in other cases, except after breathed consonants, (s) after breathed consonants, except sibilants."

That is from R. W. Zandvoort's *A Handbook of English Grammar*, a book written for foreigners learning English. Simply pronouncing *gasses, seethes,* and *hits* will demonstrate that Zandvoort's rule is true of all native-born speakers of the majority dialect (it is not true of all Black Americans, of course). If you're clever and nimble-tongued enough to violate that rule—to say *gassiss, seethss,* and *hidz*—you'll also discover how important that rule is: nobody will understand you.

Let us now take a look at the lover of language who has done the equivalent of memorizing the seventy-seven times table. Richard Mitchell, a teacher at Glassboro State College (New Jersey) is the author of a rather famous newsletter called *The Underground Grammarian,* in which he complains about the language of deans in their memos and students in their themes. In *Less Than Words Can Say,* he insists that there are some mistakes in English grammar so basic that they demonstrate incompetence in the writer no matter what his field.

To demonstrate that bad grammar equals incompetence, Mitchell quotes from a letter sent out by the executive secretary of the Michigan Board of Pharmacy: "If the death of neither man nor gnat are desired. . . ." *Are desired,* a plural verb form, is used with *death,* a singular subject. Sometimes, says Mitchell, we are in doubt about the number of the subject in English—collective nouns can give anybody trouble. But surely not here. "A man might safely spend his life using singular verbs to go with singular subjects" in sentences like this. The mistake is equivalent to a teller handing out the wrong change at a bank, or a pharmacist handing out a lethal dose of the wrong pills. In fact, it is even worse: "For our society the Secretary's mistake is *more* significant. . . . It suggests that a man in an important position . . . is careless and thoughtless in doing his work and that he seems not to have cultivated the habits of precision and correctness. . . ." It does not do to plead that the secretary was probably just not paying attention when he made this little slip. "Isn't it his job to pay attention to his job? Is this the only time he failed to pay attention? If his work is incorrect in such a small and easy matter, it seems likely that it will contain mistakes in large matters. . . . It is only a tiny indication of a much larger failure."

Mitchell goes on with this extremely bad-tempered and solemn rant for several paragraphs, presenting the case of the textbook grammarian with maximum intolerance. That is not important. What is important is that we know he is wrong. There are differences in mistakes. There are people, for example, who often make mistakes adding up long columns of figures. Yet, if we ask them to add two and two, they will always answer four. As a matter of fact, I have met several mathematicians who habitually made mistakes in arithmetic—and were in an odd way proud of them, because it gave them a chance to explain that mathematics is different than counting. Mathematics is about ideas. The people who have difficulty with long columns know how to count—just like the executive secretary knows how to write English, and learned the same rules about subject-verb concord that we did. Sometimes he violates them. Sometimes we violate them. Oddly enough, that is not likely to be when we are not paying attention; it is likely to be when we are extremely interested—in what we are saying—rather than in the way we say it.

Still, our interest in what we are saying will always demonstrate our incompetence to the grade school grammarians of the world, and there is really no way of explaining to them that they are wrong. So I have tried, in this case, to demonstrate that they are wrong by . . . well, by lying.

The executive secretary of the Michigan Board of Pharmacy quoted above did *not* write that little bit about death of man and gnat. The executive secretary *did* write a sentence in which subject and verb do not agree in number. Mitchell did take that mistake to be a demonstration of incompetence, and his argument is exactly as I have reported it. But the author of the sentence about death was Charles Darwin, and you can find the quote, along with an explanation that this is a common occurrence in English, in Otto Jespersen's *Modern English Grammar,* volume 2, page 174.

Now, if you agree with Mitchell, it seems to me that you have to suspect the theory of evolution and the mass of Darwin's observation of animal behavior. And that is not all you must suspect: "Experience is the name that *everybody* gives to *their* mistakes." The italics are mine, but the grammar is Oscar Wilde's.

Hard as it is for popular writers on language to accept, it is in fact true that in English, grammatical number frequently has as little to do with actual number as grammatical gender in French has to do with actual sex. The problem with English is not that we cannot keep numbers straight. The problem is that grammar textbooks have been trying to make our complicated and disorderly system of number into a logical and sensible one. They have been trying for several hundred years—and they have not succeeded. Because language does not change because of grammar books. Or logic.

Imagine, for example, that all the schools in France decided at this very moment to try to change the gender system of that language—the disorderly and senseless gender system—into the sensible system that we have in English. All the grammar books would point out that females were feminine, males masculine, and inanimate objects neuter. All the teachers would tell the children to simply be logical and reasonable, simply think before they spoke, simply use their heads before they wrote. . . . And everytime the natives of France began to speak their language easily and effortlessly—like natives—they would make mistakes.

Of course, writers of French grammar books do not spend their time wringing their hands in despair over the inability of the French to grasp the obvious facts of gender. Lucky French, they are allowed to leave their illogical and senseless language alone. Therefore, they do not make mistakes in gender.

Speakers of English are not as lucky. The rules of grammar in our textbooks are based on a number of eighteenth-century grammars, grammars that were written from a point of view that would seem to most of us nowadays—even to defenders of that textbook grammar—both wrong and wrong-headed. The great study of the origins of English grammar is Sterling A. Leonard's *The Doctrine of Correctness in English Usage, 1700–1800,* University of Wisconsin Studies in Language and Literature, 25 (Madison, 1929). In that book, Leonard goes back to the original grammars and describes the emergence of the doctrine of correctness in a flood of rules and prescriptions. He also makes two main points about the writers of grammars.

1. Almost all of them believed that the origins of the differences in human languages could be traced to the Tower of Babel —that is, that the Bible story was an actual historical event, and that all human language before that event was God-given, universally the same—and of course uncorrupted. "Corruption" of language was one of the punishments of the sin of building the tower. And languages had become more and more corrupt as time went

on. Hebrew was least corrupt. Greek next least. Latin next least. And so on, with English very far down on the historical scale in terms of sinfulness.

2. They believed in "the power of reason to remold language completely, and appealed to various principles of metaphysics or logic, or even made pronouncements on mere individual preference posing as authority, in the endeavor to 'correct, improve and fix' usage. . . . The prevailing view of language in the eighteenth century was that English could and must be subjected to a process of classical regularizing."

Luckily for us, the grammarians knew very little Hebrew. Luckily, they knew very little Greek. Unluckily, they knew lots of Latin—and the grammar of English was regularized and classicized along the lines of Latin grammar. Because Latin had different cases for the noun English must have the same cases. This sort of thing has not quite disappeared, and many school grammar texts still print ludicrous paradigms like this:

Declension of the noun *boy*

Singular		Plural	
Nominative	*boy*	Nominative	*boys*
Genitive	*of the boy, the boy's*	Genitive	*of the boys, the boys'*
Dative	*to* or *for the boy*	Dative	*to* or *for the boys*
Accusative	*boy*	Accusative	*boys*
Ablative	*by* or *at the boy*	Ablative	*by* or *at the boys*

Some grammars have dropped the ablative case, because they prefer to talk about the boy as "object of the preposition," and then, of course, it is in the accusative case.

Otto Jespersen, one of the greatest of the scholarly grammarians, pointed out that there is a problem with that paradigm. Except in one case, the genitive, the word itself does not change. To say that there is a nominative and an accusative case in English, said Jespersen, is to misunderstand the whole idea of case. When we talk about case in Latin we mean that in 95 percent of the words in the language, the word changes from case to case. If the words stay the same in English, then there is no nominative and accusative case for nouns in English.

Jespersen was a native Dane, and he approached English as a foreigner, interested in the language and the way that it actually worked. Questions of correctness, he said, were not his concern: he simply reported on usage as he found it and, as a foreigner, left questions of good usage to the natives, only noting, as he pointed out, that many usages condemned as wrong were either idioms of long standing or had developed out of the grammar of the language like long-standing idioms.

Jespersen, and other scholarly grammarians, tried to arrive at rules of English by studying the actual practice of speakers and writers of the language. They did not try to make English, a language where nouns do not have case, fit the rules of Latin, where all nouns have case. Jespersen not only proposed to junk the idea of case, but also proposed that there should be only one class of words, which he called particles, which would include adverbs, prepositions, coordinating and subordinating conjunctions. Think of the word *before* in the following sentences, says Jespersen:

> I have been here many times before. (In grade school grammar, *before* is an adverb.)

> I have been here many time before my marriage. (Now *before* is a preposition.)

> I have been here many times before I was married. (Now *before* is a conjunction.)

"The difference between the various functions of the word . . . is not important enough to cause it to be placed in different categories; in one employment it is like an intransitive verb (has no object); in the other it is 'transitive' and has in one case a substantive, in another a clause as an object."

To speak of an adverb as being an intransitive particle is heresy in terms of our Latinized grammar books—but it is a very sensible way to describe how the English language works.

(By the way, the sentence quoted above, in which Jespersen uses the word *between* to describe more than two functions of the word *before* is a perfect example of the traditional use of *between* with more than two objects—a use discussed and defended, since it now needs defense, on pp. 43–44).

The work of Jespersen and others—Henry Sweet, Curme, etc.

—came to be called "scholarly grammar." Scholarly grammars of English relied largely on written evidence—Jespersen is forever citing usage from English literature—and usually from the best kind of writers. During the twentieth century, after a series of studies of languages which like Native American and African tongues had no written system, linguists began to approach English in the same way. That is—they looked at the sounds of the language, as if the language were something entirely new, and as if they were trying to explain it to someone whose language was completely different.

The development of ideas like morpheme (the smallest unit of meaning in a language) and phoneme (the smallest unit of sound) made possible grammars of English that said things like:

> The morpheme /s/ is the sign of the possessive, the plural, and the third person singular of the verb in the present tense.

Of course, the morpheme /s/ could signify the phoneme (s), or the phoneme (z), or the phoneme (iz), as Zandvoort demonstrates above.

The descriptive linguist concentrated on actual usage. Sterling Leonard sent a list of sentences to editors and English teachers to ask them which they accepted and which they rejected. Charles Fries studied English usage first by taking a group of letters written to the federal government, then by recording phone conversations in Buffalo, New York. Other descriptive linguists went into the field and recorded people's voices as they told stories or read lists of words. The aim was to discover actual practice.

The aim was not to abolish standards.

On the contrary, descriptive linguists are supremely interested in differences in the way words are used and how usage differs from one section of the country to the other, from one class or subclass to another, from one ethnic group to another.

Some of those differences have been chosen by people around the country to mark lower-class or upper-class speech. Some of those differences are ignored. As an example, California talk is now getting some attention—in cartoons like Doonesbury, people talk in vague polysyllables and use odd expressions like *laid back,* and that seems very Californian to us. There is an interesting oddity of California speech that is not as often noticed.

Californians say *cot* and *caught* the same way—the way Easterners pronounce *cot*. The word *bought* is pronounced *bot,* and the word *nought* is pronounced *not.*

Now, what is a linguist to do about this feature of California speech? Say that it is incorrect? It is correct in California.

Here is another curiosity of almost all American speech. We do not pronounce the *th.* That feature has been identified for years as extremely low-class—saying *duh* is reserved in movies and on television for dumb thugs, lovable taxi drivers, and people from Brooklyn. But dropping the *th* is a feature of all our speech. We don't say *duh* in that exaggerated way. We make a small clack with our tongue: *Get outta tah way.* However, if you speak into a tape recorder and your tape is played through a voice spectrograph which is able to grasp different sounds, it will be obvious to you that in a significant number of cases you do not make a *th*-sound but this other sound. There is a difference in the way most Americans pronounce *the.*

Highly educated speakers use this clack a lot less than lower-class speakers. But they still use it. And they do not make the full *th-* sound any more often on the average than lower-class speakers—they omit it entirely and say, *uh.*

When Charles Fries published *American English Grammar* in 1940, he subtitled it *The Grammatical Structure of Present-Day American English with Especial Reference to Social Differences or Class Dialects.* He got access to thousands of letters written to the United States Army during World War I asking for early discharges for soldiers. He discarded all those that did not include this information about the writer of the letter: place of birth, education, and occupation.

He then divided them into three classes: upper class (professionals who had graduated college and had considerable standing in their community—Fries accepted newspaper editors, for example, only in towns of more than 40,000 people); lower class (less than grade school education, demonstrated difficulty with conventions of spelling and punctuation, and low paying jobs); and middle class—everybody else.

The number of college graduates before the Second World War was very small, of course, and Fries's upper class is a genuine elite. John D. Rockefeller, for example, would not have been a member. He didn't go to college—making him, for Fries's purposes, middle class.

Fries found that the expression *these kind of things,* an expression that is both prized and despised by language snobs since it allows them to bemoan the fact that a plural adjective is used with a singular noun, was used only by upper-class writers. Though it was then and is now denounced as an illiteracy, illiterate people did not use it—they used *them kind of things.* The middle class avoided the construction entirely.

What is a linguist to say about this information? That *these kind of things* is wrong? That it marks a person as uneducated? That the user will never succeed in life? That if you use it upper-class Americans will look down on you? That it is a violation of standard English? Whose standard?

Consider the problem of the person who does not want to be permissive in language, who wants to stop bad usage.

How can this be done?

By insisting that a usage is wrong, and teaching that it is wrong in school? In 1932, Sterling Leonard asked a group of linguists, editors, and schoolteachers to judge certain sentences. Among them was:

Don't get these kind of gloves.

Leonard reported. "The linguists ranked this higher than any other group of judges. The editors placed it, by unanimous consent, at the very bottom of the list of usages; the English and speech teachers rated it nearly as low."

But despite judges, despite editors, despite English teachers, the expression was in use and is in use, in the very best kind of English and in the most ordinary kind of English.

So there does not seem to be any point to arguing about it.

So why waste time teaching children that writing *those kind of things* is wrong? It will not hold them back in life. It will not mark them as illiterate among their successful future friends. It will not do anything to their lives at all—except mark them as victims of the pop grammarian.

One way to teach them not to be victims is to try to figure out the rule that makes people say *those kind of things* instead of *this kind of thing.* Even the pop grammarians of course do not recommend *this kind of things.* It just sounds funny.

And one way to discover the rule is to study the history of the language—exactly what Jespersen did when he wanted to find out how speakers of English, very adept and highly educated speakers, use *who* and *whom.* Follett says that Jespersen rationalizes bad usage; Jespersen would say that he theorizes a reason for the use.

The difference seems minor, but is important. To Follett, Jespersen is letting down the standards and encouraging chaos in language—that's why Follett keeps accusing linguists of being levelers and anarchists and panderers to the mob. To Jespersen, however, language is a system; and because it is used by humans and learned by humans, it can't be chaotic. What appears to be chaos is actually the result of "a speech instinct." English, for example, is a language that is moving away from being an inflected language—like Latin—to a language where word order determines meaning, and the words themselves do not change. Chinese is like that, too. Pronouns in English have been in a state of confusion for centuries. One of the reasons that we use the plural *you* instead of the familiar *thee* and *thou* is that no one could figure out which of those words to use when. Not because the English are exceptionally thickheaded—but because the language itself, obeying its own laws of development (*drift* is what linguists call it), is changing. As a result, there is to speakers of English a sort of subject area of the sentence—before the verb—and an object area—after the verb. That rule would help Follett understand why Americans always say *Who do you mean?* and tend to say *I remember the man whom I thought was in the know.* It would make no sense in Latin; but in discovering what modern American usage is, including the modern usage of the most educated and successful Americans, the subject area–object area rule has one important virtue: it works. Not all the time, of course—pronouns are too much in flux for anything to work all the time. Some Americans are reasonably adept at following the pop grammar rules. Many more, of course, merely think they are adept.

But discovering the rules—finding the order in what appears to someone with a strong background in Latin grammar to be chaos—is the virtue of the linguistic approach. Linguists do not "accept" every change, however crazy and illogical and barbaric;

they assume that language always changes, and that the changes therefore can't be anarchic and crazy. They have to come from "normal human speech instincts." Otherwise, people wouldn't be capable of inventing these new words and new usages.

The virtues of the pop grammar approach turn out to be specious—its information and history are wrong. The assumption of superiority by the pop grammarian is unfounded. The tone of despair is a product of ignorance.

two

Black
Vernacular English

On July 12, 1979, Charles W. Joiner, a federal judge in Detroit, ruled that the Ann Arbor school board had to recognize the existence of Black English—and not only that, but train specific teachers in the problems that speakers of Black English have with other dialects, and use that knowledge to teach Black children to read and write.

The cries of rage were predictable. Conservatives complaining that every educational innovation is a step further and further away from McGuffey's back-to-basic white American values. Ethnic populists shaking their heads over the fact that nobody ever taught kids on the Lower East Side to read in Yiddish or Italian, and wondering why the rules of the game should be suspended for Blacks alone. ("Is it really good for Blacks," they wonder, "to have education handed to them on a platter? Would you go to a Black doctor after Bakke? Or hire a Black copy editor after Joiner?") Liberals who consider themselves fair but literate agonize about the collapse of language as a form of communication. ("After all, isn't communication the whole *point* of integration? Then why set out to teach children to read different languages?") The white enemies of Black English tend to fall into patterns predictable from their attitudes to Blacks in general.

But there are also Black enemies of Black English—and they turn out to be much more interesting, because the Black critics use all the different arguments of the white critics, and spare us the more or less open embarrassment that all white Americans feel when publicly criticizing anything or anyone Black. So, of course, they can be more wrong-headed and self-righteously wrong-headed than anyone else (kind of like the woman executive who opposes ERA—because it isn't necessary).

Carl Rowan is one of the best-known and one of the best writers among the Black critics of Black English. You remember Carl Rowan—something in the Johnson administration, had his crisis of conscience over the war and eased out, wound up as a Humphrey liberal (cold war and anti-poverty programs) with a syndicated column.

"The current campaign to classify the bad English of ghetto blacks as a separate language," says Rowan, "is one of the silliest and potentially most destructive of all the terrible things done in the name of racial pride by any race of man." This is a sweeping statement, considering some of the other things done in the name of racial pride—pogroms, lynchings, genocide—but Rowan tries hard to make a case for it.

Black children who say "Do you be respected yo' motha?" instead of "Do you respect your mother?" do not need reinforcement, but correction.

> *I visit a predominantly black high school campus and a youngster says to me, "Do you be on TV?" There isn't a reason on earth why that child should not have been taught, or cannot be taught, to say, "Are you on television?" . . . The greatest burden blacks carry in America today, except for the entrenched institutionalization of racism, is that black children are not being taught the importance of communication—of using the language of the society in which they hope to succeed. . . . Black English would be a tragedy . . . it would consign millions of black children to a* linguistic separation *that would guarantee they will never "make it" in the larger US society. What black children need is an end to this malarkey that tells them they can fail to learn grammar, fail to develop vocabularies, ignore syntax and embrace the mumbo-jumbo of ignorance. . . . What we need is a massive allocation of teachers and resources to remedial programs to teach black children to speak, read and write the language of their native land.*

That's a pretty thorough survey of possible objections to teaching Black English (take the bit about learning grammar and syntax as a more intelligent and less inhumane statement of the back-to-basics argument). And the rant is better rant than we'll probably get from anybody else. Calling Black English "the mumbo-jumbo of ignorance" is especially effective.

And of course, all wrong.

First of all, no Black child says "Do you be respected yo' motha?" Rowan is ignoring the rules of syntax in the dialect. But a Black child might say, "Do you be respectin yo motha?" since dropping the *-ed* is one of the most prominent features of Black English: "He help me yesterday." Like Chinese, Black English tends to dispense with syntactic signs of the past.

Second, there is no reason why a Black child can't be taught to talk like a white child, or a white child like a Black child, or either of them like a Chinese or Spanish child. The point is that they have to be *taught* the new way. They already know how to speak in their native language when they arrive in school.

Third, we have always assumed in America that somehow the schools were supposed to function in a kind of pale and democratic imitation of the English public school. The English used to say that it took three generations to make a gentleman, but we expect our children to "make it" into middle-class American speech patterns in twelve years—though they are surrounded at home by people who they love and admire, and who they talk to much more than they talk to a teacher, and who never use those patterns.

Now it is not impossible for children to learn those patterns, and many of them do. But very few of them learn them in a classroom. The traditional aspiring working-class child or teenager simply picks a model and begins to mimic it, developing in the process a weird and sometimes almost heartrending new dialect, the product of hours of practice, that sounds merely affected to the real middle-class Americans. We all know, or have heard, Blacks with those oddly British-sounding precisionist dialects, and we are all—I am anyway—a little embarrassed by them. (Carl Rowan, whom I've heard on the radio, does not have one; he seems very sensibly to have maintained a light Southern accent from his childhood.)

The failure of the schools to teach the "Standard English" dialect isn't limited to Black children, of course—you have only to read the think pieces written by teachers of Freshman English complaining that white students come from high school with such bad grammar that they can communicate in little more than grunts and tag words, like *you know* or *like*.

But the reality is that the schools never did teach standard middle-class dialect. Schools are not even staffed by people who know what a dialect is. To the ordinary or average teacher of English, there's just *English,* which is the language of Shakespeare or Hemingway or any number of other *writers,* and *bad English,* which is the way lower-class people *talk.* Students from an upper-class background used to make up the majority of college freshmen—lots of them could skip Freshman English entirely, because they already had, from talking to people they loved and respected, a considerable proficiency in the "Standard" (that is, white and upper-class) dialect.

If we want schools to teach children all to talk the same way —I don't think we should want that, but if we do—we have to start somewhere. And surely there is no better place to start than where the child is. So recognizing the existence of Black English is a necessity, even if you want to abolish Black English.

But schools cannot abolish Black English, no matter how massive the allocation of "teachers and resources to remedial programs." Black children do not need instruction in how to speak the language of their native land—the language they already speak is the language of their native land; just as a white child born in Boston or New York or Cleveland or Los Angeles or Plains, Georgia, speaks the language of their native land—though they all sound different when they do it. There are many regional dialects in the United States, just as there are in other large countries. The interesting thing about Black English is that it is a dialect that isn't regional—a Black child born in Boston and a Black child born in Plains, Georgia, have essentially the same speech patterns and speak the same dialect. This is, as many sociolinguists have pointed out, because racism in America condemned Blacks to social and economic separation wherever they lived—so linguistic separation followed.

Now Americans are trying to end the social and economic oppression of Blacks—and, as a result, Blacks themselves are faced with a dilemma: should they blend in with the great American middle class, or should they maintain their separate identity? Many ethnic groups in this country have gone through the same crisis—and it is usually a crisis that produces a lot of literature. Think of the Southern Renaissance of the 1920s, when the Fugitives joined together to criticize industrial society and demand a return to the traditions of Southern agriculturalism. Think of the Jewish writers of the fifties and sixties, and of Lionel Trilling becoming a teacher of English literature at Columbia in the thirties (the first Jew on the staff) and having to answer, both for himself and for the administration, the question: Can a Jew assimilate and interpret the great tradition of English literature?

Blacks in America, because the question of race is so central to our history, have had this problem come up again and again. Paul Laurence Dunbar was encouraged by white editors to write in dialect. Countee Cullen chose to write traditional poetry in standard dialect; his friend Langston Hughes wrote poetry based on the blues and spiritual forms in many variations of Black English, from simple Southern to Harlem bopster. LeRoi Jones is so defiantly anti-assimilationist that he changed his name, and for a time wrote only for Black audiences.

In a sense, the struggle between assimilation and separation never ends for any American—there is hardly a person reading this who has not changed his speech in some way, to eliminate some "lower-class" or "illiterate" feature of his native dialect, whether it is ethnic or regional. And there is hardly a person who has not been criticized, at some time or other, for failing to make the change completely. We love to find flaws in our disguises.

So I defend the use of Black English in terms of the English of the people reading this—that is, by defending your right to your Boston or New York or working-class English. Because it is always difficult in America when whites talk about what Blacks need and want—no white really believes that any other white knows anything about Blacks at all.

And ironically enough, Blacks are in a position where the very language of the schools their children attend is determined by a white judge (I assume Judge Joiner is white, because newspapers would have found a way of mentioning the fact if he was Black); and the laws are interpreted by a largely white Congress, for the benefit of a white school board and a largely white group of teachers.

So it seems to me that it is important for whites—no matter how they feel about Blacks as a political question—to start to understand what dialects are, and what a dialect difference means.

In *The Irrelevant English Teacher* (1972), J. Mitchell Morse says that Black English is "the shuffling speech of slavery" taught to Blacks to make them inferior, and keep them inferior. He proposes that only Standard English can make us free—and says that it would be impossible to translate a passage from Marx into Black English.

This is an extremely peculiar test to apply to Black English. On the one hand, it assumes that, to be valid, BVE (Black Vernacular English) must be an entirely complete and separate system of English. But Morse would never worry if it was impossible to translate Marx into the Scottish or Irish variants of English. There are Scottish and Irish Marxists enough to demonstrate that people speaking these dialects are able to read Standard English well enough, and to manipulate the vocabulary of Marxism as well as any other speaker of the language.

But on the other hand, Morse assumes that, though BVE is more different from Standard than are the Scottish or Irish variants, Black children can learn Standard more easily. All they have to do is pay attention in school, especially to the irrelevant English teacher who advises them to read Edmund Waller and Samuel Beckett, and they will overcome their inadequate language and understand Marx in the original (or at least the original translation). We have all heard people from Ireland and Scotland who have never lost their accents or their peculiar divergences from Standard—even though they live in England or America, and rarely speak to anyone from their native country; and oddly enough, we think their inability to lose their native accent is charming.

In *Language,* Otto Jespersen talks about the difference between learning a language as a child and learning it in school. How does it happen that children learn their language so well, asks Jespersen. The child is very young, it has no experience of language or knowledge, it does not have the advantage of a carefully thought-out plan of learning that we can find in school textbooks, it does not have the advantage of professional teachers especially trained in language instruction, it learns only by ear and does not have the advantage of written texts or of examples of declension of the noun or even of dictionaries . . . yet the child achieves "complete command of the language as a native speaks it, however stupid the child." And an adult, learning a foreign language, with all the advantages of adulthood, gets "in most cases, even with people otherwise highly gifted, a defective and inexact command of the language."

Jespersen, who spoke many languages, thinks that we can never learn language as well as we learn it from our mothers and from our brothers and sisters:

The relation between them and the child is far more cordial and
personal, just because they are not teachers first and foremost.
They are immensely interested in every little advance the child
makes. The most awkward attempt meets with sympathy, even
with admiration. . . . The child has another priceless advantage:
he hears the language in all possible situations and under such
conditions that . . . gesture and facial expression harmonize . . .
what the child hears is just what immediately concerns him and
interests him, and again and again his own attempts at speech
lead to the fulfillment of his dearest wishes, so that his command
of the language has great practical advantages for him.

Let us take the Scots as an example of a people whose language is different than Standard English. There has been a lot of prejudice against the Scots and their "barbarisms" both in grammar and pronunciation. Boswell, a Scot, published a long list of Scotticisms—many of them, of course, Standard English words and phrases. James Beattie, another Scot, attacked Scotticisms both real and imagined. David Hume continually revised his works to take out Scottish words (many of them Standard English words). Hume believed that Scotticisms made his writing difficult and made people look down on it. Boswell thought that Scotticisms and Scottish pronunciation were social disadvantages. Boswell would never, of course, discuss the problems of getting a job —but being Scottish was considered a kind of a drawback at least equivalent to saying *pin* to mean both *pin* and *pen.*

Scots frequently tried to change their language—and Scottish schools tried very hard to teach students Standard English pronunciation all through the nineteenth century. We can get an idea of the results by looking at a biography of a very famous Scot linguist, James A. H. Murray. In *Caught in the Web of Words,* Murray's granddaughter, K. M. Elisabeth Murray, mentions Murray's language several times:

In his new school James found he had a certain amount to
re-learn. Hamilton laid stress on fluent reading and correct
English pronunciation . . . [and] cast ridicule on the teaching of
[his old teacher], when James read out for "it is a man," "eet ees
ay maan" as he had heard his former master say it. Hamilton

was at pains to point out that this was neither Scotch nor English. In fact Hamilton's own speech, *and the English generally heard in the pulpit and schoolrooms in the Borders at that time, was about as far removed from the English of the educated Londoner as the French of Strafford atte Bowe was from that of Paris in Chaucer's day [emphasis mine].*

After Murray was grown, he returned again to Scotland, thirty-three years old, after living some years in London. He wrote to his wife:

How thoroughly Scotch even literary men speak here *[my emphasis] I could hardly believe it. I never noticed it much before. I find per contra that I am taken for out-and-out English by every one. How funny, since all Londoners could tell me to be Scotch at once—and even hear you as Scotch from your contact with me—and yet here nobody suspects me to be anything but English. . . .*

Murray became a schoolmaster at an English boys' school around this time and was remembered by students as "very tall, and thin, with a large head and a sandy beard and with a careful, 'somewhat affected' Scotch enunciation."

At the end of his life, in 1909, when he was seventy-two years old, he was described by one of his assistants as speaking in "a curious Anglo-Scotch nasal accent."

A great scholar, a man fascinated with language, who is thought to be English by his own countrymen, never fools the English. They find his speech "affected" or "curious"—never natural. He could, and did, edit one of the greatest dictionaries of this or any language. He could not disguise his origins.

Is it likely that Blacks in America are going to do any better?

Let's go back again to J. Mitchell Morse and his translation of Marx. Suppose we decide to translate Marx into Basque—what will we find? Basque is—or was, according to Jespersen—a language poor in abstractions: nearly all spiritual and religious ideas are expressed in Spanish. "Basque is naturally very poor in words for general ideas, it has names for special kinds of trees, but tree is *arbolia,* from the Spanish *arbol,* animal is *animale. . . .* " Words for *thing, time,* and *law* are all Spanish. That seems to be a normal development in a language of a subjugated people. But, we can, by using Spanish words, translate Marx into Basque, and if they are Basque versions of Spanish words, so much the better—

liberty is only the English version of a French word, *liberté,* one that we didn't even need—since we have always had *freedom* available.

Many critics of BVE, Morse among them, attack it because the grammar is not subtle enough for literary and scientific meanings. But consider a language like Chinese:

> *Each word is one syllable. . . . The parts of speech are not distinguished:* ta *means, according to circumstances,* great, much, magnitude, enlarge. *Grammatical relations, such as number, person, tense, case, etc., are not expressed by endings . . . the word itself is invariable. If a substantive is to be taken as a plural, that as a rule must be gathered from the context. . . . The most important part of Chinese grammar is that dealing with word order:* ta kuok *means "great state(s)," but* kuok ta *means "the state is great," or . . . "the greatness of the state. . . ." If* ci *is placed after the subject of a sentence it makes a kind of subordinate clause:* wang poo min, *"the king protects the people";* . . . wang poo ci min, *"the people protected by the king;"* poo min ci wang, *"a king protecting the people."*

Chinese shares many features with BVE: no change in the verb for past tense; no copulative verb—*min* (people) *lik* (power) means *power to the people, the power of the people,* and *the people is power,* depending on context. Chinese is even worse off than BVE: it not only has no past tense, but no future tense, no progressive tense, no perfect tenses. It does not have the distinction between limiting and nonlimiting clauses so beloved by pop grammarians, or subtle distinctions between *shall* and *will,* or struggles about dangling participles or "barbarisms" like *hopefully* and *finalize.*

Yet Marx was very effectively translated into Chinese. And the Chinese seem able to run a very complicated society, even to serve as technical advisers to poorer countries who need engineers and scientists.

Surely it is not the relative simplicity of Black Vernacular English grammar that prevents us from translating Marx into that dialect.

It cannot be vocabulary—much of Marx's vocabulary is as foreign to Standard English as to any other dialect. And the vocabulary of Standard English can be used by speakers of BVE.

There can only really be one objection: it sounds funny to the ears of educated white Americans when Black Americans talk in their native dialect.

But that is exactly the reason given to Scottish children to make them learn Standard British English. And there are two strong arguments against trying to teach children a new dialect. First, it doesn't work. We can never really learn a new dialect, no matter how hard we try. Even though we fool our old friends, our new ones think we talk funny.

Second, insisting that Blacks talk like whites is racist.

I give one example of teaching white English which is much sillier and potentially more damaging than teaching Black English.

In Philadelphia, the city where I live, the school system is currently trying to help children read and write better by identifying "brain-damaged children"—another educational innovation which may or may not be a good one. One of the criteria used by one educationalist for determining that Black children are brain-damaged—according to my sources—is that they are unable to tell the difference between *pin* and *pen*. It is a feature of Black English that *pin* and *pen* are pronounced the same. It is very difficult for people who ordinarily make no distinction between words to really hear the distinction strangers make. Those Americans who make no distinction between *Mary, marry,* and *merry,* for example, know what they mean when they say all those different words—though they say them all the same. And they have a very hard time learning to say them in different ways. Among white Americans, Southerners also make no distinction between *pin* and *pen.* Jimmy Carter, for example, pronounces both words exactly the same. He grew up, luckily enough, in a school system where the teacher pronounced them exactly the same way, too. So his dialect never became a shibboleth, a badge of shame, or a ticket of entry into a class called "brain-damaged" or "learning disability" or "retarded educable" or "hyperactive" or any of the other phrases that seem, in the hands of teachers ignorant of language differences, to be used to designate Blacks as second-track, and second-rate.

There is really no point in arguing whether Black Vernacular English is a language, a dialect, an argot, or a slang. That's like arguing whether a particular plant is a wild flower or a weed—the distinction is meaningless to botanists. The distinction between a language and a dialect is also meaningless to linguists. English is a language related to German, both are related to Indo-European. They did not start out dialects and then get promoted to language status because they were used for great literature or great scientific discovery—anymore than a weed becomes a wild flower by being pretty.

Black English is praised (condescendingly) by Richard Mitchell because "its blithe disregard of grammatical form is as crafty as it is cocky." But Black Vernacular English does not disregard grammatical form—because it is a language, it must follow rules of grammar. These are different than the rules of Standard English—much more different than most other American dialects. But to suppose that any language can function without grammar at all is like supposing that the airplane defies the law of gravity. On the contrary, airplanes obey the law of gravity—and of thermodynamics.

Labov points out some features of Black Vernacular English that are different than Standard English: -ed is not used to mark past tense. This may lead to problems when ghetto children learn to read sentences where -ed is used. Pronunciation is completely different. For example, in the language of these children the word *trial* and the word *child* may be pronounced exactly alike. If the teacher is telling kids to sound out the word before spelling it, the ghetto kid is going to have more trouble than his white fellow students.

We may think that dialect is ugly. We may regret that it exists. It seems silly to ignore it, and silly to expect that schools —starting now—will be able to stamp it out.

I do not believe that Black Vernacular English is ugly—or that it should be stamped out. If it were possible to turn every Black child white by administering some sort of pill, I think that would be a bad idea. A loss to a pluralistic society. If it were possible to turn Black Vernacular English into Standard by administering eight years of school, I think that would also be a loss. As great as the loss of the Irish brogue, the Scottish burr, the Southern drawl, or the Yankee twang.

It also does not seem to me that schools are the best places to change dialect. Our native way of talking—the one we learned from our mothers and fathers, the one we use to cry out in pain or delight—is too much a part of our idea of self. Alfred Kazin, in

A Walker in the City, talks about how the bright Standard English taught in school was both a passport to success and a symbol to both parents and children of how shameful it was to be un-American and Jewish. Kazin's suffering because he was forced to go to language class to correct a stutter is the suffering of a child forced outside "the bright circle of the city" and abandoned as inadequate. Surely, we do not want our schools to teach children that the language of their parents and friends, of their whole culture, is inadequate and ignorant and wrong? Surely, trying to teach them that is likely to make them resist other "learning"?

The fact remains that there is a way of writing that is necessary to success, just as there are rules about which fork to use at an expensive restaurant. And preparing children for success means preparing them to manipulate those rules, just as they have to be taught to manipulate the salad fork and demitasse spoon. There is really no argument about teaching children to read and write Standard English—only about how it is to be done: with humanity and with understanding or with drills that the children cannot understand.

Finally, doesn't it seem sensible to teach children, while we are teaching them this magical language of success, that there is such a thing as tolerance—even of people so different as to say, "He ax me yesterday"? If we must change the language of our children, can't we at least try to point out to them that they have a chance, by being sensible and humane, to make it unnecessary to change the language of our grandchildren? And if the language is to be changed, wouldn't it be better to put the responsibility for the change in the hands of people who are willing to learn something about language?

three

White
Vernacular English

After recognizing the special problems of teaching children who speak Black Vernacular English, it is only sensible—and I'm sure political conservatives would say only fair—to consider the problems of teaching children who speak White Vernacular English (WVE).

The problems are severe—largely because everybody seems to think all the problems come down to only one big basic problem. And people disagree about what that one big problem is.

Some people think the problem is that the kids are just not taught good grammar. Pop grammarians, teachers of freshman and bonehead English courses, businessmen who can't find a secretary who knows the difference between *stationary* and *stationery,* conventional viewers with conventional alarm, connoisseurs of comma placement, Monday morning copy editors of the Sunday papers, jot and tittle experts of all kinds attack the way English is taught. Their solution is simple—back to basics. Get out the old-time grammar books and start parsing, declining, diagraming, and conjugating. Bring back the spelling bee and Palmer Penmanship and the good old days in general.

Other people—the College Composition section of National Council of Teachers of English, many linguists, many teachers—think that the basic problem is that Americans are afraid to write anything at all. And it is bad teaching of bad basics that has produced that fear.

For example, Charles Suhor, of the National Council of Teachers of English, reports on the 1970 National Assessment of Educational Progress. This is a series of tests given to adults who volunteer to take them—tests that show how much they

162

remember of grade school and high school work. Those tests are then compared to the results of children ages nine, thirteen, seventeen—roughly grade school, junior high, and high school graduates. And they show how successful teaching is now, and has been in the past. The adults were all happy to take the tests, in subjects they could hardly be expected to remember much of—chemistry and physics. (What *is* a valence? Think back and see if you can remember.) But "when asked to compose a short essay in the form of a letter to a public agency, 29% of these otherwise cooperative and well-disposed adults flatly refused to do so. . . . The fact is that our society is severely hung up on the pursuit of picayunish perfection in writing. So much so, that many adults are in absolute dread of putting their ideas on paper."

Even given the fact that fear is the problem, some pop grammarians say, the solution is still a simple one: just teach people not to be afraid, by teaching them to write right. Back to basics. Bring back the spelling bee, and diagraming, and all that other right stuff.

The problem with that solution is there is no evidence that it works. Suhor reports: "In 1969 John Mellon did an exhaustive study of 20th century research on the relationship of formal grammar instruction to writing skill. Unlike research in many other important (educational) areas—methods of teaching reading, for instance—the results of Mellon's investigation were unambiguous. He couldn't find a single study to support the idea that instruction in grammar improves writing."

That statement surprises some people—we all assume that we are learning to write when we learn the difference between a noun and a verb and a gerund and a gerundive. But there is lots of evidence that drill in the traditional grammar of English has nothing to do with writing well.

Paul Roberts, in *Understanding English,* points out that

> there are those [students] who can learn to read and write
> without very much instruction in reading and writing. They learn
> through a more or less unconscious imitation of other writers,
> slowly building up a feeling for sentence structure that doesn't
> depend much on any ability to analyze sentences. Such students
> have no obvious need to study English grammar, though they are
> often the only ones who enjoy it.

163

But this does not answer the question: what shall we teach children about language?

First of all, whether they speak BVE or WVE, it would seem to be a good idea to teach them *not* to be afraid of writing. Many strategies have been proposed for this. One of the best is by Kenneth Koch in *Wishes, Lies and Dreams* (New York: Vintage, 1971). Koch, himself a poet, says that he was struck by the fact that children's drawings were so gorgeous and children's writing seemed so stilted and appalling. He went into the public schools of New York and began asking children to write wishes, lies, and dreams. Essentially, as Suhor points out, there is built-in punctuation instruction as well as invitation to use imagination in Koch's formulas:

> I used to be a *peanut butter,* but now I'm *a hot dog.*
> I used to be *a kitten,* but now I'm *a fox.*
> I wish I was a (color item) on a (place item).
> I wish I was *a gold star* stuck on *all my good papers.*
> I wish I was *a red mountain in my back yard.*
> *Ocean,* where did you get *those waves?*
> *Radio,* where did you get *that music?*
> *Rose,* where did you get *that red?*

Koch's method, encouragement, and delight are, incidentally, identical to the method that Jespersen says mothers use to teach children to speak. Koch's students learned about commas and question marks—and did it without learning what discourages most children: that all you get on an English composition, no matter how good, is red pencil marks from a teacher who is never satisfied. Suhor also points out that, as adults, we almost never write without an audience in mind—but students write solely for the purpose of having their writing corrected by the teacher. He suggests that "the teacher can serve better as a technician, advisor, and midwife to the process if there is a real honest to god reader for what the student is writing. That's why the most energetic and expressive writing nowadays is coming from class newsletters, jokebooks, graffiti boards, letter-writing clubs, and anthologies."

Parents lucky enough to have kids in a school that uses these little mimeographed newsletters—usually nothing more than a couple sheets—know how important they are to the children. They are the only other thing, besides those gorgeous finger paintings on brown wrapping paper, that the kid ever wants to hang on the refrigerator.

Koch has expanded his method to include senior citizens and produced a book with poems as stunning as the ones the children made—an indication that inviting the student to invent may be the best way to teach writing.

But there are limitations to this method: we do not want our college freshmen coming home with a mimeographed sheet for mom to hang up on the refrigerator. Having taught children that writing is fun, and an invitation to invention at least as strong as a set of watercolors, we want them to learn to manipulate Standard English.

As has been pointed out in the chapter on BVE, the problem here is that most grammar books, and many teachers of composition in high schools and colleges, demand an English which is not standard at all—but a hyper-correct dialect largely unknown outside the classroom. Martin Joos, in *The Five Clocks* (1967), says this best: "The community prefers the center of the scale: *'good'* usage, not 'best.' It routinely rejects morbidly honest candidates for office, and the best English counts as the disqualification that makes a teacher."

So let's consider that center of the scale. And let me propose that there is a standard of English, which our grammar books have been trying to correct—fortunately without success—that is now, as it has been for centuries, the best speech available.

I'm going to do this by describing the language of Daniel Defoe and Jane Austen. The descriptions are not my own, they are taken from *The Evolution of the English Language* by George H. McKnight.

In Defoe, "one finds the difference from modern accepted good usage apparent," for example, the double negative, "was not true neither"; use of *or* with *neither,* "neither man or beast"; flat adverbs (without *-ly*), "nothing near so anxious"; irregular use of personal pronouns, "Why does God not kill you and I. . . ." "Between Friday and I"; *who* for *whom,* "The old goat who I found expiring"; *had best,* "What I had best do"; indicative for subjunctive, "as if he was bound for"; the use of the collective followed by a plural pronoun, "every thing at large in their places"; plural without *-s,* "eight year"; use of words later condemned, "a more *healthy* spot of ground" (the proper word in this instance is *healthful,* says the *Harper Dictionary of Contemporary Usage,* and finds the answer so obvious that it doesn't even bother to ask the panel what it thinks).

Besides this, McKnight lists "many tense forms since abandoned": *awaked* for *awoke, eat* for *ate, took* for *taken, situate* for *situated, run* for *ran, laid down* for *laid himself down* or *lay down, had drank* for *had drunk, sunk* for *sank,* and *while this was doing* instead of *while this was being done.*

"In general Defoe's language represents a stage before the discipline of the English grammarian had been applied," says McKnight. I invite the reader to look over the list again—is it so bad? Have any of those "mistakes"—actually, it seems more sensible to call them standard idioms—really been removed from the language? Surely all of us have been exposed to these usages at one time or another. They make up a great part of the pet illiteracies of pop grammarians, and they have taken up centuries of classroom time.

It is possible that they will not die because they *are* the language. They *are* correct. It is possible, if you prefer it, that they will not die because all the people who speak English are too thickheaded to pay attention to logic and sense when they talk and write. But in any case, they will not die.

So let's stop trying to kill them.

McKnight picks *Mansfield Park* to analyze because in it Austen contrasts a lower-middle-class family, the Prices, "the abode of noise, disorder, and impropriety," with the upper-class family of Mansfield Park, where all was "elegance, propriety, regularity, harmony." The Price family "betrays its social class" by using *lay* for *lie*—but it is not the lowest class: the Price family keeps two servants. At Mansfield Park, says McKnight, "we find a language governed less by the grammarian than by social custom and native idiom." The distinctions between *shall* and *will,* and *should* and *would* are "fastidiously made."

But there is lack of pronoun concord at Mansfield Park: *"nobody* put *themselves* out of *their* way"; "I would have *everybody* marry if *they* can"; "while *each* of the Miss Bartrams *were* meditating."

Who is used for *whom: "Who* have they got to meet us?"

The phrase *it is me* is employed: "Depend upon it, *it is me."*

There is a lack of concord between subject and verb in number: "Miss B——'s attention and opinion *was* evidently his chief aim."

Double negatives occur: *"not* so bad with you *neither."*

The superlative is used with only two: "the youngest and eldest [of the two Miss Bartrams]."

"An expression disapproved of by grammarians" occurs: *"these* sort of hours . . . *these* sort of hopes."

There is redundant conjunction: *"but, however,* I soon found. . . ."

"Verb forms later superseded" are used: *learnt* for *learned, bid* for *bade, broke* for *broken, drank* for *drunk, ate* for *eaten.*

Anxious is used to mean *eager;* and *apt, allow, confess,* and *furnish* are employed in "ways objected to by later rhetoricians." The *Harper Dictionary,* for example, will only say that *apt* and *liable* are "considered by many to be interchangeable" (without mentioning that Jane Austen was one). *Allow* and *confess* and *furnish* I cannot find criticized in either Harper's or Fowler, so I assume that whatever objection was made, it was momentary—as many pop grammar objections are.

And other "widely disapproved forms" are used: *aggravation* for *irritation* (57 percent of Harper's panel would edit this out of Austen); *demean* for *lower* (only 31 percent would change Austen, a clear victory for clear prose in our time); *parties* for *persons* (a "vulgarism," say the editors of the *Harper Dictionary,* again, without bothering to ask the panel to join in condemning the speech of the English aristocracy).

Once again, I look at all those things and they do not seem so bad. McKnight seems to agree:

> *The citations here given are from a single one of Miss Austen's novels. Her other works afford abundant illustration of the form of language, controlled by social usage rather than by book rules, that prevailed in England a century ago. They also serve to illustrate a stage in the continuous stream of cultivated colloquial English and help to make clear the irregularities, the absence of bookishness, persisting in the cultivated colloquial speech of England at the present time.*

And in the speech of cultivated Americans at the present time.

Once again, why not leave it alone? It is obvious that no matter how hard the schools try, they have not been able to stamp out these vulgarisms and errors. In fact, the rest of society does not see them as errors or vulgarisms. And those students who learn to write "almost unconsciously from other writers" are likely to use just these expressions because they find them in the books they read, and hear them in the language they speak, the language McKnight calls "cultivated colloquial English," that is, WVE.

Many English teachers, English teachers who can see the necessity of treating BVE speakers in a special way, refuse to believe that there is such a thing as WVE. But it does exist—in a long tradition of clear and sensible expression. Feminists have revived interest in the journals and letters of ordinary women—unpublished and not meant for publication—and we are now discovering more and more about the real language of our ancestors. In *Diary of an Edwardian Lady,* for example, a book published in facsimile of the elegant handwriting of its upper-class author, the possessive *its,* as in "the flower lifted its head," is routinely written *it's.* No copy editor got a chance to mold the book into publishing house standard, so this is one of the few glimpses we have of actual practice of upper-class writers at the beginning of this century.

Feminists have revived interest in the writing of women—but Thomas De Quincey was there before them:

> The idiom of our language, the mother tongue, survives only amongst our women and children; not, Heaven knows, among our women who write books—they are often painfully conspicuous for all that disfigures authorship; but amongst well-educated women not professionally given to literature. . . . Would you desire at this day to read our noble language in all its native beauty, picturesque from idiomatic propriety, racy in its phraseology, delicate yet sinewy in its composition—steal the mail-bags, and break open all the letters in female handwriting.

Would you like to see WVE disfigured? Read an American edition of an English author. About this, Randolph Quirk writes in *The English Language and Images of Matter:*

> The original London edition of Graham Greene's novel, The End of the Affair *(Heinemann 1951) contains the following two sentences:* The world would have said he had the reasons for hate, not me *(p. 3).* She did not believe in anything, anymore than you or me *(p. 166). In the American edition by Bantam Books we find* me *replaced by* I *in each case. Such examples*

sharply contradict the image of American speech as tough, creative, convention-flouting, and imbued with the virility of the frontier spirit.

In *The People's Almanac* # 2, edited by Irving Wallace and David Wallechinsky, there is a section called "The Wit of Oscar Wilde"; and Wilde's famous epigram:

Experience is the name everyone gives to their mistakes.

appears as:

Experience is the name everyone gives to his mistakes.

This section was compiled by Irving Wallace, one of the two editors of *The People's Almanac,* and I have always thought he should keep his correction of Wilde's WVE intact, because it would have made Wilde laugh—but he should also change the title of the section to something more descriptive: "Half Wisdom of Oscar Wilde, Half Wit of Irving Wallace."

Once again, laughing at the false corrections of pop grammarians does not change the fact that they exist—and have power. Copy editors at Bantam Books, publishers of other people's wisdom like Irving Wallace, and professors like Wilson Follett are members of an elite—and a very hardworking elite. Asking the teacher to encourage his students to write with "idiomatic propriety" is, in one sense, asking for trouble. Parents object. Other teachers object. Many professors in college believe that one of the purposes of bonehead English, and of all introductory English composition classes, is to protect them from ever having to deal with idiomatic propriety—they try to stamp it out wherever they see it.

But the alternatives are even worse. Bonehead English is possibly the least respectable, intellectually and academically, of all the courses in college. It is taught, almost exclusively, by teaching assistants—graduate students who work for a pittance and a scholarship. And these graduate students are themselves English majors—almost entirely ignorant of the history, the syntax, and the grammar of English. They are overworked, underpaid, and attending classes full-time besides. They are usually white, middle-class, and academically oriented. They are often confronted with classes that are Black and Spanish and white working class or lower class—and students who are not used to responding to what teacher says with awe or respect or even attention. The TA's have no training, and no experience in teaching, and they are almost as likely as the boneheads to have difficulty writing in correct academic style.

In fact, teaching assistant is not only a bad job—it is often the worst kind of scholarship, reserved generally for the worst of the graduate students. Better students get fellowships (no work at all), or research assistantships (a few hours in the library a week). Many TA's are of course brilliant and genuinely concerned with their students—but even then, in many cases, a TA trying to teach academic style to working-class students is nothing more than the well-intentioned blind leading the blind who are eager to follow.

The results are often appalling. Paul Roberts (in *Understanding English*) provides a sample of how to write a 500-word freshman composition: You start with a simple idea and expand it:

> *"Why College Football Should Be Abolished"*
> *College football should be abolished because it's bad for the school and also bad for the players. The players are so busy practicing that they don't have any time for their studies.*

Not a bad start, says Roberts—but it's only thirty-two words.

> *You still have four hundred and sixty-eight to go, and you've pretty much exhausted the subject. . . . Make a pot of coffee and start to fill out your views on college football. Put a little meat on the bones:*
> *"Why College Football Should Be Abolished"*
> *In my opinion, it seems to me that college football should be abolished. The reason why I think this to be true is because I feel that football is bad for the colleges in nearly every respect. As Robert Hutchins says in his article in our anthology in which he discusses football, it would be better if the colleges had racehorses and had races with one another, because then the horses would not have to attend classes. I firmly agree with Mr. Hutchins on this point, and I am sure that many other students would agree too.*
>
> *One reason why it seems to me that college football is bad is that it has become too commercial. In the older times when people played football just for the fun of it, maybe college football was all right; but they do not play football just for the fun of it now as they used to in the old days. Nowadays college football is what you might call a big business. Maybe this is not true at all schools, and I don't think it is especially true here at State but certainly this is the case at most colleges and universities in America nowadays, as Mr. Hutchins points out in his very*

interesting article. Actually the coaches and alumni go around to the high schools and offer the high school stars large salaries to come to their colleges and play football for them. There was one case where a high school star was offered a convertible if he would play football for a certain college.

And so on. And on. Teachers of freshman composition despair over stuff like this—unjustly, it seems to me. Getting students to produce this kind of work is what they are trying, unconsciously, to do, and what the school is employing them, unconsciously, to do. No idiomatic propriety, no grammatical errors, no spelling errors, no thought, no energy, no invention, no fun—and no way to correct it. Compare this composition with:

Rose, where did you get *that red?*

Compare the original passage about hunting seal in the Follett chapter with Follett's correction. Is this what we want our freshmen to learn about prose? Is this how we want them to write?

Compare the *Foxfire* books—a project in which high school students interviewed elder craftsmen in their areas, and printed directions on how to cane chairs and other such folk crafts—the diction is clear, precise, accurate, and full of sense and meaning: idiomatic propriety.

Actually, the Roberts composition is not the worst that traditional methods of teaching students to write can produce; Suhor provides a worse example, written by a student in a highly respected prep school:

It is not for me to determinate whom was right; however, it is neither the individual's decision.

Only an English teacher—a very serious and dedicated English teacher who was also a lover of the language—could produce a student who writes prose like that.

Surely if the purpose of bonehead English is to teach the students how to write academic standard, it is misdirected from the start? Most students do not need to know academic standard —they will never go on to graduate school, and even if they do, there is a very small chance that they will wind up being college teachers, and an even smaller chance that they will ever write very much—statistically, as Suhor points out, the average Ph.D. writes only two articles after getting his degree.

And if the student needs to know academic standard so that

the full professors can understand him, surely it would be cheaper and better and easier to simply teach the professors what idiomatic propriety is, in both BVE and WVE. After all, students have to be taught all over again every four years. Professors stay on forever—professors are interested in language, used to learning, delighted by new information. . . . I imagine these classes, taught by somebody like Geneva Smitherman, of Wayne State University, an articulate and energetic user of both BVE and academic standard.

She sits at the desk, shaking her head in a firm but kindly way, at a professor who might be Mitchell Morse, or at least look like him: white-haired, trim, natty, articulate in academic standard . . . and eager to learn.

"No, no no, Professor Morse," says Geneva Smitherman. "We do *not* say on entering the room, *Hello motherfuckers;* what we say is *Hay Muhfuhs.* You are just going to have to try a little harder to *think first,* and then put your thoughts in words."

That will never happen.

But an introductory English curriculum based on the students' actual language is at least a possibility. To show how faint that possibility is, however, I have only to point to what Otto Jespersen wrote in *The English Journal* in 1924 ("The Teaching of Grammar"): language teaching in schools, said Jespersen:

> should deal first and foremost with the sounds found in the
> pupils' own speech and in the language which they hear everyday.
> Their own local dialect, and the "received" or "standard"
> pronunciation of their teachers must be taken as the basis of
> analysis; but then that basis, if examined in true scientific spirit
> —though without the use of the learned terminology of the
> scientific phonetician—will form an extremely valuable
> fundament on which to build. . . . If there is one thing I dislike
> in grammar, it is definitions (of parts of speech) too often met
> with in our textbooks. They are neither exhaustive nor true; they
> have not, and cannot have, the precision and clearness of the
> definitions found in textbooks of mathematics, and it is extremely
> easy to pick holes in them.

Jespersen proceeds to pick holes in several definitions: A sentence is a group of words that makes sense: Why a group of words? Isn't *Go!* a sentence? Why "makes sense"? *He is older than his father* is a sentence.

And thus we might go on to the definitions found even in the best grammars: they are unsatisfactory all of them and I do not think they are necessary. When children begin to learn about cats, and dogs, they do not start with the definition of what a cat or a dog is, but they are shown first one cat and told that is a cat, and then another, and so on, till they have no difficulty in recognizing a cat when they see one, and the want of a definition does not prevent them from learning a good many facts about cats. . . . If grammar is to be real grammar, it must face the realities of life: we cannot teach grammar in the abstract, but we can and must teach English grammar, that is to say, the way in which English-speaking people express their thoughts and build up their sentences.

That is to say: we must teach the rules of the vernacular. And a classroom lucky enough to have both speakers of BVE and the many forms of WVE will be able to teach more rules more easily.

four

Who Changes Language

A Primer of Language Politics

The proper pop grammarian attitude to change is to see it as ugly, unnecessary, illiterate, obscurantist, illogical, alien, ignorant, and threatening not only to the language but to the maintenance of the social order.

In almost all cases, there is an unpleasant edge to the pop grammar complaint—it sounds a little like the way realist painters used to refer to modernists, and the way modernist painters now refer to the young realists. It is as if the pop grammarian was saying, "I learned this new and difficult dialect. I changed the way I spoke, lost my accent, submitted myself to all sorts of humiliation by my wonderful English teachers. Now I've made it—and I'm going to make sure that nobody else makes it without going through the same thing." Language is seen as a skill anyone can acquire (like painting in perspective, or painting in broad abstract brush strokes), if they care enough.

Not to care is to attack the pop grammarians' whole life, and their hard-won position in the writing business.

This helps to explain why pop grammarians frequently say that they have a vested interest in correcting errors—after all, they are writers, and they feel that television (from above) and careless ignorance (from below) are combining to destroy their wonderful, supple, eloquent medium, the standard dialect of English. After all, what is thinking but making distinctions—and every time the word *flaunt* is used to mean *flout*, or *hopefully* to mean *it is to be hoped*, or *disinterested* for *uninterested*, a distinction dies, and with it a possible thought in English.

Let's try to answer this by talking about language change—who does it, and how is it done. It is easiest, perhaps, to separate the changers from the defenders by means of a political metaphor: the Left, and the Right:

The Left (Language Changers)

1. Illiterates, semiliterates, occupiers of ethnic or cultural ghettos. Most speech by the very poor or very isolated (by geography or by prejudice) is not adventurous *in form*. Grammatical structures are essentially old-fashioned, unchanged sometimes for centuries. Donald J. Lloyd, in *Snobs, Slobs and the English Language*, has this to say:

> Them things *was once standard, so were* he don't, guv, clumb and riz. *The common speech of the uneducated is comparatively static, though it varies from place to place it is everywhere conservative.*
>
> *The changes made by the poor are likely to be in vocabulary —slang. Seldom written because its users seldom write, it is capable of great literary beauties, uncomplicated force, compact suggestion and moving sentiment.*

2. The new educated class. Lloyd points out that in the nineteenth century the concentration of schools, colleges, publishing houses, and print shops in New England and New York helped establish a written standard, "native only to those who grew up near the Hudson River or east of it. Elsewhere in America this written standard has been a learned class dialect—learned in the schools as the property and distinguishing mark of an educated class . . . an heirloom handed down from the days when the whole nation looked to the school masters of New England for its book learning."

One interesting example of this is the spelling of *uh*, that little pause we all make in our speech from time to time. *Uh* is frequently spelled *er*—because *uh* is the way *er* is pronounced in the *r*-less standard New England dialect. If you speak a dialect where the *r*'s are pronounced, as I do, you may also remember how odd it sounded when you read the word *er*—and pronounced it to rhyme with *her*. Slowly, as standard pronunciation in the United States is demanding that *r*'s be pronounced—largely because it is pronounced in radio and TV announcer standard—the word is being spelled in the new dialect, *uh,* a fact that would have horrified Henry James, who insisted in an address to the graduating class of Harvard that the United States would never be capable of a real literature or a beautiful speech until it stopped pronouncing its *r*'s, an "ugly sound" that James insisted was "a morose grinding of the back teeth."

The domination of the East was a long one; as recently as 1959, according to *The New York Times* (July 23, 1979), 75 percent of the Ph.D.'s in America came from the East Coast. The educational explosion of the past twenty years has changed all that: in 1979, only 20 percent of the Ph.D.'s came from the East.

The new educated class is large, self-sufficient, and writes the language it knows. "Most," says Lloyd,

> *take their diplomas and go to work among their own people. They form a literate class greater in numbers and in proportion to the total population than ever before. Speaking the speech of their region, they mingle naturally and easily with its people. When they write, they write the language they know, and they print it, for the most part, in presses close at hand. Everywhere they speak a standard literate English—but with differences: a regional speech derived from the usages of the early settlers.*

Many of these people invent new words—out of their own experience. Nowhere is this more apparent than in contemporary physics—a science that seems always to be inventing new words for almost invisible phenomena. In the nineteenth century, scientists made up new words—out of Latin and Greek. Fowler complains that scientists could never be convinced to keep these two languages separate, and thus produced "barbarisms" like *Pleistocene, pliocene, miocene*—in each case the prefix is Greek and the suffix Latin. Fowler mourned that it was impossible to stop these words. "A barbarism is like a lie; it has got the start of us before we have found it out, and we cannot catch it; it is in possession, and our offers of other versions come too late. . . . It is worthwhile to mention this . . . on the chance that the men of science may some day wake up to their duties to the language—duties much less simple than they are apt to suppose."

That day has arrived. The newest words do not come from mixed Latin and Greek—because Latin and Greek are no longer studied by scientists. *Quark* is the name given newly discovered subatomic particles, and quarks come in colors; among the colors is *beauty.* Thinking of beauty as a color is a little odd—but apparently attractive to physicists who seem to enjoy the fact that their discipline requires them to think about things in an odd way. *Quark* as a word first appeared in *Finnegans Wake,* but the inventor of the scientific term, Murray Gell-Mann, is frequently quoted as saying that he did not know that at the time. He just wanted a funny-sounding word for a funny-acting particle. The newest particle or substance that physicists claim to have discovered is the stuff that holds the atom together, and it is called *gluon,* from the word *glue,* and the suffix *-on.*

This delightful kind of invention is responsible for the use of words like *finalize, input, unsave* (in computer terminology, this does not mean the same thing as *destroy,* rather, it means not actually to throw something away but simply refuse to collect it —a fine and subtle distinction that should delight pop grammarians), *gigo* (garbage in, garbage out—give a machine nonsense instead of true data and you get only nonsense back), *mego* (*m*y *e*yes *g*laze *o*ver—indicating boredom, and in combination with *garbage* in *garbage out*—as, *what is all this gigo and mego?*—the strongest possible condemnation).

3. Linguists. Frequently accused of being "anything goes" linguists. Or destroyers of Standard. Actually, linguists frequently insist that anything does not go—that in certain situations the Standard of the grammar books is wrong because it is alien and alienating.

This comes down to saying, in effect, *whatever is is right,* which is not usually considered a leftist statement (and resembles Hegel's conservative dictum—The *real is the returned*)—but in language, even conservatives are to the Left.

The Right (Language Preservers)

1. Real conservatives. This book is in favor of true conservatives. People who still say *icebox,* and who still use old-fashioned

constructions. Conservatives are walking history books of the language, and they keep to old words and old ways out of a kind of instinct of preservation.

Titles of organizations frequently stay the same, and act as a way of dating the organization. For example, certain kinds of word chains are relatively new in modern English. So, simply from the titles of the two groups, we could tell that the National Council *of* Teachers *of* English is an older organization than the National Educational Association, or the Modern Language Association.

In "The Possessive Apostrophe in Names" (*American Speech,* October 1958), Robert L. Cord points out that "not one of the teachers colleges in the United States takes an apostrophe in its name. . . . Years ago, the apostrophe seems to have been employed in the form. . . . Old editions of the Encyclopaedia Britannica write of the *Teachers' College* of Columbia University."

A conservative almost never corrects others, however. For example, your aunt who still says *icebox* does not have a sign on her door that says, "The word fridge must not be used in this house. Violators will be humiliated."

And a language conservative is not necessarily conservative in any other matters. For example, as Lounsbury points out, Browning as a poet used many new words and new constructions in his work—he was what linguists today call an advanced speaker. Tennyson used almost none—a language conservative. That says something about them as poets—and nothing wrong about either of them. It is interesting that Tennyson, the language conservative, was interested in the newest scientific thought of his day—and was extremely modern in ideas; while Browning seems not to have bothered too much with scientific discovery, or worried about dealing with the new problems science presented to educated nineteenth-century readers. But however interesting that is as literary criticism (any graduate student will see the essay staring him in the face: "Advanced Thought and Advanced Language in the Nineteenth Century—A Study of Contrasts in Browning and Tennyson"), it is important here only to help point out that we are all conservatives in some matters. I really can never bring myself to say *film* for *movie.*

The Far Right

Editors and teachers of English who are, or consider themselves, masters of that school-mastered dialect called Standard. They frequently consider themselves guardians of the Standard—without the good sense of Fowler, who points out that trying to stamp out barbarisms is impossible.

For example, take the apostrophe. The state of Colorado by declaration of a joint session of its congress decided in 1978 to drop the apostrophe from its motto. *Pike's Peak or Bust* became *Pikes Peak or Bust*. *The New York Times* deplored that decision in an editorial, declaring that this was just one more instance of permissive grammar, and praising the apostrophe in general as an outstanding felicity of English typesetting.

Of course, the state of Colorado was only following—belatedly—the advice of the American Cartographic Association, which recommended in the early 1950s that the apostrophe be dropped in place names because it made maps extremely hard to read. That advice is followed by all modern atlases I have checked, by all dictionaries that print a gazetteer—and by *The New York Times* itself, which has, for at least fifteen years, been printing towns like Harpers Ferry, Virginia, and Toms River, New Jersey, without the apostrophe.

When Webster's Third International first appeared, it frightened the Far Right out of its collective mind—and many publications, *Life* and *The New York Times* included, declared that they would not use Webster's Third, since it was too permissive. They would insist on Webster's Second as the dictionary of record. Bergen Evans, in the *Atlantic Monthly* (May 1962), had a little fun doing a word count of both publications:

> In the issue in which Life *stated editorially that it would follow the Second International, there were over forty words, constructions and meanings which are in the Third International, but not in the Second. The issue of* The New York Times *which hailed the Second as the authority to which it would adhere . . . used one hundred and fifty-three separate words, phrases and constructions which are listed in the Third but not in the Second and nineteen others which are condemned in the Second. . . . The* Washington Post, *in an editorial captioned "Keep Your Old Webster's," says in the first sentence, "don't throw it away," and*

in the second, "hang on to it." But the old Webster's labels don't
colloquial and doesn't include hang on to *in this sense at all.*

One example of Far Right language attitudes can be found in
the stylebooks published by leading papers, like *The New York
Times* and *The Washington Post*. Certainly, there is a value to the
paper in always printing the box scores of baseball games in a
simple and rigorous way. The spelling of words transliterated
from languages that do not have our alphabet is also a problem,
and stylebooks choose for the harried reporter and copy editor an
arbitrary "correct" form: *succoth* or *succah* or *sukkah* from the
Hebrew; *kif* or *kef* or *kief* from the Arabic; *Kruschev* or *Chrus-
chev* or *Khrushchev* from the Russian—the list is long and the
decisions are usually made without fuss or *hutzpah* (or *chutzpa*).

Most stylebooks are as innocuous, and as ineffective, as the
pronouncements of editors in editorials—like declarations that
only Webster's Second will be used, they represent policy. The
reporters and writers represent practice; and practice ultimately
wins.

The Yahoo Right

The yahoos are, of course, the pop grammarians—who offer
the same strictures that the Far Right do, but with even less
intelligence and understanding—without mastering the standard
dialect themselves in many cases—and who publish interminable
death of English despairs and private lists of language peeves.
Professional busybodies and righters of imaginary wrongs, they
are the Sunday visitors of language, dropping in weekly on the
local poor to make sure that everything is up to their own idea of
Standard, not because they care about the poor, of course, but
because the diseases the poor contract from inadequate sanitation
can be catching.

The Center

The Center is made up of those people who are the doers and
achievers of the world—hard workers, worried about the impression they make, and determined to rise in life.

They don't have the assurance of the taxi driver, the ghetto

Black, or the teenager speaking his high school slang. They care what people think about the language they use.

They do not have the power of print that the indigenous Ph.D. does—or the same capacity to delight in their own invention and their own dialect.

They don't have the mastery of Standard that comes to people who have spent years and years in the classroom—years that members of the Center have spent out on the streets humping for a living.

So they are the victims of the yahoos who frighten them with words like *illiterate* (back to the factory) and *ignoramus* (you'll never make it in the middle class, no matter how much money you earn). Randolph Quirk, in *The Use of English,* points out that at both ends of the social scale, the upper and lower classes, no one worries about language.

People of position and status do not need to worry about their language—"no fear of being criticised or corrected is likely to cross their minds, and this gives their speech that characteristically unself-conscious and easy flow which is often envied. Their nonchalant attitude to language was epitomised in the nineteenth century in the words of Bulwer Lytton: 'I am free to confess that I don't know grammar. Lady Blessington, do *you* know grammar?' "

The very poor, or the isolated, or speakers of nonstandard dialects also speak with "a similar degree of careless ease." They know their speech is condemned, and don't care.

In between is the Center.

> *They live their lives . . . in some degree of nervousness over their grammar, their pronunciation and their choice of words; sensitive and fearful of betraying themselves. . . . It is all too easy to raise an unworthy laugh at the anxious. The people thus uncomfortably stilted on linguistic high heels so often form part of what is, in many ways, the most admirable section of any society; the ambitious, tense, inner-driven people, who are bent on going places and doing things. The greater pity then if a disproportionate amount of their energy goes into . . . this shabby obsession with variant forms of English—especially if the net result is (as so often) merely to sound affected and ridiculous.*

One of the purposes of this book is to try to get everybody, especially the anxious Centrists, to relax about language, and not to listen to the yahoo pop grammarians. But this book is not likely to accomplish that. This is a sad thing for the people in the Center who will endure lots of suffering and worry.

But not so sad for the language. As Quirk points out, the people in the Center, by trying to follow the unreasonable and silly dictates of the yahoo pop grammarians, sound affected and silly—and as a result, ironically, they are changing the language. In fact, as many studies by William Labov have shown, changes in pronunciation are most frequent in members of the upper working class and lower middle class—exactly those highly motivated movers and doers who are likely to change the way they talk. They may be searching for a new and more elegant way to disguise their origins, but they are changing the language nonetheless. Labov has found that the *r* is coming back into New York speech—among the anxious Center, of course. The poor do not attempt it, and the rich never bother to try. Nelson Rockefeller, for example, spoke in a rich r-less accent all of his life. In Philadelphia, where Labov has been working for years, he has found a truly amazing kind of shift in white speakers:

baby	becomes	*beebee*
me	becomes	*may*
Ann	becomes	*Ian*
fight	becomes	*foit*

and the sentence *City streets are often straight* is pronounced *Shitty shtreets are often shtraight.*

The more the person is a climber and doer and the wider their circle of acquaintances, the more they are likely to join in these shifts. Older working-class speakers, or middle-class speakers, do not participate.

So we look back over our list of people grouped by language attitudes, and we find the ones who change language and the ones who do not.

The poor and speakers of nonstandard dialects are likely to hold onto old grammatical forms—and introduce new slang.

The members of the new educated class are likely to hold onto varieties of Standard grammar but introduce new words from their professions, or make up new words for their professions.

The editors and writers and other media people are likely to be sure that they are holding onto the good old ways of Standard

English grammar—and to use new words and new constructions from both the poor and the new educated class without realizing it.

The yahoo pop grammarians insist on logic and grammar and etymology and actually introduce change themselves. Edwin Newman insists, despite everything we know about the history of the word, that *culprit* means "guilty culprit," and the word *guilty* is therefore a redundancy. John Simon takes him at his word, and a new citation is added to the list that will eventually change the word to mean "guilty culprit." Theodore Bernstein, in an excess of zeal about a language he knew all too little about, insisted that *the hoi polloi* is redundant, since *hoi* means *the* in Greek. Bernstein admits that *hoi polloi* without *the* sounds awkward and advises everyone to simply avoid the construction. Every citation in every dictionary I am able to find lists *the hoi polloi*—but John Simon, once again, takes Bernstein at half his word, and drops *the* from *hoi polloi,* a phrase he loves to use: another new citation —eventually, perhaps, *hoi polloi* will need no *the* in English.

The anxious workers in the center of language listen to all the fuss raised by the pop grammarians and strain to bring their language under conscious control, producing sounds never heard before: more change comes from anxiety than from complacency.

And change is life. The slang of the poor, the new technical terms and jargon of the professionals, the cant of journalism, the simplistic language notions of pop grammarians—all keep language from going stale.

Samuel Johnson, in the preface to his dictionary, put the case for change very strongly:

> . . . *The language most likely to continue long without alteration, would be that of a nation raised a little, and but a little, above barbarity, secluded from strangers, and totally employed in procuring the conveniences of life; either without books, or, like some of the Mahometan countries, with very few: men thus busied and unlearned, having only such words as common use requires, would perhaps long continue to express the same notions by the same signs. But no such constancy can be expected in a people polished by arts, and classed by subordination, where one part of the community is sustained and accommodated by the labour of the other. Those who have much leisure to think, will always be enlarging the stock of ideas, and every increase of knowledge, whether real or fancied, will produce new words, or combinations of words. . . . As any custom is*

disused, the words that expressed it must perish with it; as any
opinion grows popular, it will innovate speech in the same
proportion as it alters practice.

You want language stability, says Johnson—primitive communism is the best way to guarantee it. There seems to be nothing to add to that as far as the politics of language attitudes goes— but there is still another justification for language change, and it is an important one: language change is a product of language instinct, and it comes about because it is based on the same attitudes to language that produce poetry. This idea was advanced by Kittredge and Greenough in *Words and Their Ways in English Speech.*

The ordinary processes by which words change their meanings are essentially the devices of poetry, say Kittredge and Greenough, and those processes go on as long as the language is alive:

> *. . . There is no device we are accustomed to call poetical, no*
> *similitude so slight, no metaphor so strained or so commonplace,*
> *that language has not seized upon it to make new forms of*
> *expression as the needs of advancing thought have required them.*
> *Even when the resultant words appear intensely prosaic*
> *[*stonewalling, plumbers, laundering cash, *for example], the*
> *processes which created them are identical with those of artistic*
> *poetry.*

The richness of our speech was not produced merely by the capacity of the English to borrow words from other languages, say Kittredge and Greenough—"such a result was achieved only when this great mass of variously derived material had been subjected for centuries to the language-making instinct; that is, to the poetic faculty of man."

This last theory, a very old one (*Words and Their Ways* was first published in 1901), is especially attractive because it helps explain why people like new words so much, and not only new words, but new ways of making sentences, new sounds, new combinations—it is because "All language is poetry."

Test

Your

Own

Language

one

Test
Your Language

(What These Common Overcorrections Reveal about You and Your Friends)

Forget about Edwin Newman and Theodore Bernstein and the *Harper Dictionary of Contemporary Usage.* Forget about permissiveness and wonderful English teachers and the importance of speaking and writing in your own dialect.

Just take this simple test. And compare your own ideas of grammar and word usage with the great writers of English literature—and with the editors of the *Oxford English Dictionary.*

If you happen to know a wonderful English teacher—or someone who can't resist acting like one—have them take the test, too. You probably won't change them; but at least you can show them just who, and what, they're messing with.

1. *(I/me)*

a. All debts are cleared between you and *(I, me).* Shakespeare, *Merchant of Venice,* III.ii.321

b. So let you and *(I, me)* come to an understanding. Meredith, *The Ordeal of Richard Feverel,* p. 180

2. *(between/among)*

a. The space *(between, among)* the three points . . . force a pencil *(between, among)* the petals of a flower . . . the treaty *(between, among)* the three powers. *Oxford English Dictionary*

b. With a shake of her head *(between every, between every other)* rapid sentence. Dickens, *Tale of Two Cities,* II, p. 279

3. (Pronoun Agreement)

a. Experience is the name everyone gives to *(their, his)* mistakes. Wilde, *Lady Windermere's Fan,* III

b. Nobody does anything well that *(they, he)* cannot help doing. Ruskin, *Crown of Wild Olives,* No. 38

c. Each House shall keep a journal of its proceedings, and from time to time publish the same, excepting such parts as may in *(their, its)* judgment require secrecy. *Constitution of the United States,* Article I, section five, subsection three

d. No man goes into battle to be killed—But *(they do, he does)* get killed. Shaw, *Three Plays for Puritans,* p. 138

4. (Agreement of Subject and Verb)

a. *(There's, There're)* two of you. Shakespeare, 2 *Henry VI,* III-.ii.303

b. Neither Coleridge nor Southey *(is, are)* a good reader of verse. De Quincey, *Confessions of an Opium-Eater,* p. 219

c. Neither the morning nor the evening star *(are, is)* so fair. Coleridge, *Biographia Literaria,* p. 61

d. Really good talk is one of the greatest pleasures there *(are, is).* Arthur W. Benson, *From a College Window,* p. 75

5. *(like/as)*

a. He talks *(like, as)* Brunswick did. Southey, *Letters,* I, p. 12

b. It is astonishing how they raven down scenery *(like, as)* children do sweetmeats. Keats, *Works,* V, p. 75

c. She'll never be *(like, as)* she was. Brontë, *Wuthering Heights,* p. 123

d. Nobody will miss her *(like, as)* I do. Dickens, Letter, July 1, 1841

e. Unfortunately, few have observed *(like, as)* you have done. Darwin, *Life and Letters,* III, p. 58

6. *(different from/different than)*

a. Things will be made different for me *(than, from)* for others. Wilde, *De Profundis,* 41

b. See that you use no word in a different sense *(than, from)* it was used a hundred years ago. Walter Page, letter to his son, quoted in Evanses, *A Dictionary of Contemporary American Usage,* p. 135

c. It has possessed me in a different way *(than, from)* ever before. Cardinal Newman, quoted in Evanses, *A Dictionary of Contemporary American Usage,* p. 136

7. *(lie/lay)*

a. There let him *(lay, lie).* Byron, *Childe Harold,* Canto 4, line 180

b. "What is the use," he said, "of *(laying, lying)* in bed when one has enough of sleep?" Trollope, *The Belton Estate,* quoted in Lounsbury, *The Standard of Usage in English,* p. 140

c. But Maria *(laid, lie)* in my bosom. Sterne, *Sentimental Journey,* quoted in Lounsbury, *The Standard of Usage in English,* p. 140

8. (Dangling Participles—simply indicate whether the sentences are right or wrong)

a. In the Library, taking up, by merest chance, a finely bound book, it proved to be Ticknor's. Macaulay, in *Life and Letters* by Trevelyan, II, p. 291

b. Looking out of the window, there were the flower beds in the front garden. Butler, *The Way of All Flesh,* p. 385

c. But, lying in my bed, everything seemed so different. Galsworthy, *On Forsyte 'Change,* p. 32

d. It rained hard coming back. T. Huxley, *Life and Letters,* I, p. 190

e. Wanting to be alone with his family, the presence of a stranger . . . must have been irksome. Austen, *Mansfield Park,* p. 174

f. Talking of war, there'll be trouble in the Balkans this spring. Kipling, *The Light That Failed,* p. 82

g. Yet, Jenny, looking *(= when I look)* at you, the woman almost fades from view. Rossetti, "Jenny," pp. 90–91

9. *(this kind of/these kind of)*

a. *(These, This)* kind of knaves I know. Shakespeare, *King Lear,* II.ii.107

b. If you read *(these, this)* kind of things. Swift, *Journal to Stella,* p. 150

c. The impertinence of *(these, this)* kind of scrutinies . . . Austen, *Sense and Sensibility,* p. 246

10. Typhus fever *(decimated, killed a large number in)* the school periodically. Charlotte Brontë, Letter, in Mrs. Gaskell's *Life,* p. 276

11. Consider first, that Great and Bright *(infers, implies)* not excellence. Milton, *Paradise Lost,* VIII, 91

12. All these three, like, went together. (or "All these three went together.") Richardson, *Pamela,* I, p. 238

13. The whitish gleam was . . . conferred by the *(enormity, enormousness)* of their re-motion. De Quincey, *The System of the Heavens,* III, p. 183

14. That last foul thing Thou ever *(author'dst, wrote).* Chapman, *Iliad,* I, 231

15. Ilka ain to be liable for their ain *(input, contribution).* Scott, *Heart of the Midlothian,* xii

16. We drove very *(slow, slowly)* for the last two stages of the road. Thackeray, *Vanity Fair,* viii

17. The gentle heart, *(anxious, eager)* to please. Blair, *The Grave,* 94

18. *(Who/whom)*

a. *(Who, whom)* are you speaking of? Hardy, *Far from the Madding Crowd,* p. 170

b. *(Who, whom)* do you think? Idiomatic

c. The Lord knows *(who, whom)*! Idiomatic
  And as a special bonus, for the extra careful user of language; fill in the blank:

19. a = [the prefix meaning "not or without"] should be prefixed only to Greek stems. . . . "Amoral" being literary, is inexcusable. _____ should be used instead. H. W. Fowler, *Modern English Usage,* p. 1

two

Answers

1. *I* is correct in both sentences. The OED cautiously notes that both are "now *considered* [my emphasis] incorrect" but supplies a rule: You can use *I* in the accusative when it is separated from its preposition or verb by another word or words. See pp. xvi, 44 for more examples.

2. The OED says you must use *between* in all cases of (a). Bergen Evans says "between every" is right in (b). See pp. 43–47 for more.

3. Correct answers are (a) *their;* (b) *they;* (c) *their;* (d) *they do.* Bergen Evans says of the quote from the Constitution:

> *This is not bad grammar which must be smilingly excused because of the ignorance of the Founding Fathers. It is good English. It doesn't even prove that things have changed, because such sentences are being written every day and by literate people. It simply proves that the "laws" of grammar are something different from the laws of the land or the laws of the physical sciences.*

The OED insists *they* or *their* is correct when referring to a single person who could be of either sex. If everyone adopted this sensible rule we would be spared all those clumsy self-consciously liberated *he and she* constructions.

4. Correct answers are:

(a) *There's* is correct; the singular copulative with plural predicates is exceedingly common in the Shakespeare folio of 1623, and in standard northern dialect, "though much altered," notes the OED with some asperity, "by editors ignorant of its history." The rule is: you may use *is* when the subject is a relative, even though the predicate is a plural: "Here's two dollars."

(b) *is* is correct; **(c)** *are* is correct. Speakers of English have never bothered to reach a consensus on singular or plural verb with *neither/nor*. Do what you want—who's to stop you?

(d) Arthur W. Benson is not a great writer—but I use him to illustrate a popular idiom: *are* is correct idiomatic English. *Is* sounds funny (i.e., is merely logical).

5. *Like* is correct in all cases, says the OED. There is nothing wrong with saying, "Winstons taste good—like a carcinogen should." All the wonderful English teachers, and all the purists, and other criers of alarm who said that sentence was wrong . . . were wrong themselves. Among writers of standing who have used *like* this way, the OED lists Shakespeare, Southey, Newman, and Morris. Even Fowler in *Modern English Usage* backs off from this one: "The reader with no *instinctive* [my emphasis] objection can now decide for himself. . . ." For "instinctive objection," of course, you should substitute "objection learned from the wonderful English teacher."

6. *Different than* is right in all cases. The OED notes that the usual construction in the 1890s was *different from*. But, says the OED, the construction with *than* is found in Addison, Steele, Defoe, Richardson, Goldsmith, Coleridge, Southey, De Quincey, Carlyle, Thackeray, and Newman. Use *different from* if you like, but criticize *different than* and you're messing with the big guys.

7. Correct answers are: **(a)**, *lay;* **(b)**, *laying;* **(c)**, *laid.*

Jespersen notes that the OED considers *lay* in the first sentence illiterate—and then simply comments—"Byron illiterate!" Lounsbury says that Sterne was savagely attacked in a leading review for using a vulgarism characteristic of "a city news-writer."

"Our readers," wrote the reviewer, "may possibly conclude that Maria was the name of a favorite pullet."

Sterne's indifference to the criticism all through his writing career, seems to indicate, says Lounsbury, that "Sterne was one of those who regarded the usage as proper." And so do I.

8. Dangling participles. All the dangling participles in all the sentences are correct—not as far as any grammar book you've ever read is concerned, of course. But as far as Macaulay, Butler, Galsworthy, Thomas Huxley, Austen, Kipling, Rossetti, Shakespeare are concerned. A pretty strong recommendation. Jespersen says that some "loose participles" (he doesn't use the phrase "dangling participle") are widely accepted: *speaking of, judging by, generally speaking.* In the phrase "three or four of us, counting me" (Dickens, *David Copperfield,* p. 145), *counting me* is a dangling participle.

9. Shakespeare wrote *these kind.* The OED remarks that it is "now considered incorrect"—but Jespersen doesn't think so. He notes the use in Goldsmith also, and lists the construction under "seeming irregularities of number"—right after *all manner of things,* which is just as irregular, and hardly ever criticized.

10. Charlotte Brontë used *decimate* to mean "kill a large number, not necessarily a tenth." The OED says that this use has been common since the seventeenth century.

11. Milton used *infer;* the OED lists *imply* as a standard meaning of the word *infer.* The wonderful English teacher spent a lot of time convincing us that there was a distinction which is extremely important to the language. But it wasn't important to Milton, and it isn't to the rest of us.

12. I am a little ashamed of this one. The first sentence is as Richardson wrote it, and considered correct by the OED—with one small exception. I dropped the *be-* from *belike.* But the OED says that *belike* means "to appearance, likely ..." and that seems the same sort of usage as the contemporary *like.* If purists persist in being offended, I suggest we make them happy by restoring the syllable: "All this grammar, belike, is getting heavy."

13. De Quincey used *enormity.* The OED remarks that this use (*enormity,* for "great size," not "a great crime"), though an old one, is now *"regarded* [my emphasis] as incorrect ... though many examples could be found in recent authors."

14. *Author* as a verb is correct. Actually Chapman is using the verb to mean "caused." The supplement to the OED says our current use of *authored* is a revival. It seems like one that is destined to last. It is difficult to say of many authors that they *wrote* a book. Many don't write but type (though *type a book* means something different). Many more authors simply talk into

Answers

a tape recorder—or hold conferences with the people who put the actual words on paper. Nixon authored his memoirs. There doesn't seem to be another word to describe his relationship to the book.

15. *Input* is correct. It means contribution. Bernstein calls the word "computer cant . . . laymen sometimes take it over to sound impressive. . . ." Actually, computer scientists borrowed the word from ordinary language, where it has been used at least since 1753. But the computer people don't need the word all to themselves. We can borrow it back.

16. Thackeray wrote *slow*. There are some people, among them the experts of the *Harper Dictionary of Contemporary Usage,* who feel that *slow* is always an adjective, and the only adverb is *slowly.* The Evanses wrote: *"Drive slowly* may also be used, but anyone who claims that this is 'better grammar' misunderstands the nature of language. And in this particular case, he is also unfamiliar with English literature over the past four hundred years."

17. Blair wrote *anxious;* Newman insists that *eager* should be used in all cases where the outcome is favorable.

18 (a). Hardy used *who.* And the OED called him wrong, listing it as a grammatical error. But by 1928, the *Shorter Oxford Dictionary* said, "Whom is no longer current in unstudied colloquial speech," meaning that you should never say it, and only write it in very formal situations. The great American scholar G. L. Kittredge defined *colloquial* clearly when he said, "I always speak colloquial, and often write it."

(b) and (c). *Who* is listed as correct by the OED—though surely some readers, if they had not by this time figured out that the first word was the right word in every case, would have been tempted to say *whom*—for the first time in their lives. It is odd that many of us think that what we would never say is much better grammar than what we always say.

19. This question is only included to show where the principles of logic and etymology applied to language can lead. Fowler, who thought the word *paleolithic* a barbarism, insists that the proper word should be *nonmoral,* which is a nice word. Fowler must have had fun using it. But it doesn't mean *amoral* to me. Does it to anyone?

But that hardly matters. Just as the relative correct or incorrect grammar of the quotations hardly matters. What matters is that they're all certifiably literary and old. These are not new errors creeping into our speech, killing language, overturning standards, making us all into grunting morons.

It could be argued instead that these sentences demonstrate that grammatical rules fail when they set out, wrongheadedly, to improve the language rather than describe it.

Anyone is free, of course, to side with the grammar books and the wonderful English teacher against the authors (and ordinary speech). You can say what you want and believe what you want about language. But using grammar books to prove that great authors are wrong is troublesome. As Thomas Lounsbury said, "This leads to the dismal conclusion that correct language is not found in authors everyone reads with pleasure, but is reserved exclusively for those whom nobody can succeed in reading at all."

But that hardly matters. What matters is that Shakespeare said "between you and I," and "There's two of you," and English did not die. So English is likely to keep on living, even if I decide to talk like him.

three

Surprise
Extra Bonus!

The Reader Unmasked!

Common grammatical overcorrections do reveal something about
you. Disregard the bonus question (you could only have got it right
if you read it in Fowler—and it's meaningless as far as the English
language is concerned), and give yourself five points for every
question you answered correctly (by agreeing with a great writer
of the past or the OED). Where there is more than one sample
(a,b,c, etc.) you must have got a majority right to get the five
points.

Now look up your score in the handy table below, and see
what your attitudes tell about you.

Zero

What—not even one? You are either Edwin Newman or a wonderful English teacher—in either case, all but hopelessly intolerant, and proud of your tin ear. You either carry some fussy little
grammar book to torture adolescents with, or else write them.

Five to Twenty-five

Some hope here. You are a copy editor for a very stodgy publication. You would never dream of criticizing anyone for their laziness, alcoholism, or disgusting sexual practices—but you think
nothing of ridiculing the language they learned at their mother's
knee. Read more new novels—and William Carlos Williams.

Thirty to Fifty

Working journalist—it's hard keeping up with the kids, and they keep coming all the time: new journalism, participatory journalism, advocacy journalism—sometimes you wish they'd just leave you alone with *The New York Times* stylebook. But you keep trying. It's a living.

Fifty to Eighty

Highbrow novelist, New York poet, or linguistic sociologist— with tenure at a good little college that deserves to be Ivy League, even if it isn't. You know what to listen for, right? If only you got to the city more often. . . .

Eighty to One Hundred

Ordinary speaker. Congratulations! Good writers listen to you.

Notes

Preface

Shakespeare, Defoe, Dickens, Swift, and Hardy Examples: *The Oxford English Dictionary* (Oxford: Oxford University Press).

***Part One* The Road to Ruin**

***chapter one* The Standard of Nineteenth-Century Usage**

Lounsbury on language corruption: Thomas R. Lounsbury, *The Standard of Usage in English* (New York: Harper & Brothers, 1908), pp. 1–2.

Lounsbury on the persistence of language worry: Lounsbury, ibid., pp. 2–3.

On the melancholy of language correctors: Lounsbury, ibid., p. 3.

On language purity in the past: Lounsbury, ibid., pp. 3–4.

Newman on the 1960s: Edwin Newman, *Strictly Speaking: Will America Be the Death of English?* (Indianapolis and New York: The Bobbs-Merrill Co., 1974), p. 11.

Lounsbury on ethnicity and class: Lounsbury, *The Standard of Usage in English,* p. 26.

Lounsbury on Scotticisms: Lounsbury, ibid., pp. 26–27.

Lounsbury on artificial restraints: Lounsbury, ibid., p. 38.

Lounsbury on the experience of the past: Lounsbury, ibid., pp. 9–10.

Lounsbury on fixed language: Lounsbury, ibid., p. 5.

Lounsbury on excuse for past forebodings: Lounsbury, ibid., pp. 4–5.

Johnson quotations: OED.

Dear Abby excerpt: January 31, 1978.

Shakespeare and Dryden examples: OED.

Williams on teaching English: L. Pearce Williams, *The Washington Post,* September 22, 1977.

Editorial on giftable: "Unpalatable," *The Washington Star,* November 29, 1977, p. A2.

chapter two Edwin Newman

Newman on y'know: Newman, *Strictly Speaking,* pp. 14–15.

Newman on rhetoric: Newman, ibid., p. 29.

Newman on -ize words: Edwin Newman, *A Civil Tongue* (Indianapolis and New York: The Bobbs-Merrill Co., 1976), p. 54.

Bacon, Tait's magazine, Cudworth, and Bentham examples: OED.

Newman on optimizing: Newman, *A Civil Tongue,* p. 55.

Newman on priested: Newman, ibid., p. 74.

Newman on -ing words: Newman, *Strictly Speaking,* p. 16.

Newman on different than: Newman, ibid., p. 35.

Shakespeare example: OED.

Newman on supportive: Newman, *A Civil Tongue,* p. 90.

Nashe example: OED.

Newman on to decimate: Newman, *A Civil Tongue,* p. 85.

Posture, remind, and anxious examples: OED.

chapter three John Simon

Simon on Paul Owens: John Simon, "Language: Attack and Counterattack," *Esquire,* December 1977, p. 20.

Simon on chair: Simon, "Language," *Esquire,* April 25, 1978, p. 36.

Simon on linguistic change: Simon, "Language," *Esquire,* March 28, 1978, pp. 86, 88.

Simon on changes based on ignorance: ibid., p. 88.

Simon on standard excuses: Simon, "Language," *Esquire,* March 28, 1978, p. 88.

Simon on writers' grammar: Simon, ibid., p. 88.

Simon on lapses: Simon, ibid., p. 88.

McKnight discussing White on their: George H. McKnight, *The Evolution of the English Language* (New York: Dover Publications, 1968), p. 528.

Simon on between and among: Simon, "Language," *Esquire,* July 1977.

Simon on academic jargon: Simon, ibid.

Evanses on what: Bergen Evans and Cornelia Evans, *A Dictionary of Contemporary American Usage* (New York: Random House, 1957).

Simon on uprooting language horrors: Simon, "Language," *Esquire,* March 28, 1978, p. 88.

---

chapter four Harper Dictionary of Contemporary Usage

The Morrises on the idea for the Harper dictionary: William Morris and Mary Morris, *Harper Dictionary of Contemporary Usage* (New York: Harper & Row, 1975), p. x.

Leonard on actual usage: Albert H. Marckwardt and Fred G. Walcott, *Facts About Current English Usage* (New York: Appleton-Century-Crofts, 1938), p. x.

D. H. Lawrence example: OED.

Shakespeare, Jonson, and Hughes examples: OED.

Collins, Sackville-West, and Dickens examples: Otto Jespersen, *A Modern English Grammar on Historical Principles,* vol. 7, p. 597.

Lees example: OED.

Fielding and Browning examples: OED.

Arthur, Merlin, and Arnold examples: OED.

Shakespeare, Milton, and Thackeray examples: OED.

Asimov example: OED.

Milton and Ruskin examples: OED.

---

chapter five Theodore Bernstein: Mind Your (Native) Tongue— A Word from Mr. Thistlebottom

Bernstein on Hoi Polloi: Theodore M. Bernstein, *Dos, Don'ts & Maybes of English Usage* (New York: Times Books, 1977).

Bernstein on redundancy: Theodore M. Bernstein, *Watch Your Language* (New York: Atheneum, 1965), p. 49.

Bernstein on mortgage burning ceremony: Bernstein, ibid., p. 35.

Bernstein on between and among: Bernstein, *Dos, Don'ts & Maybes of English Usage*, p. 29.

Bernstein on aggravate: Bernstein, ibid., pp. 9–10.

Bernstein on intrigue: Bernstein, *The Careful Writer: A Modern Guide to English Usage* (New York: Atheneum, 1965).

Bernstein on officer: Bernstein, *Watch Your Language.*

Bernstein on verbal: Bernstein, *The Careful Writer.*

Bernstein on critique: Bernstein, *Dos, Don'ts, & Maybes of English Usage*, p. 56.

Bernstein on couple: Bernstein, ibid., p. 55.

chapter six Safire: William the Few

Safire on advertising: William Safire, "On Language: The Fumblerules of Grammar," *The New York Times Sunday Magazine*, November 4, 1979.

Burman on language snobbery: Ben Lucien Burman, in Morris and Morris, *Harper Dictionary of Contemporary Usage*, pp. xi–xii.

Safire on the guardians of the language: William Safire, "On Language," *The New York Times Sunday Magazine*, August 26, 1979.

Safire on centers around: Safire, "On Language," *The New York Times Sunday Magazine*, October 7, 1979.

Part Two The Joys of Watergate—How to Stop Worrying and Love the Language

chapter one The Joys of Watergate

Pound on bad writing and thinking: Ezra Pound, "101," *Literary Essays of Ezra Pound*, edited by T.S. Eliot (New York: New Directions, 1954), p. 21.

Newman on Watergate: Newman, *Strictly Speaking*, pp. 7–8.

Notes

The Morrises on stroke, go the hangout road, launder the money, and plumber: Morris and Morris, *Harper Dictionary of Contemporary Usage*, p. 629.

Newman on Gulf of Tonkin Affair: Newman, *Strictly Speaking*, p. 7.

chapter two Detestable Words

Lounsbury on language care: Lounsbury, *The Standard of Usage in English*, p. 11.

Lounsbury on language purifiers: Lounsbury, ibid., p. 9.

Lounsbury on purists' unnecessary misery: Lounsbury, ibid., p. 10.

Lounsbury quoting Swift: Lounsbury, ibid., p. 12.

Lounsbury quoting Scott: Lounsbury, ibid., p. 17.

Swift to Earl of Oxford: Lounsbury, ibid., p. 15.

Lounsbury on the language of Swift's letter: Lounsbury, ibid., p. 16.

Lounsbury on Swift's exaggerated forebodings: Lounsbury, ibid., pp. 16–17.

Coleridge on talented: Samuel Taylor Coleridge, from *Table Talk*, in *A Coleridge Reader*, edited by Kathleen Coburn (New York: Minerva Press, 1951), pp. 100–101.

Lounsbury quoting Locker-Lampson: Lounsbury, *The Standard of Usage in English*, p. 197.

Macaulay to his sister: Thomas Babington Macaulay, letter to Hannah Macaulay, May 30, 1831.

Lounsbury on Landor as an exception: Lounsbury, *The Standard of Usage in English*, pp. 38–39.

Landor on island: Lounsbury, ibid., p. 46.

Landor on execute: Lounsbury, ibid., p. 43.

Landor on I had better: Lounsbury, ibid., pp. 150–151.

Poe on Fuller: Edgar Allan Poe, "The Literati of New York: Sara Margaret Fuller," *The Works of Edgar Allan Poe*, vol. 8 (Philadelphia: J. B. Lippincott, 1908), p. 165.

Poe on Fuller's poetry: Poe, "The Literati of New York: Sara Margaret Fuller," ibid., p. 165.

Reviewer attacking Americanisms: *The European Magazine and London Review*, 1787.

Webster on the false passive: Lounsbury, *The Standard of Usage in English*, p. 179.

Lounsbury on the usefulness of the idiom: Lounsbury, ibid., p. 179.

Lounsbury on Brown: Lounsbury, ibid., p. 181.

White on the progressive passive: McKnight, *The Evolution of the English Language*, p. 511.

Lounsbury on Webster: Lounsbury, *The Standard of Usage in English*, pp. 76–77.

Landor on prefixes and roots: McKnight, *The Evolution of the English Language*, pp. 509–510.

Fowler on barbarisms: H. W. Fowler, *A Dictionary of Modern English Usage*, 1st ed. (Oxford: Clarendon Press, 1926), p. 130.

Fowler on coastal: Fowler, ibid., p. 81.

Mitchell on noun combination: Richard Mitchell, *Less than Words Can Say* (Boston: Little, Brown, 1979).

Follett on controversial: Wilson Follett, *Modern American Usage: A Guide*, edited and completed by Jacques Barzun (New York: Hill & Wang, 1966), p. 109.

Lounsbury on tireless: Lounsbury, *The Standard of Usage in English*, p. 200.

Lounsbury on back-formations: Lounsbury, ibid., p. 198.

Lounsbury on none: Lounsbury, ibid., p. 162.

Scott on Scotticisms and Solecisms: Lounsbury, ibid., pp. 106–107.

---

chapter three You're Welcome to Using My Idiom

Follett on infinitive and participle: Follett, *Modern American Usage*, p. 180.

Publisher's note: Follett, ibid., p. vi.

Follet on different to: Follett, ibid., pp. 172–173.

Follett on rules of syntax: Follett, ibid., pp. 13–14.

Rewritten sentence: Follett, ibid., p. 65.

Evans on between each: Evans, *Comfortable Words*, pp. 52–53.

Follett on faulty parallelism: Follett, *Modern American Usage*, p. 120.

Follett on number and person: Follett, ibid., p. 136.

Evanses on lack of distinction: Evans and Evans, *A Dictionary of Contemporary American Usage*, p. 149.

Follett on preserving the distinction: Follett, *Modern American Usage*, p. 136.

Follett on ineptitude: Follett, ibid., p. 136.

Follett on of and in: Follett, ibid., p. 177.

Follett on insignia: Follett, ibid., p. 183.

Follett on jargon: Follett, ibid., p. 189.

Follett on more preferable: Follett, ibid., p. 219.

Johnson and Hawthorne examples: OED.

Dirac columns: Follett, *Modern American Usage*, p. 229.

Proximity columns: Follett, ibid., p. 230.

Missile columns: Follett, ibid., p. 235.

Jonson, Dickens, Kipling, Thackeray, and Twain examples: Otto Jespersen, *A Modern English Grammar on Historical Principles*, vol. 2 (London: George Allen & Unwin, 1948), pp. 340–341.

Follett's use of string compound: Follett, *Modern American Usage*, pp. 254–255.

Evanses on ownership and personification: Evans and Evans, *A Dictionary of Contemporary American Usage*, p. 197.

Follett on possessives: Follett, *Modern American Usage*, p. 254.

Fries on the use of 's: *American English Grammar*, p. 75.

Evanses on the genitive: Evans and Evans, *A Dictionary of Contemporary American Usage*, pp. 15–16.

Evanses on dismissing genitive as possessive: Evans and Evans, ibid., pp. 197–198.

Follett on hanging and hung: Follett, *Modern American Usage*, p. 180.

Follett on human: Follett, ibid., p. 170.

Follett on level: Follett, ibid., p. 197.

Follett on verbiage: Follett, ibid., pp. 341–342.

Follett on defects: Follett, ibid., p. 342.

---

chapter four Worst Words Defended: Thunderbore and the Instinct for Poetry

---

Evans on correct use: Evans, *Comfortable Words*, p. 244.

Evans on fun: Evans, ibid., p. 165.

Evans on actual usage: Evans, ibid., p. 26.

Evans on prescription: Evans, ibid., p. 229.

Fowler on alright: Fowler, *Modern English Usage*, p. 16.

Evans on alright: Evans, *Comfortable Words,* p. 24.

Evans on alright: Evans, ibid., pp. 24–25.

Evanses on dangling participles: Evans and Evans, *A Dictionary of Contemporary American Usage,* pp. 354–355.

Jespersen on loose participles: Jespersen, *A Modern English Grammar on Historical Principles,* vol. 5, pp. 407–413.

Evans on between: Evans, *Comfortable Words,* p. 53.

Nicholson on between: Margaret Nicholson, *A Dictionary of American-English Usage* (New York: Oxford University Press, 1957), p. 55.

Example of exaggerated courtesy: Evans, *Comfortable Words,* p. 20.

Take you along example: Evans, ibid., pp. 75–76.

Don't be surprised example: Evans, ibid., pp.125–126.

Newman on presently: Newman, *A Civil Tongue,* p. 170.

Greenough and Kittredge on words of delay: James Bradstreet Greenough and George Lyman Kittredge, *Words and Their Ways in English Speech* (New York: Macmillan, 1916), pp. 292–293.

Millay example: Edna St. Vincent Millay, "Passer Mortuus Est," *Collected Lyrics* (New York: Washington Square Press, 1959), p. 56.

Evans on the draft: Evans, *Comfortable Words,* p. 286.

Macdonald on ain't: Dwight Macdonald, "Sweet Are the Uses of Usage," *The New Yorker,* May 17, 1958, p. 144.

Bernstein on ain't: Bernstein, *Dos, Don'ts & Maybes of English Usage,* pp. 13–14.

Chaucer example: Geoffrey Chaucer, *The Canterbury Tales,* "Prologue," 11. 70–71.

Evanses on double negative: Evans and Evans, *A Dictionary of Contemporary American Usage,* p. 143.

Evanses on double negative: Evans and Evans, ibid., pp. 143–144.

Austen and Darwin examples: OED.

Follett on hopefully: Follett, *Modern American Usage,* pp. 169–170.

Stafford on hopefully: Morris and Morris, *Harper Dictionary of Contemporary Usage,* p. xviii.

Bernstein on hopefully: Bernstein, *The Careful Writer.*

Follett on hopefully: Follett, *Modern American Usage,* p. 170.

Bernstein on hopefully: Theodore M. Bernstein, *Miss Thistlebottom's Hobgoblins: The Careful Writer's Guide to the Taboos, Bugbears, and Outmoded Rules of English Usage* (New York: Farrar, Straus & Giroux, 1971).

Bernstein on hopefully: Bernstein, *Dos, Don'ts & Maybes of English Usage.*

Knight on hopefully: Andrew Knight, "News in Review," *The New York Times,* May 7, 1978, p. 23.

Robinson on hopefully: Paul Robinson, "Lost Causes," *The New Republic,* January 26, 1980.

Simon on language deterioration: John Simon, "The Corruption of English," in *The State of the Language,* edited by Leonard Michaels and Christopher Ricks (Berkeley: University of California Press, 1979), p. 38.

Hudson on premodification: Kenneth Hudson, *The Dictionary of Diseased English* (New York, Hagerstown, San Francisco, and London: Harper Colophon Books, Harper & Row, 1977), p. xiii.

Howard on U.S. ethnic dialects: Philip Howard, *New Words for Old: A Survey of Misused, Vogue and Cliché Words* (New York: Oxford University Press, 1977), p. xii.

Lounsbury on self-explaining compounds: Thomas R. Lounsbury, *History of the English Language,* rev. and enlarged ed. (New York: Henry Holt and Co., 1926), pp. 109–110.

Quirk on compounds: Randolph Quirk, *The Use of English* (New York: St. Martin's Press, 1962), p. 164.

Jespersen on compound making: Jespersen, *A Modern English Grammar on Historical Principles,* vol. 2, p. 327.

Part Three Does Anything Go?

---

chapter one A Democratic Approach to Grammar

Bernstein on linguists: Bernstein, *The Careful Writer,* p. ix.

Follett on antigrammarians: Follett, *Modern American Usage,* p. 29.

Follett on Jespersen: Follett, ibid., pp. 29–30.

Mitchell on incompetence: Mitchell, *Less Than Words Can Say,* pp. 67–70.

Leonard on usage: Sterling A. Leonard, in Albert H. Marckwardt and Fred G. Walcott, *Facts About Current English Usage, Including a Discussion of Current Usage in Grammar from "Current English Usage" by Sterling A. Leonard* (New York: Appleton-Century-Crofts, 1938), p. 97.

---

chapter two Black Vernacular English

Joiner decision: *The New York Times,* July 13, 1979.

Rowan on black English: Carl Rowan, " 'Black English' Isn't 'Foreign,' " *The Philadelphia Bulletin,* July 11, 1979, p. A15.

Jespersen on language learning: Otto Jespersen, *Language: Its Nature, Development and Origin* (New York: W.W. Norton, 1964), pp. 141 ff.

On Murray's language learning: K. M. Elisabeth Murray, *Caught in the Web of Words: James A. H. Murray and the Oxford English Dictionary* (New Haven: Yale University Press, 1977), p. 21.

Murray to his wife: Murray, ibid., p. 92.

On Murray's appearance and accent: Murray, ibid., p. 109.

On Murray's accent at seventy-two: Murray, ibid., p. 298.

Jespersen on Basque: Jespersen, *Language,* p. 210.

Jespersen on Chinese: Jespersen, ibid., p. 369.

Mitchell on Black English: Mitchell, *Less Than Words Can Say,* p. 164.

---

chapter three White Vernacular English

Suhor on written English: Charles Suhor, "Creative Writing and the Pursuit of Picayunish Perfection," *Louisiana English Journal,* vol. 16, no. 2, 1977.

Suhor on the writer's audience: Suhor, ibid.

Joos on hyper-correct English: Martin Joos, *The Five Clocks* (New York: Harcourt Brace, 1967), p. 18.

McKnight on Defoe: McKnight, *The Evolution of the English Language,* pp. 337–338.

McKnight on Austen: McKnight, ibid., pp. 520–521.

De Quincey on women and language: McKnight, ibid., p. 519.

Quirk on WVE disfigured: Randolph Quirk, *The English Language and Images of Matter* (New York: Oxford University Press, 1972), p. 31.

Roberts on freshman composition: Roberts, *Understanding English,* pp. 405–406.

Suhor example: Suhor, "Creative Writing and the Pursuit of Picayunish Perfection."

Notes

---

chapter four Who Changes Language—
A Primer of Language Politics

On the language of the uneducated: Donald J. Lloyd, "Snobs, Slobs and the English Language," *American Scholar*, Summer 1951.

Fowler on barbarisms: Fowler, *Modern English Usage*, p. 49.

Quirk on upper-class English: Quirk, *The Use of English*, pp. 69–70.

On the center: Quirk, ibid., pp. 69–70.

Kittredge and Greenough on poetry and language: Greenough and Kittredge, *Words and Their Ways in English Speech*, pp. 9, 12.

Part Four Test Your Own Language

---

chapter two Answers

Evans on the Constitution: Evans, *Comfortable Words*, p. 8.

Fowler on like: Fowler, *Modern English Usage*, p. 325.

Bernstein on input: Bernstein, *Dos, Don'ts & Maybes of English Usage.*

Evanses on slowly: Evans and Evans, *A Dictionary of Contemporary American Usage*, p. 460.

Index

Index

Birkett, N., 50

Blacks (and Black English), 8, 22, 119, 150–61

Blair, Robert, 29, 69, 190, 195

Borland, Hal (*Harper Dictionary* panelist), 46, 51, 52, 124

Boswell, James, 156

bridegroom, 90

British critics of American English, 87–8, 129–30

British English: *ain't*, 119–20; in Scottish schools, 156, 159; slang, 8; *them, their, they*, with singular pronouns, 34; *unpractical*, 106

Brontë, Charlotte, 28, 103, 113, 188, 190, 194

Brooks, John (*Harper Dictionary* panelist), 46

Broun, Heywood Hale (*Harper Dictionary* panelist), 43, 46, 91

Brown, Goold, 89

Browne, Sir Thomas, 51

Browning, Robert, 85–6, 89, 178

Buchwald, Art, 57

Bunyan, John, 29

Burgess, Anthony (*Harper Dictionary* panelist), 43, 44, 53, 57, 116

burgle, 93

Burke, Edmund, 87, 89

Burman, Ben Lucien, quoted in *Harper Dictionary*, 68

Burrows, Abe (*Harper Dictionary* panelist), 46, 52, 53

Butler, Samuel, 35, 189, 193

Byron, George Gordon, Baron, 59, 89, 104, 189

C

California speech, 145–6

capability, 28–9

Careful Writer, The (Bernstein), 12, 122, 136

Carlyle, Thomas, 36, 69, 93, 193

Carter, Jimmy, 25, 159

center around/center on, 70–1

chair, for *chairman*, 31–2, 38

Chapman, George, 86, 190, 194

Chaucer, Geoffrey, 22, 65, 86, 120

Chesterfield, Philip Stanhope, Earl of, 33

Chinese, 127, 148, 152, 158

Ciardi, John, 43, 57

Civil Tongue, A (Newman), 29

class differences, in speech patterns, 24–6, 145, 146–7, 152, 175, 181–2

clearly, 69, 127

coastal, 91

Coleridge, Samuel Taylor, 37, 55, 83, 89, 188, 193

college English courses, introductory, 169–71; at Cornell, 14–15

Collins, Wilkie, 113; example of *between each* by, 46

colloquial, definition of, 119, 195; "cultivated," 168

Comfortable Words (Evans), 47, 65, 98, 109–11, 114, 115, 117

communism, 76

complected, 65

componentry, 65

compounds, 103–4. *See also* word chains

computer words, 177, 195

Concise Oxford Dictionary, 119, 125, 127–8

confess, 167

Congreve, William, 33

Constitution of the United States, 188, 192

controversial, 92

Cooper, James Fenimore, 59

copy editing, examples of, 168–9

Cord, Robert L., 178

Cornell University, 14–15

Cowper, William, 23, 86

critique, 64

Cronkite, Walter (*Harper Dictionary* panelist), 46

Cullen, Countee, 154

culprit, 27, 183

Current English Usage (Leonard), 10, 40

D

dangling participles, 112–14, 189, 193–4

Darwin, Charles, 121, 141, 188

De Quincey, Thomas, 35, 83, 89, 168, 188, 190, 193, 194

Dear Abby, 13, 14

decimate, 28, 190, 194

Defoe, Daniel, 33, 99, 113, 165–6, 193

demean, for *lower*, 167

dialects: distinction between language and, 159–60; regional and ethnic, 153, 154

Diary of an Edwardian Lady, 168

Dickens, Charles, 42, 88, 89, 99, 187, 188; dangling participles in, 113, 194; *David Copperfield*, *super* as

right, 111; on *amoral,* 191, 195–6; on "barbarisms," 90–1, 176, 179; on *like,* 193
Foxfire books, 171
Franklin, Benjamin, 87, 88, 113
French, 141, 142
Fries, Charles, 104, 145, 146–7
Fuller, Margaret, 86, 87
fulsome, 47–8, 49
fun, as adjective, 109–10
furnish, 167

G

Galsworthy, John, 113, 189, 193–4
Gann, Ernest (*Harper Dictionary* panelist), 50
Gay, John, 86
Geismar, Maxwell, 57
Gell-Mann, Murray, 177
genitive *'s,* 104–5
gentlemanly, 85
George III (king of England), 6
German, 130, 160; *hoffentlich,* 122, 124–5
gift, as verb, 16, 48–9
giftable, 15–16
gigo, 177
Gladstone, William, 84
gluon, 177
go jump in the lake, 14
golden age, 5–6
Goldsmith, Oliver, 33, 89, 113, 193, 194
Gowers, Sir Ernest, 69
graduate/was graduated, 91–2
grammar, scholarly studies of, 10, 11, 16, 142–5
grammar instruction, and writing skill, 163
grammar textbooks, traditional, 137–8
Greek, 143; English words from, 59, 132, 176–7, 191; *hoi polloi,* 58–9, 183
Greene, Graham, editing of novel by, 168–9
Greenough, James, 116, 184
guilty culprit, 27, 183
Guthrie, A. B., Jr. (*Harper Dictionary* panelist), 124

H

Haley, Alex, 20
Handbook of English Grammar, A (Zandvoort), 140, 145
Hardy, Thomas, 34, 103, 190, 195

Harper Dictionary of Contemporary Usage (Morris and Morris), 12, 21, 39–57, 68, 69; on *apt* for *liable,* 167; on *different than,* 26; on *enthuse,* 93; example of dangling participle in, 113; on *graduate,* 91–2; on *healthy/healthful,* 166; on *hopefully,* 122, 123–4; on *I could care less,* 114; on *identical to,* 96; on *parties* for *persons,* 167; on *presently,* 116, 117; on *slow/slowly,* 52–3, 195; on Watergate, 77–8
Harrison, Richard Edes (*Harper Dictionary* panelist), 51
Hart, James D., 95
Hawthorne, Nathaniel, 101
Hayakawa, S. I. (*Harper Dictionary* panelist), 47
healthy/healthful, 165–6
Heart of the World (Haggard), 55
Hebrew, 143
Hegel, Georg Wilhelm Friedrich, 76
Hemingway, Ernest, 111
Henry, O., 65
History of the English Language (Lounsbury), 131
hoi polloi, 58–9, 183
hopefully, 12, 13, 69, 82, 121–8
Horgan, Paul (*Harper Dictionary* panelist), 43
Hoss, Norman (*Harper Dictionary* panelist), 55–6
host, as transitive verb, 53
Howard, Philip, 130
Hudson, Kenneth, 129
Hughes, Langston, 154
human, for *human being,* 105
Hume, David, 156
Hutchens, John (*Harper Dictionary* panelist), 46
Huxley, Thomas, 113, 189, 194

I

I/me (after verb or preposition), 44, 187, 192
I could care less, 114–16
I had better, I had best, 85, 165
identical to, 96
ignore, ignoramus, 86–7
impractical/unpractical, 106
in/into, 14
in/of (describing a material), 99
incumbent on me, 29
infer/imply, 190, 194
influential, 84–5

Index

Sanders, Leonard (*Harper Dictionary* panelist), 50, 51

Schoenbrun, David (*Harper Dictionary* panelist), 43

Schonberg, David (*Harper Dictionary* panelist), 53

Schonberg, Harold (*Harper Dictionary* panelist), 44, 53, 54

schools: Black English in, 152–3, 159, 160; grammar instruction in, 162–3; grammar textbooks in, 137–8

Schorer, Mark (*Harper Dictionary* panelist), 43

scientific words, 176–7

Scott, Sir Walter, 33, 88, 94, 117, 190; quoted by Lounsbury, 81–2

Scottish dialect (and Scotticisms), 7, 48, 94, 155, 156–7, 159

sensuous/sensual, 55–6

sentence(s), 139; definition of, 172; rewritten by Follett, 96–108; subject and object areas of, 148

Shakespeare, William, 26, 29, 34, 37–8, 89, 104, 113, 188, 193, 194; *between you and I* in, 44, 187, 196; example of *in* instead of *into* by, 14; example of *slow* as adverb by, 53; *these kind of* in, 190, 194

Shaw, George Bernard, 33, 38, 57, 76, 113, 188

Shelley, Percy Bysshe, 33, 104, 113; example of *precipitous* by, 56

Sherrill, Robert (*Harper Dictionary* panelist), 43

Shorter Oxford Dictionary, The, 195

Silberman, Charles (*Harper Dictionary* panelist), 53

Simon, John, 4, 8, 12, 30–8, 62, 63; disapproves of *hopefully,* 122, 124; disapproves of word chains, 128; writes *hoi polloi* without *the,* 183

slow/slowly, 52–3, 190, 195

Smith, Red (*Harper Dictionary* panelist), 44, 47

Smitherman, Geneva, 172

Smollett, Tobias George, 26

solstice, 131

Southern Renaissance, 153

Southern speech, 159

Southey, Robert, 29, 88, 89, 90, 91; *like* as conjunction in, 188, 193

Spencer, Edmund, 86

Spender, Stephen, 76

Stafford, Jean (*Harper Dictionary* panelist), 46, 57, 121–2, 124, 125, 127

Stahr, Elvis, Jr. (*Harper Dictionary* panelist), 44

stamina, 99

Standard of Usage in English, The (Lounsbury), 3. *See also* Lounsbury, Thomas R.

Stein, Gertrude, 111

Stephens, James, 35

Sterne, Laurence, 189, 193

stonewalling, 27

Strictly Speaking (Newman), 3, 12, 29, 76, 113, 129

string compounds (word chains), 103–4, 128–32, 178

stylebooks, 12, 180

success, 29

Suhor, Charles, 162–3, 164, 171

super, as adjective, 29

supportive, 27–8

Sweet, Henry, 44, 144

Swift, Jonathan, 5, 6, 33, 63, 81–3, 89, 190

Swinburne, Algernon Charles, 23, 51, 52, 103

Swinnerton, Frank, 35

Swope, Herbert Bayard, 91

T

talented, 83

Taylor, Davidson (*Harper Dictionary* panelist), 56

Taylor, Harold (*Harper Dictionary* panelist), 124

Tennyson, Alfred, Lord, 89, 103, 104, 178; example of *precipitous* by, 56

Thackeray, William Makepeace, 24, 33, 42, 62, 90, 193; example of compounding by, 103; *slow,* as adverb in, 190, 195

the, pronounced *duh,* 25, 146

thee and *thou,* 148

their, they, them, with singular antecedent, 33–5, 38, 188, 192; in Austen, 166; in Defoe, 165; in Wilde, 169

these kind of/this kind of, 147–8, 190, 194

tireless/untiring, 93

titles, 129; of organizations, 178

Tomorrow Is Sunday, 94

Trilling, Lionel, 95, 153–4; as *Harper Dictionary* panelist, 41, 42

Trollope, Anthony, 189

Index

Twain, Mark, 65; example of compounding by, 103
twat, 86

U

uh/er, 175–6
Underground Grammarian, The (Mitchell), 140
unpalatable, 16
unsave, 177
used to, 86

V

Vanity of Vanities, 86
Veblen, Thorstein, 63
verb(s): definition of, 139; passive, 88–9; past tense (*-ed* endings), 82, 152, 158, 160; superseded forms of, 166, 167; third-person singular present (*-s* endings), 139–40. See also *is/are* (agreement of subject and verb)
verbal/oral, 63–4
"verbiage," 106–7
Vietnam War, opposition to, 78–9
Viorst, Judith (*Harper Dictionary* panelist), 49, 57, 124

W

Walcott, Fred G., 10, 16, 40
Wallace, Irving, 169
Wallechinsky, David, 169
Walpole, Horace, 52
Washington, George, 87
Watch Your Language (Bernstein), 60, 122
Watergate, 67, 76–8. See also Nixon, Richard M.; Ziegler, Ron
Webster, John, 86
Webster, Noah, 87, 89, 90
Webster's New Collegiate Dictionary (1976), 124

Webster's New World Dictionary, 128
Webster's Third New International Dictionary, 179–80; words listed in, 71, 111, 112, 118, 119, 123, 128
Weeks, Edward, 95
welcome to, 96
West, Rebecca, quoted by Evans, 110
what, with plural verb, 37
Whipple, A. B. (*Harper Dictionary* panelist), 50, 51
White, Richard Grant, 34, 89
who/whom, 34, 136, 148, 190, 195; in Austen, 166; in Defoe, 165
Wilde, Oscar, 38, 141, 169, 188; example of *what* with plural verb by, 37
Williams, L. Pierce, 14–15
Williams, T. Harry (*Harper Dictionary* panelist), 124
Williams, William Carlos, 197
witness, 86
Wittgenstein, Ludwig, 76
women: as grammarians, 63; letters and diaries of, 168
word chains, 128–32, 178. See also compounds
Wouk, Herman (*Harper Dictionary* panelist), 44, 49, 116
Wright, Richard, 76
writers (great authors), as standard of English usage, 4–5, 8, 11, 145, 196. *See also* journalists
writing, teaching of, 162–5; grammar instruction and, 163

Y

Yeats, William Butler, 75
you know (y'know), 8, 21–2
youth, as language corruptors, 7–8

Z

Zandvoort, R. W., 140, 145
Ziegler, Ron, 26–7

Jim Quinn

is a poet, satirist, and the food columnist for Philadelphia Maga-zine *and* The Soho Weekly News. *He is the author of* The Cam-paign Alice, *a satire on the 1972 presidential election, and* Word of Mouth, *a restaurant guide to New York City, and a contributor to* The Poet's Encyclopedia.